THE COMFORT OF SIN
PROSTITUTES & PROSTITUTION
IN THE 1990s

Naturam expellas furca, tamen usque recurret
'You may drive out nature with a pitchfork, yet she'll be
constantly running back

HORACE – EPISTLES X.24

About the author

RICHARD GOODALL is a lawyer with some 40
years experience. He was born in London in 1933
and read Law at the University of London, being
called to the Bar in 1961. He subsequently chose
to qualify as a solicitor and in 1967 he opened his
London office, making commercial litigation one
of his specialities.

Before pursuing his career in law, he sampled
life as a telephonist, shorthand typist, customs
clearance clerk and travel agent. He married his
first and only wife in 1963. They have three
children – two sons and a daughter – and the
family home is in Buckinghamshire.

The other constants in his life are his love for
food and wine, responsive cars and the Mediterranean. He is also fond of music, animals and
gardening.

His other books include *The Myth of Divorce*, a
full-length study of the nature and implications of
marriage, also to be published by Renaissance
Books in 1995.

THE COMFORT OF SIN

PROSTITUTES &
PROSTITUTION IN
THE 1990s

RICHARD GOODALL

RENAISSANCE BOOKS

THE COMFORT OF SIN
Prostitutes and prostitution
in the 1990s

First published 1995 by Renaissance Books Ltd
PO Box 219, Folkestone
Kent CT20 3LZ, England

© 1995 Renaissance Books Ltd

ISBN   1–898823–05–7 (paperback)
       1–898823–10–3 (hardback)

All rights reserved. No part of this publication
may be reproduced or transmitted in any form or by
any means without prior permission in writing
from the Publishers.

British Library Cataloguing in Publication Data
A CIP catalogue entry for this book is available
from the British Library

Set in Bembo roman 12 on 12.5 point
by Bookman, Slough
Printed in England by Cromwell Press Ltd, Melksham, Wiltshire

Contents

Foreword

I think I am fairly resilient. As a practising lawyer for 40 years I have always subscribed to the view that I could cope with the greed, the brutality, the foibles and the sexual perversions that I have been called upon to deal with from time to time. I have always thought that I had a strong stomach, since one has to develop a fair degree of insensitivity when practising our profession. I believe I have taken poverty, abuse, famine, organized crime, disregard of human rights and freedom, genocide and man's general inhumanity to man in my stride, as ordinary occurrences in our sad world.

But nothing, nothing at all, is more shocking and sickening to me than to read, as one does nowadays ever more frequently, of the rape of elderly women (some of whom have been in their eighties) by teenagers. When, some years ago, I read for the first time of a similar occurrence, I thought that the age of the victim had been wrongly recorded. But no: these inexplicable, perverted acts seem increasingly common. And just as common is the manner in which we receive the news; it has become almost routine. After all, if younger women are raped daily, why should not women in their seventies and eighties also be submitted to the same brutality and indignity.

We read about it, but we do not appear to be unduly troubled. We take these occurrences for granted in the same

way as, for example, we accept that people can divorce and remarry at such a rate that today one marriage in two, at least in
the United Kingdom, ends in divorce.

On the rare occasions that sociologists and psychologists try
and provide some kind of explanation for the sexual violence
used on women in their seventies and eighties, the answer is
put forward that these are manifestations of masculine power.
It must be readily admitted, of course, that some rapes
committed by men on women are motivated primarily by a
desire for self-assertion. But this rather facile explanation,
which is very fashionable at present, is in my view not entirely
correct, and cannot be put forward to explain all sexual
violence. It is unlikely to apply, for example, to what in the
1990s is commonly known as 'date rape', and even less likely
to be the cause of the kind of disgusting assault which, as I said,
makes me feel physically sick.

I have spent some time trying to determine why, in a
society where sexuality appears to have been freed from all its
so-called 'taboos' and is given the opportunity, some might say
fairly unrestricted, to manifest itself in all its multifarious forms,
the relations between the sexes should be *more unsatisfactory*,
judging by the results, than, say, fifty years ago. And I have
come to the conclusion that, for a number of reasons*, we
appear to have made a mess of our sexual relations. Indeed, I
am one of those people who believe that instead of having
progressed in this activity, we have seen regression, simply
because the unrestrained exercise of any right is the antithesis
of freedom – it creating chaos by ignoring the corresponding
duties. I believe that this question of the relationship between
the sexes in the general sense, but above all in the specific
sexual context, is one of the most important issues of our time.
And I believe, too, that the reason why we are witnessing an

---

* These reasons will be referred to in greater detail later on, but for present
purposes, suffice it to record that the principal ones are the spread of reliable
contraception brought about by the development of the Pill, what I would call
moral consumerism, a general lack of discipline, and the elimination of the family as
a social, economic and moral unit.

ever-increasing disrespect by man of woman is to be found in a context which has little if anything to do with the exercise of power.

The reader should consider (official statistics will be quoted later) that throughout the United Kingdom there were, in 1938, just under 3,000 reported violent offences of a sexual kind on women and children. The equivalent figure for 1993 was in excess of 1.5 million.

In my view, the principal reason for this escalation is the blurring of the line of division between love and lust, between the sacred and the profane. The clarity that we had in the past, which enabled us to call things by their proper names and use the right colour to describe concepts and activities, has been lost. Black and white have moved into grey: and the resultant opaqueness causes real, fundamental problems.

I am looking at it from the standpoint of a heterosexual male, but the same consideration applies from the woman's standpoint; for all I know, but I am less experienced in those emotions, the same may be said for homosexuals, male and female. Whichever way one looks at it, however, the reader will see that in recommending legalization of brothels I do not distinguish between men and women, heterosexual or homosexual.

What is forgotten nowadays is what French writers used to refer to as 'nostalgie de la boue' (lit. 'longing to be back in the mud'), namely the well-established tendency of man to debasement, to wallowing in mud, in the same manner as some animals still do. As far as I am concerned, and I do not suppose that I am different from other members of the male species, there are women you marry and there are women with whom you simply have sex. There are women whom one loves and there are women over whom one lusts. To me, this division is perfectly clear; but it seems that the universality of role that modern woman is arrogating to herself is causing some confusion in this context. That is a pity because the sufferer, ultimately, is woman. The amount of violence currently being displayed against her and against children is so

great that few women walk the streets of the Western world
without looking over their shoulder if they sense that there is a
persistent and uniform step behind; few women travel in their
cars without locking themselves in; even fewer enter into an
underground compartment if they realize that they would
have to travel in it alone but for a man; and a great many
modern women have a low or very low opinion of men.

I am not moralizing, and I am not philosophizing, but I
consider myself a keen observer of human nature and I have
tried to set out, in the same way as if I were arguing a case in
court, my thoughts as to a possible way of overcoming the
present-day problems of escalating violence against women
and children, and of restoring some validity to the distinction
between love and lust. My case for the decriminalization of
the activities of prostitutes and the legalization of brothels,
which I hope I have put forward with conviction and
without pruriency, presupposes that the State will wish to
intervene, because the solution of the problem with which I
intend to deal cannot be left to human beings, whether male
or female, who have already made such a mess of their sexual
relations.

This intervention by the State is much less unusual than the
reader might think. After all, it is now very rare indeed to see
anyone even attempting to smoke on the railway and
underground networks. True, it needed a high-powered
Government-led public relations campaign against smoking,
and the traumatizing fire which killed many people at King's
Cross underground station, London, to jolt the authorities into
action. It would be more difficult to provoke a reaction from
officialdom in a field where hypocrisy reigns supreme. But
speaking for myself, I would much prefer to know that
brothels exist than to have to read at regular intervals in the
papers that another self-appointed guardian of morals had been
caught with his pants down in perverted sexual circumstances.

I wish to make it clear to the reader, however, that I am not
sufficiently conceited to believe that what I propose will be
readily acceptable or, if accepted, would be an immediate

panacea. But I feel strongly that the matter is important enough to require public debate.

Those who will be violently opposed to what I say can be classified into two broad categories. To the first category belong do-gooders, theoreticians of matters sexual and ardent feminists who will no doubt clamour about immorality and complain of the restrictions which the re-definition of a woman's role would appear to impose. To them I say that the system which has resulted from the application of the principles in which they believe has proved an absolute failure, so it is time that we should give someone else a chance. To the second category belong all those who, each in their own different form, derive substantial economic benefit from the maintenance of the status quo. I have in mind in particular lawyers, newspaper owners and writers, and purveyors of pornography in the broadest possible sense. To these latter I say that it is time that they stopped abusing a gullible and corruptible public.

One final point. I have carefully considered the most recent writings, statistics and pronouncements concerning the increase in crimes of sexual violence and rape in England and Wales (now standing at about 33,000 and 5,000 for 1993–1994), in the number of lone parents claiming benefit (now standing at 1,013,000, and costing £3.7 billion a year in income support), in the number of children of lone parents (which now exceeds 1.3 million and is costing the State a sum well in excess of £5 billion even excluding non-income-related aid such as free National Health Service prescriptions), about recent, worrying trends in pornographic writings by women and, more recently (September 1994) by the Principal of St Anne's College, Oxford.

This 'confession' by Ruth Deech, a member of the Law Commission which formulated the Divorce Reform Act 1969 (which effectively, no matter what else you may hear about it, made divorce on demand available in practice in England and Wales) that she made a mistake in voting for that Act and that the 'existing divorce law should be strengthened' and 'an education for marriage' should be drawn up for schools, I found very interesting. It follows on certain pronouncements by the Lord Chancellor's Office to the effect that divorce should be made more difficult. It seems to me that we are tinkering with the problem at its periphery but we are not dealing with the fundamental issue. I was reminded of the situation that arose when Marthe Richard, who pushed through the law that abolished brothels in France in the late 1940s, (which I consider in Chapter 10) five years after the law was passed, retracted her support for it and admitted that she had been wrong.

It is my firm opinion that there is a clear connection between the uses of and the social approach to prostitution, on the one hand, and the rate of divorce on the other. This aspect, too, is considered at some length; but the reader should know that the present volume is a companion to my forthcoming analysis of marriage, entitled *The Myth of Divorce*.

Of the reader I ask only one thing, and that is that he or she should approach the subject with an open mind. If this is done I am convinced that, whether or not there is agreement with my conclusions, the reader may, as I fervently hope, still believe that what I have tried to express was worth saying.

R.G.
December 1994

Acknowledgements

The subject matter of this book makes it difficult for me publicly to acknowledge the assistance I have received, especially from my male friends who, for one reason or the other, understandably prefer to remain anonymous. To all of them go my sincere thanks for their interest and support and for the insight so provided into their reactions which are not always understood, either by their wives or by society as a whole, and which do not necessarily find a correct echo in the comments on their performance and their attitudes made by those girls whose case histories are recorded here.

I should make it clear that my views and commentaries regarding certain situations which are analysed in these pages have always been double-checked, if that be the right expression to use, by a cross-section of both men and women. The same anonymity, however, has no place as far as my publisher, Paul Norbury, is concerned. He has shown faith in what I have tried to say, over and above the proverbial course of duty, not to mention his editorial skills that were so effectively brought to bear on my original manuscript; and for all of that, I am exceedingly grateful.

My thanks are similarly due to Beth Macdougall and to her team at MGA for all the work done on promoting *The Comfort of Sin*, thus displaying a belief in the necessity of a debate on the issues canvassed in this work which, if I may be forgiven for saying so, is rather unusual among emancipated women of the late twentieth century. I owe no lesser a debt to my very helpful staff, either for the painstaking efforts involved in research or for their typing and assembling skills, especially my personal assistant, Valerie Simpson.

In conclusion, I should record the debt that I owe, in the first place to my wife, and secondly to all the women with whom I have discussed these issues and who have served as a valuable and vital sounding board for my own views and beliefs. I also owe no lesser a debt to my very helpful staff, either for the painstaking efforts involved in research or for their typing and assembling skills, especially my personal assistant, Valerie Simpson.

The ultimate responsibility for all conclusions reached is mine, obviously, and mine alone. Yet it is always comforting for a man to know that his views, beliefs and prejudices are shared by women whom he respects and trusts. Such sharing has enormously strengthened my belief in the strongly-held view that the time is right for a debate on the issues that are raised herein.

Introduction

The invention of the Pill by Doctors Pinkus and Roth in the early 1960s must surely rank as one of the most important discoveries in the evolution of man. Not unlike the atomic bomb invented by Enrico Fermi and others, a generation earlier, the effect of this first, extremely practical contraceptive device·was to be both earth-shattering in its immediate impact and stupefying in its long-term implications for mankind.

Yet, in a strange sense, it could be said that the mechanics and the consequences of the A-bomb's first-time use on Hiroshima and Nagasaki were probably better understood than those that would follow from the handing over to woman herself of the control of her reproductive cycle.

There is no doubt that, at the time, the Pill was widely considered to be a major step forward in social development since, by relieving woman (and society) of unwanted pregnancies, it could release her for different and avowedly higher purposes in her quest for self-fulfilment, as well as liberalize sexual relations to the benefit of humanity as a whole, not least the over-populated third world.

Less than two generations later, however, the position is far from clear-cut. Indeed, I believe that sociologists who, fifty years from now, look back at Western society in the second

xvi   THE COMFORT OF SIN

half of the twentieth century, will be struck by three apparently inexplicable phenomena.

In the first place, they will find that our sexual relations seem to have gone awry at the very time when woman's progressive emancipation at home and in the work place, which followed the introduction of the Pill, should have made relationships between the sexes very much easier. It is arguable that, by creating a climate of sexual *laisser faire*, the Pill may have dulled man's hunting instinct, since woman became a much more willing prey in one sense and, in a totally different one, herself the hunter.

Some of the consequences of this switch in the gender of the hunter are considered in greater detail later, but in my view the single most traumatic effect is the growing tendency amongst men to prefer the dominance (and company) of other males, thus noticeably increasing the number of homosexuals throughout Western society.

Secondly, at the moment when female emancipation should have ensured equality of rights and treatment and thus greater respect for her as an individual, sexual violence on women and children of all ages has increased at a rate never before witnessed in our recorded history, the crime of rape becoming almost a routine daily occurrence. It is equally true that the focus on sex, fostered by the profit motive of the media and the publishing industry, principally for the purposes of entertainment and indulgence, has reached staggering proportions with the equivalent of soft porn material vigorously promoted even in 'classy' women's periodicals.

Finally, our twenty-first century sociologists may find it somewhat difficult to understand why, far from being reduced, the number of prostitutes is increasing in our society when the satisfaction of sexual needs of both sexes is very much easier than it ever was when early feminists, campaigning for the dignity of woman, argued that prostitution would disappear as soon as the inalienable rights of women were recognized by the law.

It would appear that, instead of representing a panacea for

all women's problems, the Pill has actually created severe social difficulties and sexual imbalances which can only be redressed by acknowledging that one of the avowed aims of Western policy, namely the abolition of prostitution, is incapable of ever being achieved in a free society.

The essence of this book, therefore, is a defence case for decriminalizing the activities of prostitutes and the logic of creating licensed establishments, supervised by State or Local Authorities, where sexual services by and for both men and women are provided, subject to stringent hygienic safeguards. My case would also extend to prostitutes the right of association in trade unions and other recognized workers' organizations in the same way that other providers of services receive union recognition.

My proposals are, in practice, much less far-reaching than they may first appear; in fact, to some extent, they have already been put in place, at least in part, even in countries like Britain and the United States which officially reject legalized prostitution. In other countries, such as Germany, Holland and Denmark, they have already become embodied in the law of the land.

As a practising lawyer for nearly forty years I have had to deal with a wide variety of litigation, including, of course, matrimonial cases, and in the last ten years I have taken an exceptional interest in the subject of prostitution, not least because of my growing awareness and concern about the nature of social change outlined above. During this period, I have read practically all that has been written (in English) on prostitution, I have followed correspondence in newspapers and magazines and watched much of what has been televised on the subject (in Britain); I have also monitored a great many 'agony aunt' and so-called 'sex experts' columns, and have conducted dozens of interviews with prostitutes.

This is not intended to be, nor is, a scientific study. But as in any court that I have attended, I have done my best to present the evidence and argue my case. It will be for others to determine the outcome.

Chapter One

The law, the facts of life and prostitution

For the purpose of this book, the following definition shall apply:

'A prostitute is any person whether male, female or hermaphrodite, who earns a living wholly or in part by the more or less indiscriminate, willing and emotionally indifferent provision of sexual services of any description to another, against payment, usually in advance but not necessarily in cash; and prostitution is the rendering of the services defined.'

(For the record, there does not appear to be a statutory definition of the word 'prostitute'; and until the decision of the Court of Appeal in Regina -v- McFarlane (20 December 1993) there was not even a definition of the word 'prostitution', except in dictionaries. An interesting, if not curious fact, since Section 30 of the Sexual Offences Act 1956 (referred to hereafter) provides that 'it is an offence for a man to live wholly or in part on the earnings of prostitution'.)

Many authors who have attempted any kind of definition are probably proud of their work. In my case I am not sure. Nevertheless, I believe the above definition does overcome all difficulties of a practical, psychological, social and emotional nature, as well as any problem of semantics. Readers will no doubt tell me otherwise if they disagree; indeed, I fully expect disagreement, if not heated debate, to be engendered by many of the issues raised in the pages that follow.

In setting out to write this book I became convinced about two fundamental canons:

Firstly, that prostitution is ineradicable because the sexual urges, frustrations and deviations of human beings, whether male, female or hermaphrodite, demand satisfaction more or less continuously. I quite appreciate that this is a broad and, some might say, ridiculous generalization. It can be argued, for instance, that a human being is not a slave to his passions and that he can make use of his free will to avoid satisfying his sexual urges, frustrations and deviations. One can go further and say that a number of people (priests and nuns, for example, and all those who live a celibate life) have achieved just that.

Of course they have. But to argue that the exercise of free will will be sufficient to deny the need to satisfy sexual urges and frustrations is much the same as saying that the exercise of free will will ensure that there is no crime in society. If only it were so. The principle is absolute, but the practice is something different and not within the scope of this book. If human beings were capable, by exercising their will-power, to eliminate particular sexual requirements, there would certainly be no need for prostitutes; in the same way, thieves would be encouraged to exercise their will-power. Thus, there would be no need to lock up our houses and cars. But the fact is, we live in a hard and unpleasant world of greed, crime, passion and lust. And that is why I make the point that because human beings are made equal in some respects or many respects and have particular urges or deviant interests, prostitution is always going to be an essential element of the human condition.

If that is the case, and I have absolutely no doubt that it is, is it not extraordinary and sad that over the past 50 years not a single Western government has had either the courage or the wisdom to acknowledge the consequences of a failure to admit this first premise?

The second premise follows with inexorable logic from the

first, which is that it is preferable that prostitutes should be recognized by the State as performing a useful social function and should be controlled and regulated in the most efficient manner, in the same way that horse-racing or casinos or the provision of public parks are. Accordingly, the activities of prostitutes should be decriminalized, they should be allowed to have their own trade unions, and brothels should be licensed by the State or the Local Authority.

Feminists, optimistic sociologists, theoreticians of sexuality, church leaders, do-gooders and hypocrites of all nationality and class will be up in arms over the statements made above. But once the first premise is proved, the regulation and taxation of the activities of prostitutes would be no different, conceptually, from betting levies or taxes on football pools, or the national lottery.

The problem of how to deal with prostitutes and the human condition on which they thrive has effectively been with us for millennia. It is quite naïve to say that 'prostitution is the oldest profession'. Those who simply hide behind the expression tend to ignore the true meaning of the words. Let us try and analyse its implications. In the first place, a statement of fact: prostitution is undeniably the oldest profession known to man.

This is not a fact which this book challenges in any way; on the contrary, it is fully accepted as a starting point. That prostitutes have existed from time immemorial goes to support the first of the two premises. We have never been able to get rid of prostitutes and never will. But more about this later.

At this point, some might say that to argue that prostitution is the oldest profession is to use language too loosely. Traditionally, there is a limit to the number of those who can call themselves 'professional people'. Quite so; thus, a prostitute is no more a 'professional' than a soldier or a farmer. I fully accept that it is only when certain requirements are satisfied (e.g. a recognized course of learning, instruction and training, a code of conduct, disciplines to enforce that code, and a recognized supervisory body) that one could claim to have 'a profession'. Nevertheless, 'the oldest profession' is an effective, and widely understood expression of almost venerable antiquity. I hope, therefore, that the reader will not mind if I appear to elevate the standing of a prostitute by referring to her as a professional. I am not putting her on the same pedestal as that of a lawyer, a doctor, an architect, or an engineer (though many a prostitute might argue otherwise).

Qualitatively, of course, there is no comparison; quantitatively, too, it is difficult if not impossible to make an appropriate calculation. Yet it is a fact that prostitutes are professionals in the same way other providers of services may be. After all, what a prostitute does, amounts to an occupation, for certain; and by some, it may even be perceived as a vocation. Some prostitutes actually take pride in what they do, in the same way as a surgeon rejoices over a job well done or an architect over a successfully completed design. And there are undoubtedly women who are naturally adept at being prostitutes, who are born to be good at it.

So, in the final analysis, I can find only two contexts in which the activities of a prostitute do not appear to qualify for the definition of being a so-called 'professional'; the first is where there is transmission from prostitute to client of any kind of venereal disease; the second is the prostitute's inability at common law to sue for herself.

As to the first point, if a professional in the execution of his tasks makes a mess of it for his client or damages his client's interest, he is liable to compensate that client. However, there seems to be no recorded occurrence in either the USA or the United Kingdom where a client has successfully sued a prostitute for having communicated a venereal disease. This is presumably because the client has consciously or unconsciously recognized the wisdom of the Latin maxim 'Volenti non fit iniuria' which translates as: 'If you go out looking for trouble, you should not complain when you find it'.

However, there are some indications already, particularly from the USA, that this situation may well change and that the communication of a venereal disease is of itself actionable and gives rise to a claim for damages. If ever such a principle were to become established in Anglo-American jurisprudence, the comparison of the prostitute's activities with those of other 'professionals' would be practically complete. Here, it is interesting to note in passing that the Irish Court of Appeal, way back in 1878, had forcefully rejected the argument that communication of a venereal disease was actionable (Hegarty v Shine (1878) 4 LR IR page 288).

As to the problem raised by the prostitute's inability to sue for her fees, on the basis of the Latin maxim '*Ex turpi causa non oritur actio*', i.e. you cannot sue to recover what is the fruit of illegality, it is probably an academic point. Most whores insist on payment in advance anyway. In fact, in the USA it is now customary in some establishments for payment to be made by credit card. This is exactly what would happen in the UK once it were decided to treat the provision of sexual services as no different from that of any other service. (The question of tax on the prostitute's earnings is considered on page 105.)

Another feature that endorses the description of at least some prostitutes as professionals is the almost universal trait which distinguishes the real tart, the better type of prostitute (and, one may remark in passing, the woman who is capable of holding on to her man, married or not); that is to say, the 'professional' desire to please another in the provision of a particular sexual service.

Whether this desire is truly felt by the prostitute or is purely artificial must often be a matter of debate and no doubt depends upon the circumstances of each relationship. In actual fact, it matters little how or why it arises, for the important thing is that it should be there at all. On the other hand, the prostitute's client will certainly not be too bothered about matters of legal principle and semantic definition and is likely to be too far driven by desire or passion as to be able to afford any noticeable display of critical sense. What matters is that the prostitute should please and should provide satisfaction as any other 'professional' would wish to do.

This desire and, indeed, ability to please is not, of course, exclusive to prostitutes: some 'honest' women also display it. How often may a husband or partner who is particularly pleased by his wife's or woman's sexual performance think, and perhaps even say to her: 'You really are a proper tart', or words to that effect. Such a remark, whilst flattering of her ability, is clearly provoked by the wife's desire to please the man and by his appreciation of that desire. In the man's eyes, the woman is turning herself into a professional of sexual matters.

If this analysis be correct, it is sad to record that the number of men who will feel the need of something more than their normal sexual relationships with their women, (whether wife, mistress, co-habitee and so on) can but increase unless, of course, such men should wish to find 'pleasure' in homosexual relations. This presumed increase in the need for supplementary sexual activity surely stems from the fact that the desire to please man is not foremost in the mind of modern woman (but you may also rightly ask, was it ever?). It seems to me that woman today is primarily motivated by the desire to seek self-assertion and her own way, to ask, crudely or sweetly, for whatever may fulfil her orgasmic, if not orgiastic, needs, to be in charge of a relationship, to take the initiative in matters sexual as in others. In effect, to prove herself and her dominance over the male of the species who is believed to be, and is just as often described as, and indeed is, a weakling in need of support and direction.

So strong is this tendency among women today, one rapidly comes to the view that within her ethos is the conviction that she has a duty to give herself pleasure. The desire to please is usually not there, for it presupposes a submission to man at least at the superficial and practical levels which modern woman, intoxicated by her ever-increasing grasp of power over an ever-weakening and impotent male, is not prepared to entertain. This greater power is one of the results of the availability of the Pill. At this point, it is worth remembering that in 1951 Dr Pinkus, with progesterone in his mind, set to work to discover whether this hormone could be taken with the deliberate purpose of controlling fertility. What he wanted to do was to verify whether the introduction of progesterone could control the release of egg cells for a prolonged period.

In 1952 he consulted Dr John Roth, a Director of the Fertility Clinic at the Free Hospital for Women in Brooklyn. Together, they chose a group of female volunteers for a trial period, which was generally satisfactory, although it did show that one in five women did not respond to progesterone. The two doctors then set to work for four years to find more efficient methods. In 1956 they discarded progesterone and replaced it with a synthetic material manufactured in the laboratory, which was called Norethynodrel.

The tests were repeated and they found that small doses of this synthetic chemical were, in fact, quite efficient. In April 1956 Dr Pinkus set up a contraceptive field-trial and selected a product manufactured by G.D. Searle Limited which was afterwards called Enavid. The field-trial was set up in Puerto Rico. In 1957 a further field-trial took place in Haiti. Meanwhile, in the United Kingdom some progress had been made but it was only in 1959 that the Council for Investigation of Fertility Control undertook to conduct trials on oral contraceptives. By 1960 the Medical Advisory Council and the Family Planning Association decided that it was safe to carry out larger-scale trials and, as a result, over 1,000 women in Birmingham, Slough and London tried out the new product called Conovid. A full report on these trials emerged in June 1961, the year in which Conovid and the additional product Anovlar, were added to the list of approved oral contraceptives.

The year 1961, therefore, was the one during which, at least as far as the United Kingdom is concerned, the contraceptive pill became of age and freely available. (In the United States it was somewhat earlier. Elsewhere in the industrialized world it was adopted in the years following. However, in Japan it was never adopted on medical grounds – some would argue on cultural grounds – and its use – except in rare cases – continues to be against the law.)

Over the past 30 years or so it is plain to see that, thanks to the Pill, women have become increasingly assertive and more knowledgeable as to matters sexual generally. But no amount of technical knowledge, picked up either through early sexual experiences or sex education literature of one form or another, is sufficient to offset the basic psychological imbalance which exasperated feminism, coupled with ever-decreasing male potency, has brought about. (The increasing number of Western whites who marry girls from other ethnic back-grounds e.g. Asia, the Philippines, the West Indies, Latin America etc. in the belief that they will be more 'submissive' and less bossy and dominating than white women, highlights this point.)

The reader who, at this stage, feels that my remarks are somewhat extreme, is reminded of certain findings of the first Kinsey Report. (Kinsey & Others *The Sexual Behaviour of the Human Male* and *The Sexual Behaviour of the Human Female*, Philadelphia 1948 & 1953; W.B. Saunders Company). Allow me to explain. These two reports, although somewhat out of date, are still the principal scientific studies into the sexual habits, foibles and deviations of Western man. It is true that they have been criticized on a number of grounds of which the two more important ones are first, that people who volunteer to be interviewed about their sexual behaviour are probably cranks in any event and should not be believed and, second, that what happens in the USA is not necessarily typical of what happens in the Western world generally.

As regards the first criticism, it should be stated that the Kinsey team were keenly aware of the risks of being fobbed off with figments of sick imaginations: accordingly, they developed extremely careful and controlled interviewing techniques. As to the second, the USA seems to me such a melting pot of races, that it is probably fair to say that the opinions recorded in the two Kinsey Reports are representa-tive of a very good section of humanity. Particularly, as far as Britain is concerned, we are entitled to assume that there is some correspondence between the American findings and English attitudes, since at least in the post-Second World War period British culture and sexual 'mores' have been greatly influenced by the American pattern.

Given the greater sexual freedom that has developed since the second Kinsey Report was published (1953), one is entitled to assume that the Kinsey figures are extremely conservative. Consider, for example, their finding that only 4% of males are practising homosexuals: this is without question a major understatement of the true position at the present time and, as figures show elsewhere, totally inapplicable in the 1990s.

I have taken the view, therefore, that Kinsey is a reliable source of information, not so much because 20,000 people were interviewed, but simply because the two reports discovered nothing new: they merely confirmed in scientific fashion what those with experience of life have always known. For present purposes, they provide an authoritative record of minimum standards of human conduct or failures, and of its perversions. Furthermore, they are very thorough: the amount of detail is staggering, there are numerous graphs and the information is conveyed clearly and objectively. I am not ignoring other published reports into sexual activity. In the 1960s, we had Masters and Johnson in the United States and in 1992 the Welcome Report in the United Kingdom. In 1993, we saw in Britain 'The Janus Report on Sexual Behaviour'. Numerically, the Janus Report seems the more thorough since nearly 8,000 Americans were interviewed. However, I still think that the Kinsey Reports represent a milestone.

Allied to the point I made earlier regarding the State and prostitution, it should be noted here that no Western government has ever supported or undertaken any investigation into prostitution – never mind the scale of the Kinsey Report involving 20,000 people.

The most relevant finding of fact for present purposes is found on page 580 of Kinsey. It states: 'For perhaps three-quarters of all males, orgasm is reached within two minutes after the initiation of the sexual relation and for a not inconsiderable number of males, the climax may be reached

within less than a minute or even within 10 or 20 seconds after
coital entrance.' Partial verification of the Kinsey findings had
come in 1938 from Terman and his colleagues (*Psychological
Factors in Marital Happiness*) who, rather more optimistically for
American women, found that the estimate of the mean
duration of intercourse made by 41% of the husbands they
interviewed and 46% of the wives was 'seven minutes or less'
(table 98 in figure 20 on page 296).

These optimistic data collated by Terman clash somewhat
with those recorded seven years earlier by Dickinson and
Beam (R.L. Dickinson and Laura Beam – *A Thousand
Marriages*, Baltimore, 1931; Williams & Wilkins). Dickinson
and Beam reported on the estimates given by 362 wives as to
the usual duration of their copulations. Forty per cent of the
estimates were of three minutes or less and the median were
reported as five to ten minutes. Terman was obviously aware
of the Dickinson and Beam findings and explains them away
by stating that when Dickinson's patrons reported these
estimates, the average date thereof was probably 20 to 30 years
before Terman's own investigation.

Accordingly, of course, 'a cultural change seems to be
taking place in the direction of higher evaluation of the erotic
aspects of sexual love'. Evaluation is one thing, but duration of
erection is a more permanent one.

Terman and his colleagues probably had greater faith in the
ability of the American male to satisfy his female counterpart
than any other American writer who has subsequently
considered the problem. Nearly 20 years after Terman,
Kinsey showed that Dickinson and Beam were more likely
to be correct, except in one respect. It is true that Terman
correlated the duration of performance in intercourse with
marital happiness; since he found the factor of a mere .02 for
the husband and .04 for the wife, he deduced from the figures
that the duration of intercourse had no significant effect on
marital happiness and that it was merely a factor in the overall
marital relationship.

Whilst one must agree that sexual satisfaction is not the

most essential element in a marriage, one wonders whether the wider sample of Kinsey (12,000 men and 8,000 women) may not give greater authority and weight to the Kinsey findings when compared with Terman's calculations. The 1990 update of the Kinsey Institute findings does not deal with the duration of erections.

Whichever way one looks at the American data, it is arguable that modern woman is not being satisfied by her man and may well feel some contempt for him. As a result, man may well find it easier to go with a prostitute who by definition will not be too interested in standards of performance. Indeed, the cynic might argue that a female prostitute is likely to be only too pleased if her client's requirements are less than herculean. As one of them was heard to remark: 'It's true that it kind of kills you, but it doesn't last long. It's over fast, otherwise there wouldn't be a girl left to do this job.' An observation which surely endorses both the points that have just been made.

* * *

The definition I gave at the beginning uses the technical noun 'prostitute' as all-embracing. It includes all other terms in Anglo-American language and jargon that identify the kind of person defined: whore, wench, bawd, trollop, tart, harlot, hooker, hustler, courtesan, broad, 'scrubber', street-walker, strumpet, night-walker, bar-girl, call-girl, 'hussy' etc. Some, like wench and whore, are of considerable antiquity; others, like call-girl, are much more modern and reflect a change in the way in which prostitutes have operated. They also show a move away from the condemnatory note which is inherent in the older terms.

It is perhaps less offensive to be considered a call-girl rather than a prostitute: this is in line with the wider modern tendency to use euphemisms to describe activities which are unpleasant or unpalateable, such as rodent exterminator instead of rat-catcher.

The word prostitute is of Latin origin. Etymologically, it is derived from '*pro*' meaning 'in front' and '*statuere*' meaning 'to stay' and it identified initially those religious prostitutes, (see Chapter 3) who stood in front of temples displaying themselves in order to offer their services, not for money, but as part of certain religious functions. The term then came to describe a woman who stood, whether at street corners or in front of taverns, showing what she had to offer for sale.

From whichever angle one approaches the noun, however, it is interesting to observe that it is almost an oddity in the English language. The English nouns which identify the performing of functions end in either 'er' or 'or' (like adviser and doctor) sometimes in 'ian' (like beautician and mortician) or in 'ist' (like physicist and analyst); and there are other forms with which we need not be troubled for present purposes. Suffice it to say, however, that there are few nouns in the English and American languages ending in 'stitute'. There may be a few verbs, e.g. constitute, and a few adjectives, such as destitute, but the nouns are exceptionally limited in numbers. It is almost as though, by choosing a noun from a limited category, one were adding to the contempt felt for the woman who provides sexual services in return for payment. Others might remark, not altogether flippantly, that 'a prostitute is an institute without substitute'.

In Britain, we have gone further. We have also, at least for the purposes of legal definitions, pejoratively qualified the noun by adding the adjective 'common'. The expression 'common prostitute' appears to have been first used in the Metropolitan Police Act 1839 [2 & 3 Victoria C.47 section 54(11)] where the 'common prostitute' is associated with a night-walker. It reads as follows: 'Every common prostitute or night-walker loitering or being in any thoroughfare or public place for the purpose of prostitution or solicitation to the annoyance of the inhabitants or passengers...'. I interpret the addition of the adjective 'common' in this way. On the other hand, it could be argued that it identifies her free availability, namely her cheapness. Either way, it carries a pejorative connotation.

The Victorians were, of course, far from happy with what the prostitutes were doing and a few years later, in 1846, the first Contagious Diseases Act was passed. Although the Act itself does not use the words 'common prostitute' or 'prostitute', it is a landmark in the United Kingdom's attitude to prostitutes, for it highlights the association between the whore and venereal disease which was to become a distinguishing feature of the approach to prostitution in most European countries, and which persists to this day. One year later, the Police Clauses Act 1847 repeated the term 'common prostitute' and also qualified the term 'night-walker' by the addition of the adjective 'common'.

The second Act on contagious diseases was the Public Health Act of 1875 which, in line with its predecessor, did not specifically use the word 'common prostitute' or 'prostitute', nor did it specify what were infectious diseases. However, the Criminal Law Amendment Act of 1885 did use the term 'common prostitute'. Overall, the legislation passed in the period 1839 to 1885 represents the high watermark of Great Britain's contempt for women who sold their bodies for pleasure, since its essential purpose was to identify them as vehicles for the transmission of disease. The moral criticism of them was camouflaged in medical considerations. The situation remained largely unchanged until the mid 1950s when the government appointed a committee chaired by Sir John Wolfenden. Its report is considered in detail in Chapter 15.

So, I come back to the point that the terminology used in current speech is important. As Bacon reminds us, words govern us rather than we them; one has only to think of Orwell's 1984 and the official language 'Newspeak'. After all, the essence of my argument is that the activities of a prostitute should be immediately decriminalized except in cases regarding children or minors. It is true that the definition of what is a child or minor for the purposes of prostitution may vary from country to country, but for the sake of simplicity, one could adopt the same age as is adopted for marriage. If a

person is allowed to marry at 16, he/she would cease to be a
minor for the purposes of the laws on prostitution at that same
age; but more about that later (Chapter 16).

I would also argue that it is an insult to the dignity of the
female sex that a certain category of women should be singled
out as being a black sheep of the family simply because
pseudo-religious or pseudo-moral considerations lead us to
adopt a hypocritical stance in matters sexual. A prostitute is a
provider of services. Our society (the industrialized world as a
whole) is one that is increasingly reliant upon the provision of
all kinds of services. The prostitute's activities, therefore,
should be taken out of the sphere of the criminal law and,
insofar as they represent a problem, should be treated as a
social and not as a penal problem.

It has been said, especially by some churchmen, that one
cannot develop a rational public policy as regards prostitutes
but one has to do the best one can with regard to cleaning up
the mess for which they are responsible. At best, this is totally
defeatist attitude, and at worst, it is not very Christian. Our
society makes provision for the mentally ill; why should it not
make similar provision for the sexually ill? I hasten to add, of
course, that no suggestion is being made here that all men who
frequent prostitutes are sexually ill. There must be many
perfectly normal and comparatively healthy (in mind and in
body) men who may, from time to time, have need to visit
prostitutes. The principal focus of the present argument,
however, is that the majority of people who frequent
prostitutes have some sexuality 'dysfunction' and for this
reason they require the assistance of, what one may term, sex
therapists. If my interpretation is right, no amount of wishful
thinking will cause prostitutes to disappear.

In making this statement, I wish to make clear that I part
company from the American historian, A.W. Calhoun (*Social
History of the American Family*, Cleveland 1919, volume 3 page
80) who says: 'The future of prostitution is clearer, it is certain
practically to disappear. This prediction does not mean that
irregular sex relations will necessarily disappear but that the

mercantile element will be eliminated. . .'. It is true that one has to be exceptionally careful when dealing with forecasts of sexual activity: but clearly Calhoun read the future wrongly. On the other hand, in an article published in the late 1920s, another American, Dr W.J. Robinson, is on record as stating that 'If in spite of all the humiliations, risks, obstacles, atrocious punishments, ostracisms and fear of Hell, prostitution has continued unabated up to the present time, it is fair to assume that it will continue to persist in the future; but it will persist not because it always has: it will persist because it satisfies a definite and biological need and answers it in a way that no other present arrangement does'.

However, in the United Kingdom, as a result of the Wolfenden Report, we have legislated, unsuccessfully, to ensure that prostitutes are driven off the streets. The Street Offences 1959 Act attempted to do just that by defining the offences of loitering and soliciting 'in public places', as the commentary to the Act puts it. But the nuisance element remains, as anyone who lives in 'red-light areas', e.g. King's Cross in London, Balsall Heath in Birmingham, or other areas much frequented by prostitutes in all the major cities of the UK knows only too well. After dark, there is shouting, swearing, slamming of car doors; in the morning, condoms, syringes. Law enforcement, as far as prostitutes are concerned, has become so uneven and so different from city to city as to be considered a lottery.

Furthermore, despite the legislation, anyone who knows the streets of the major cities is aware of the fact that prostitutes have not disappeared; indeed, quite the opposite has taken place, as is well known. The result is contempt for a law which is not applied or which is applied differently in different parts of the same country. In London, a prostitute may be prosecuted for soliciting, in Manchester she may merely be warned. This is absurd but it is surely typical of everyday experience, in Europe and the Western world generally, including the United States, France, Spain and Italy.

For example, one need only go to present-day Rome and

see what happens, especially in the evening, along the embankments of the Tiber, or to Barcelona to see 'the sights' in the Ramblas; and so on. It is only in Holland and Germany that the position seems more clearcut in the sense that there are areas set aside for prostitutes and the licensing of brothels is delegated to local authorities.

Here again, one is forced to conclude that the activities of prostitutes should cease to be illegal – a view that has the support of some feminists and ought to have that of most liberal-thinking people. In addition, I am entirely convinced that once such decriminalization takes place, the acknowledgement and supervision of brothels or some similar establishment, would follow as inevitably as night follows day. But this would not necessarily please all feminists.

There is one further consideration to be addressed regarding the usefulness of the services rendered by prostitutes. In certain circumstances, their 'beneficial' effect cannot possibly be doubted: they have, as it were, proved their worth through the centuries. Indeed, as a remedy to concupiscence, they could be said to be almost unrivalled. But what is constantly forgotten is that the sexual appetite, in so far as it represents primarily a physical need – and only secondarily a psychological one, – is satiated by its satisfaction in the same manner as the pains of hunger are assuaged by the intake of food. It is hardly a coincidence that the two essential human drives are, preservation (eating) and reproduction (sexual activity), in that order.

We are becoming increasingly unable, it seems to me, to understand that in the sexual sphere we can separate physical from mental activity to a fairly considerable extent and that it is conceivable that by so doing we may even strengthen our mind. It can obviously be argued that, inasmuch as lust is an activity which does not meet with social approval, it should be controlled in the same manner as violence or theft. I do not share that view. There is nothing anti-social *per se* in lust. It is only when it is coupled with violence or nuisance or interference with the freedom of others that lust can be objectionable as a matter of law.

Whichever way one wishes to view it from the philosophical standpoint, however, it is a fact that our (Western) society has been unable to find an adequate outlet for lust. It is undoubtedly true that woman now comes to sexual relations much more knowledgeable, at least in the technical sense, than her grandmother. When girls decide, at an increasingly early age, that they want to have sexual intercourse, they have already had available to them through magazines, books, films and television, a substantial amount of technical knowledge. They know the meaning of words and actions (of which many of their forebears were quite ignorant throughout their lives) and they therefore feel that they can cope well with whatever relationship, whether cohabitation or marriage, they embark upon. And, of course, they have the Pill to prevent pregnancies.

The reality, however, is that no matter how technically proficient young women might be, they are probably emotionally immature, at least in the sense that the shift from matron to whore – as those concepts will be described in later pages – is somewhat more difficult than modern feminists and psychologists seem to believe. The attempt of the wife or cohabiting female partner to replace the prostitute is not entirely successful.

In effect, one can distinguish two extreme situations, in any kind of marital or cohabiting relation, as far as female sexuality is concerned. The first is where the spouse or partner is not too efficient in bed; and the latter, where she is quite efficient. In the former case, either through education or lack of experience or environment, it is conceivable that what the young girl may have lacked in sexual tuition, she may have gained in other contexts. Maybe her mother taught her how to truss a chicken or to cook or wash clothes or rinse plates or even sew; the ability to cope with such matters was taught at an early age by grandmothers to their daughters. So that what the 'wife' lacks in sexual experience she makes up by being a good 'housewife' and mother.

In the second situation, the odds are that the woman who comes with a certain amount of sexual experience to either a steady cohabitation arrangement or marriage is not quite so proficient in the other domestic virtues that, menial though they may be in the eyes of certain modernists, are nevertheless an essential adjunct to the success of any man/woman stable relationship. Put differently, some men may find it difficult to accept that their woman performs in bed almost as successfully as a whore, but is otherwise deficient in other respects.

This is a dilemma for modern society. We are witnessing an increase in the assertion of individual freedoms and political personality, from the break-up of the Soviet Union, the emancipation of minorities in Eastern Europe and, closer to home, the increase in the feelings of Welsh and Scottish Nationalists. This is not a problem which is exclusive to the United Kingdom, since most other countries in Europe have had to face the assertiveness, whether justified historically or not, of its minorities, whether ethnic, linguistic or religious. One can think of the Austrians in the Trentino Alto Adige of Italy, the Basques and the Catalans in Spain, the ethnic groupings in the former Yugoslavia, the Greeks and Turks in Cyprus. A reaction to these claims is to try and bolster individual freedoms, at least nominally.

The climate of our society is on the whole in favour of the upholding of individual freedoms. But it is exactly at that point that our approach to prostitutes becomes ambiguous. If it is true, as feminists claim, that woman is at last mistress of her body and her destiny, it is difficult to see how the right to dispose of one's body freely can possibly be denied to prostitutes when our society has granted it, without too much compunction, to both homosexuals and lesbians. It is sometimes said that the reason for the differentiation lies in the fact that the prostitute sells sexual favours, thus converting herself into a 'professional' or a businesswoman; but such argument lies uncomfortably in the mouth of Western society which has made money its god.

The reluctance on the part of woman to acknowledge that there are some members of the female sex who are in fact, whether by nature or necessity, inclined to a life of prostitution, may be understandable, since we none of us wish to acknowledge publicly our worst faults. But it is untenable. What is more, it is not clear how much modern woman cares for the institution of marriage; but if she does, she ought to consider that in many cases the existence of a prostitute (male or female) is a safety valve, where the spouse either has naturally or develops through circumstances, a leaning towards deviation from the so-called path of righteousness.

For example, one could ask any wife whether, assuming for the sake of argument that she had to cater for some deviant requirement in her husband and was unwilling to provide it herself, she would prefer him to go with another man, to find himself a mistress, or visit a prostitute.

The answer, of course, may vary but the great majority of wives would unquestionably consider the prostitute the least damaging of the three options (evils?), especially if certain guarantees, albeit in theoretical form, could be provided by the State which was effectively controlling, supervising and medically examining the women who rendered such sexual services.

Of course, the deviant might have to go without. That is also an answer to the problem; but human nature being what it is, such an option is likely to bring more benefit to the psychiatrist than to the marriage.

Before taking the discussion any further, however, it may be helpful to look at some case histories, which I believe are reasonably representative. The names of the prostitutes interviewed have been changed and specific geographical locations that might in any manner assist in identifying the interviewee, have also been avoided. The general geographic indications given, however, are correct.

Chapter Two

Case histories

Janice

Janice is 27 years old, but looks younger. She is an attractive brunette about 5'5" tall, with dark brown, almost Mediterranean eyes. She has a pleasant smile but the eyes themselves are not smiling. She is neatly dressed, her silk shirt has the two buttons undone to reveal in part not-too-solid breasts and no bra; black trousers disappear into calf-high, elegant, black boots. She wears no jewellery, little make-up, save around the eyes, and no perfume. Her hands are well-manicured.

She is soft spoken, with a Midlands accent, is extrovert and confident ('I could sell sand to the Arabs'). Nothing in her appearance marks her out as someone who has been a prostitute for 10 years. Nor has she ever taken drugs. She smokes a maximum of six cigarettes a day and enjoys lager beer. She left school at 16 and went to the hairdressing college in a small town in the Midlands. She did not complete the course because, she said, there would be no scope in her home town for such qualifications, particularly since no less than 30 girls from her school went on the hairdressing course.

Her mother divorced when she was fairly young, and remarried. Janice claims to come from a very good and quite

20

wealthy family but did not get on too well with her stepfather. There was no question of any abuse from him, sexual or otherwise; they were simply incompatible.

At 17 she decided to leave home and went to the nearest large Midlands town where her grandmother had lived all her life. She did not, however, go and stay with the grandmother, but started sharing a flat with another girl and, as she puts it, 'got in with the wrong crowd'. There had never been any problems at home; indeed, during the interview, Janice stated more than once that she had had a very happy childhood, going on holidays at least three times a year, and spending a lot of time with her grandmother of whom she seems incredibly fond even now. She also claims that, as a child, she was spoilt even though she had a younger brother.

She first had intercourse with a boy from her own school when she was 15 and she considers that totally irrelevant to her present way of life, which she ascribes to the fact that she mixed with girls who, for one reason or the other, had jewellery, clothes and elegant homes: she wanted all that from a very early age. In her own words, she wanted to repeat at 17 what her mother (who was more than twice her age) had at home.

She had little money, no clothes and certainly not enough to live on. As soon as she set up on her own she took on odd jobs (at a newsagent, tobacconists etc.) but soon found that she was getting nowhere. She then decided that she would try what other girls whom she knew were doing. She had her first experience as a prostitute when aged 17. She took to walking down the street and was picked up by a man in his late 30s driving a very large American car. She got on very well with him, although she was a little scared at the particular first encounter. However, she assumes she must have performed quite well, as she puts it, since he paid her £15.00, which, in the early 1980s, was quite a lot of money.

She claims she has never looked back and considers that the prostitute's lifestyle suits her because she is an independent spirit. Nevertheless, she is quite prepared to give it up when the time comes, and to marry 'if the right guy comes along'. She certainly would not marry for money.

Janice has nothing against men; as a matter of fact, she admits to liking some of her customers. She tries to avoid those she does not like. On the whole, she is not too fond of coloured men but has mixed with Arabs whom she considers difficult to please. Her 'menu', as she puts it, is fairly limited: 'straight' intercourse and oral sex, always using condoms. She is not prepared to do anything else, does not really know much about sado-masochistic practices, and was asked once to perform in the presence of a child of 11 and refused. She has never indulged in any lesbian practices, but on one occasion only she recalls that, with a friend, they both entertained one man.

She has never had any kind of venereal disease although she has been to prison two or three times for non-payment of fines. She considers that, apart from being a good judge of men, she has been exceptionally lucky. She has no means of personal self-defence because she claims she does not need them. She operates mainly in saunas in north London. She claims that operating from a sauna also makes for greater cleanliness because all her customers have to be 'clean'. According to her, 90% of all prostitutes start out on the street and only 10% start in saunas or massage parlours but she does admit that, ideally, a prostitute who starts on the street would wish to graduate to better standards by changing from street-walker to call-girl.

She does not work every day but only when she needs money. If she needs extra money, she would just 'pop out' on to the street. She charges on a half-hourly basis: minimum £50.00, maximum £150.00. She has never had a pimp. She classifies her customers into two very clear-cut categories: firstly, there is the average married man, happy or unhappy with his wife; and secondly, there is the young single guy who earns perhaps too much or has had a dare with his friends, or seeks the excitement of a new experience or perhaps wants no commitment. She feels that quite a few youngsters like the excitement inherent in the partial illegality of an encounter with a prostitute and, for both youngsters and married men, she considers that saunas can provide an addictive environment.

Amongst her customers she counts police officers, judges and one pop star and she has known Englishmen, Italians, French, Spaniards, Portuguese and Arabs but was not prepared to find any distinguishing feature amongst them other than the more exacting nature of the requirements of the Arab. Her 'menu' has never varied. As she says, you can have starters and a main course but not more than that: 'Either you do it my way or you don't do it at all'. She takes good care of herself, eats well, and tries to keep up to date with developments concerning prostitution, particularly anything to do with VD and AIDS. She is not too fussed about AIDS on the basis that she only indulges in protected sexual practices.

Janice draws a clear distinction between street-walkers and girls who operate in clubs, on the one hand, and those who operate from saunas. She claims that in a sauna the customer is limited to half an hour unless he wants to pay a lot more and there is no sadomasochistic equipment available there. That makes for simplicity. On the other hand, street-walkers and girls who operate in clubs are more tempted to indulge in 'kinky' practices. 'Some girls will do anything, the more morbid the requirements, the higher the fee charged.'

On at least two occasions during the interview she said: 'I have standards'. When asked to explain why, she feels that perhaps they are related to her upbringing, which was fairly strict until she left home. She recalls that when she used to go out, her mother and her grandmother used to warn her not to speak to strangers and actually gave her a pepperpot with which she was supposed to spray anybody who tried to molest her.

She was asked specifically whether she had any view on whether the daughter of a whore would, as a matter of course, follow in her mother's footsteps. She said that although she could not speak from personal experience because she came from a reasonably normal family, she had noticed, speaking to colleagues and friends in the profession, that this was so. She had not heard of the Kinsey Reports. When the Kinsey figures concerning the duration of male erections were put to her, she thought perhaps they were even on the high side. 'Especially if a guy likes you, he may get over-excited and too eager and last a lot less than that.'

She has very seldom, if ever, derived any pleasure from contacts with her customers. She has had a regular boyfriend for the past five years and he has known of her activities. The relationship went sour very recently and, when interviewed, she had no boyfriend at all.

She considers that if prostitution were legalized, although she herself would not be personally affected, 'it would help quite a few of the girls I know'. She claims that street-walkers have a very sad life, they look terrible and need improvements in their working conditions. After some thought, she said that she would also approve of brothels. The reason given was not only the improvement in the working conditions of the street-walker but mainly because 'too many people are now at it; housewives when the husbands are out of work, women who have to do it during the day for the sake of their children, or the bored housewife who indulges in lesbian practices'.

She attributes the fact that she became a prostitute to her ability to separate her spiritual from her physical side. Again, she had definite views: 'There are a million-and-one reasons why a woman becomes a prostitute, but only one out of a million-and-one applies to any one woman.'

She has no doubt that Cynthia Payne is right when she claims that the degree of sexual corruption in high places is very marked. She is exceptionally conscious of the fact that she is fulfilling what she calls a 'very useful social function'. There would be many more sexual offences 'if it weren't for us working girls', as well as many more divorces. She went further and claimed from direct personal involvement, that the happiness given by a whore could, in some cases, actually alleviate the unhappiness of a marriage and ensure its continuity.

She believes that legalizing prostitution would make a little difference to VD, but not very much and ascribes this conclusion to the fact that 'youngsters would be unaffected and they are very promiscuous'. She only had to face violence once in her life, when she was with a customer inside a cubicle in a sauna and two armed men entered the premises and robbed the cashier. She could hear what was going on from inside the cubicle. She herself was not troubled.

* * *

Lyn

Lyn claims to be 22 years old, but looks older. There is nothing unusual in her attire save for a shortish skirt which reveals a shapely pair of legs. She walks with an undulating gait which highlights both the strength of her hips and the shortness of her skirt. She has almost no breasts at all, however. Her hair is blond, but dyed. Her natural hair colour is probably light brown. She has grey eyes with a far-away look to them.

She wears cheap plastic earrings, what looks like a gold chain and a Swatch watch. She smokes constantly ('I buy one packet a day but expect to be offered another half') and she admits to being very fond of Bacardi and rum. She denies she is on drugs, although she admits to having tried cannabis.

Lyn's accent is nondescript, certainly low-class, almost Cockney. She herself comes from Suffolk. She says she ran away from home when she was 16 after being raped by her father. She claims she never told her mother nor her two brothers. She has an elder sister, in her forties, who is married and lives in Ireland.

Lyn is a street-walker and operates in the King's Cross area of London, but only during the daytime. After she ran away from home she found herself in London practically alone and met Brian, with whom she lived. During this time, a daughter was born, but Lyn is not absolutely sure who the father is. Apparently Lyn was also sleeping with two of Brian's friends and when Brian found this out, he left her.

She went on the streets but was not prepared to give up her daughter. She had developed a fairly close attachment to a married lady living in the locality, with two children of her own. The present arrangement is that in the morning Lyn leaves her daughter with her friend, who has a council flat, and then walks about the area touting for business. Lyn herself has a bedsitter in the same general locality which she uses for her customers. She works until about 5.30 and then goes to collect her daughter from her friend and returns home; they are always together in the evenings. She claims that she has a few friends and she never goes out on the streets in the evening. She would like to, because she would make more money, but she is not prepared to leave her daughter alone at night.

She is not at all fastidious as to the type of customer. She claims they are all alike to her regardless of age and colour. Her only concern is that they should pay and get out of her flat quickly. She is certainly not shy about the services she offers. She says she will do anything provided she is paid well enough. Her minimum charge is £25.00 but on occasions she has performed for less than that. She can in fact, or so she says, deal with practically any requirement no matter how deviant, except that she has never indulged in any sado-masochistic practices. She prefers customers to use condoms but, as she put it, 'If they pay me well enough, I don't mind the odd occasion without Durex'.

She does not seem to have rationalized either what she is, or why she prefers this kind of life to any other type of work. To her, one man is very much like another and one formed the impression that she did not particularly like men. Asked to speak more about this aspect, she said that it was probably true that she preferred the company of women, but she denied she was a lesbian. She did say, however, that she was very close to her friend who babysat, so to say, for her.

Lyn was heavily made up, quantity appearing to be more

important than either quality or technique. She wore a rather strong, cheap-smelling perfume and had short, unkempt hands; she kept her fingernails very short, almost as though she chewed them, and coloured them with darkish nail polish.

She claimed that operating in the daytime was easier because the police were not so active. She said that it needed a particular kind of mentality for a policeman to go on night duty seeking out prostitutes and spoke of the police with a sneer. She had never been either arrested or cautioned. She had, however, caught gonorrhoea three times but, as she put it, it is easy to cure. She did not seem too concerned about AIDS. 'I'm not a drug addict and I don't do it often enough without a condom to have to worry.'

She claims that there are quite a few girls like her, namely abandoned by their man with one or more children, who would prefer to do something else, but find it convenient to work in this way. She was very reluctant to disclose her income, almost as though she feared that the interview were aimed at getting her to pay tax. Throughout, she was ill at ease, either refusing to answer questions or giving replies accompanied by a little nervous laughter. She said she had never derived any pleasure whatsoever from what she did. All she was interested in was the money. She preferred what she called 'businessmen'. The explanation of her preference was that, firstly, they had less time to spare and therefore were soon out of the flat; secondly, they were less fussy about paying her what she wanted, and as she put it: 'They are more likely to be clean and not smelly.'

She has not been back to her family home but has kept in fairly constant touch with her mother who comes up to London to see her regularly. The mother knows that Lyn is a prostitute, is not happy about it but looks upon it as inevitable. Lyn is convinced that her mother has no idea what caused her to leave the family; nor would she tell her. She is also very close to her sister, who comes to London every now and then to see her with her own family.

She had no overall view of prostitution, had never heard of

the Kinsey Reports, and seemed to have no particular interests in life other than smoking and drinking. When invited to comment about the average duration of intercourse, she said she had never thought about it. Although it did not last long, for her it was much too long anyway and she would do anything she could to shorten it, or even avoid it. She claimed to make fairly frequent use, when allowed to do so, of mechanical aids that expedited orgasm in her customers. When asked whether she would still be doing this sort of work in ten years time, she replied: 'I don't know. I don't want to know' and almost clammed up, with a hurt look on her face. And immediately proceeded to light a cigarette.

She did not think she would ever marry and did not even have a regular boyfriend. She did admit to one or two 'affairs', which for her meant going out in the evening with a man and then having intercourse with him without being paid. She said she would only do that if she really liked the fellow. She stated that that could be nice, because every now and then she met a decent bloke. However, she appeared to be more appreciative of the company and of being treated gently, than of the sexual component of the outing.

Asked whether she was in favour of decriminalization, she expressed the view that there were so many women who to all intents and purposes were prostitutes and got away with it, that it was unfair that the street-walker should be persecuted. Asked whether she was in favour of licensed brothels, she said that she knew that all the street-walkers with whom she mingled, who were not on drugs, would have been only too pleased to work in a brothel. Those who were on drugs were not so keen because they felt that this was a way in which the authorities were controlling their addiction. She herself would not go and work in a brothel simply because, as she put it, 'I don't look upon myself as a full-time prostitute'.

* * *

Carla

Carla claims she is 40, and looks it. Analyzing the timetable of events mentioned during the interview, one would have to say that she must be at least 47. But she is well preserved, slim, black (certainly dyed) hair cut rather short, pale complexion, light blue-green eyes, and long, pointed, well-manicured hands. She wears quite a lot of jewellery, most of it probably being of little value except her rather large diamond ring which, if genuine, must be all of a carat-and-a-half. She drives about in a convertible blue BMW and lives in a small terraced house in Kensington, London.

The visitor is received by her with an open, fairly pleasant smile and shown into the drawing-room which fronts the road. It is discreetly furnished with one or two expensive items. A large French-type window overlooks the road with a rather attractive doll positioned in the centre of it.

Carla approaches customers very gently. As she explains, she usually offers them tea or coffee or drinks. She is not in a hurry since most of her customers come through recommendation so they know what is involved, as she puts it, and have money to spend.

She started out in the profession when she was 30. She had married seven years previously and the marriage had ended in divorce when she found out that her husband, a successful architect, was committing adultery with one of her friends. There were no children. The divorce was, according to her, a fairly friendly affair and she came out of it quite well financially. It was as a result of the divorce settlement that she became the unencumbered owner of the terraced house in Kensington.

She claims that she started out on the streets but soon realized that there was much more money to be made exploiting men's deviant tendencies. She was introduced to a 'governess' who operated in south London and claims that she actually paid her a fairly substantial sum of money to be taught the tricks of the flagellation trade. She cannot remember when she last had intercourse with a customer. She indulges in no real sexual practice other than masturbating those customers who are insistent that she should. Apart from that, the facilities she offers are extensive, but confined to sado-masochistic practices.

The purpose of her entertaining the client in her drawing-room is really to try and understand whether he has any particular requirement that should be catered for and to fix a fee which is proportionate to the oddity or level of deviancy required. The fee is a minimum of £100.00 for what she terms 'simple birching'. She admits to having charged as much as £500.00 per session.

Once the fee is agreed upon and paid, the client is taken upstairs to a bedroom which has been set aside for the purpose. It is not her own bedroom: that is at the other end of the corridor with its self-contained dressing-room and bathroom areas. Her 'operating room' is quite a comfortable one with a double bed and with a small array of implements on show. She claims she has others which she can bring out as required but was not too keen to display all her equipment. She admits to having highly respected members of the community as customers. She talks quite casually, but convincingly, about doctors, architects, pop stars, QCs and Judges.

She herself is a Londoner but has no particular accent. She seems quite well educated. She claims to have a university degree but demurred from offering details about her academic qualifications. Asked whether she knew of the Kinsey Reports, she claimed that she had read both of them. Asked whether she was in agreement with them, she said that a lot of the things mentioned were common knowledge anyhow in the trade; her own experience was that the number of men who preferred flagellation to any other kind of 'sexual' practice was quite high. The only other comment was that she thought that there were many more homosexual men around than people realized. Whether this was due to a falling off in trade or a firmly-held belief, was not too easy to ascertain.

Carla lives alone. She admitted to being on intimate terms with a married woman of fairly high social status who came to visit her about twice a week. She acknowledged that this was a lesbian relationship but, as she put it, 'I don't charge for it, I wouldn't dream of charging for it'. She did admit to receiving presents regularly from her lady friend, but these were reciprocated. However, her friend had a family and lived with her husband; the relationship, therefore, had to be maintained in secret.

She was not concerned one way or the other about whether the activities of prostitutes should be decriminalized or not. She felt that it would not affect what she was doing one way or the other. She was not in favour of brothels but could not give a valid reason why.

Asked whether her first name could be connected to a continental origin, she laughed and explained that it was not her real name. It was the name that she used for her customers and she had chosen it simply because she was very fond of the works of TV scriptwriter Carla Lane.

The great majority of her customers were British. She had once had a 'well off' Spaniard as a customer over a period of two years but then he suddenly stopped coming. 'He probably went back home'. She said she was not aware of any differences between her customers, in terms of needs and responses based purely on nationality. However, she would not work with coloured people of any description. She was not willing to explain why. Asked whether she felt that she was behaving cruelly in what she did, she replied: 'Somebody's got to do it and they enjoy it'.

She was unwilling to give any details whatsoever about her family background or her childhood. She never took drugs and had given up smoking a few years ago purely because she was concerned about her health. Her principal hobbies, apart from holidaying in the south of France, were stated to be television and horse-riding. She did not think she would remarry although she claimed that she had no particular liking or dislike for her customers. She was only doing a job which made her a lot of money.

Asked how much she made in a year, she refused to answer

in detail, except to say that it was in excess of £90,000. When asked whether she paid tax on her earnings, she smiled and refused to say anymore. She had previously stated that she seldom took payment in any form other than cash. Only for one or two of her longer-standing clients would she take a cheque, provided it was not for too large an amount.

* * *

Joan

Joan was born in south London in 1975; she is still living in the area and operates there walking the streets.

When she was about 12, her mother and father split up after bitter quarrelling, mainly provoked by her father's drunkenness. Shortly after that, her mother moved in with another man and took Joan with her. There were no other children. She had no sexual problems as far as her stepfather was concerned. She was not molested by him, he did not seem to care for her very much; in any event, the second relationship established by her mother was no happier than the first and there was constant quarrelling.

She claims that she never knew what a family really is, nor a proper home. Her school performance was uneven and she left as soon as she could at the age of 16. In effect, her school leaving coincided with her abortion. She had been having sexual relations since she was about 15, her first one occurring with a boy of 18 while she was still at school. She found herself completely alone after the abortion and had no-one to turn to. Both her grandparents were dead, and her mother had her own problems with her stepfather. As she puts it, 'I slid into prostitution'.

She claims that she found it very easy to approach mainly middle-aged men in the shopping centres of south London. She first tried out a gentle smile and then asked the time, testing the man's reaction. She claims she always did it discreetly and never had any difficulty whatsoever in ascertaining whether the man was interested. Even now, she operates roughly along the same lines, except that she works longer hours than when she first started and finds it a lot less worrying to go out in the evenings and allow herself to be 'picked up'.

At present, she is living with a coloured man aged 25. She is not even sure where he comes from, she believes somewhere in the West Indies; he, as she puts it, looks after her. Sometimes they go out together and sometimes she goes out on her own. The relationship has been going on for six months and it was he who introduced her to drugs. She claims that she is very fond of him and that they sometimes have sexual relations together. She is not sure whether he is fond of her but 'he looks after me like a brother'.

Her drug-taking has steadily increased and she is now fairly heavily addicted. She has never been arrested, but was cautioned once. She has not suffered from any VD. Despite her fairly youthful age, she looks about 25. She has an unkempt appearance and her speech is hesitant. Her hands are short and her fingernails practically non-existent, chewed as far back as the quicks.

She claims that she will go with anybody and do practically anything if paid sufficiently well. She is very keen to make the point that she has never had unprotected sexual relations after her abortion. Even with her 'boyfriend', as she calls him, condoms are used. She will, however, not have anal intercourse with clients. Asked whether she did with her boyfriend, she did not answer. She looks tired and dresses unevenly in short skirt, high heels, and a brightly-coloured blouse. She wears a lot of make-up, heavily and carelessly applied; it is not pleasant. Dangling imitation coral earrings hug her neck, as does her longish blonde hair.

Asked whether she had ever tried to work at a steady job rather than at being a prostitute, she burst out laughing claiming that for a girl of her age, there is not much work available at the moment. And, in any event, she would not be sufficiently well paid. She appears to have no real appreciation of what she is doing and why. Physically well developed, solid breasts, straight legs, thinnish thighs, if well looked after and properly dressed, she might even be called attractive. As it is, there is something slightly repulsive about her.

She has no view about the men with whom she goes. She is only interested in getting paid and does not assess them either in terms of age or social class. As she puts it, 'I tell them what I charge, once they've told me what they want; and that's it. I try to get it over quickly'.

She has never been on holiday, has always lived in the same general area of London. She smokes, but not too much as she claims. She enjoys Bacardi and rum, but above all watches a lot of television during the daytime. Her pimp provides her with a fair quantity of TV films on video. She is not interested in pornographic films at all and claims to have a partiality for musicals and romantic comedies.

Communication with Joan was not easy. Apart from the poor family background and the abortion, her life, not much of which she had yet lived given her age, seemed to be fairly uneventful. In addition. she seemed to find it difficult to concentrate on the questions that were put. The only spark of enthusiasm showed up in her eyes when she was discussing how much she loved watching television.

One could not in any sense consider her mentally retarded or deficient. Her lack of education was apparent, but once she had focused on an issue, she was capable of providing a clear-cut answer. Her accent was inevitably low class but no different from the ones adopted in the TV series 'Eastenders'. Perhaps because of her age, she was the least interesting and the most difficult to interview.

*　*　*

Jenny

Jenny (not her real name) is Asian. She claims to be 40 but looks very much older. She dresses badly, wearing youthful clothes in an attempt to overcome the difficulties imposed by her almost wrinkled appearance. Her hair is dyed reddish brown, she is overweight. Her best feature appears to be her breasts.

Jenny was born in Birmingham of Asian parents and very nearly got a degree in Social Sciences. Her parents were insistent that she should marry one of three sons of a family of friends of long standing. Jenny was very reluctant to do so but her parents were so insistent that she finally gave in and got married, as she said, rather late, at 21. Rather late by Asian standards.

The marriage was a failure. It soon emerged that the husband had a vicious temperament, held orthodox beliefs and objected to anything which even remotely smacked of emancipation. As she puts it, he tried to live the life of an Asian, in Birmingham, and that was clearly impossible. She had no independence whatsoever. She could not go out on her own and whenever she did something which she herself considered quite normal when compared to young girls of her age, but which did not fit in to the Asian pattern of life, she was beaten up. She says that he was a nasty man and after two years of such life she went to a solicitor to seek a divorce. As soon as her 'family' got to know about this, they were up in arms and considerable pressure was put upon her to drop the divorce proceedings. Meanwhile, the beatings continued.

She really felt she could not cope and ran away from home. She came to London and went to live with a girl whom she had met at university. Whilst in London, she became friendly with a white man and moved in with him. That relationship was not to last either. After three months, he disappeared. The flat in which she was living was repossessed since he had not been paying rent on it and she found herself alone and on the streets.

Not knowing what to do, she went back to Birmingham and was offered hospitality by an Asian family who knew her. She was hoping that her return would not be known but, after a while, it was clear that her husband knew where she was. He started coming round, insisting that she went back to live with him. All this time, she had no money of her own and was living off firstly her university friend and secondly the man who left her and finally her Birmingham friends. She found that she could not continue like that and started looking for a job.

This proved very difficult since she had no references, no previous experience and all she could claim was that she had started taking a degree in Social Sciences but had not completed the course. She was out alone one evening walking the streets when she was accosted by a man driving, what she thought was an expensive car. He invited her in. As she puts it, 'without even realizing what I was doing, I accepted the invitation'. They drove around for a while and it soon became obvious that the man had mistaken her for a prostitute. She decided that she had nothing to lose and, as she put it 'would give it a try'.

She did and thus started her life of prostitution. She continued to live with her friends but it soon became apparent that they knew what she was up to and she was asked to leave. She found a bedsitter in one of the areas of Birmingham which were later to become very well known for the extent of prostitution activities being carried out there. She has lived there ever since.

Jenny claims that prostitution was OK when she was young. She soon got used to the life and even though she was arrested once and caught several types of VD (non-specific urethritis, gonorrhoea and herpes), they were never sufficiently serious set-backs to deter her from continuing in the business. Gradually, she became much more conscious of the need to have protected intercourse and for a while, that is to say, until she was about 30, she could afford to be fairly selective in what she did. Gradually, however, the kind of life she was leading began to take its toll. She claims that in her younger days she could have as many as 10 or even sometimes 15 encounters per night. Over the past couple of years or so, the number has decreased dramatically and now she is only too pleased if she manages two clients per day.

As she says, there are many more girls on the job these days and some of them come to it very young indeed. It is very difficult for her to compete, especially now that she is no longer so attractive. She claims that, when she was young, her dark features made her more interesting but having put on weight and having grown perhaps not old, but having aged prematurely, she is no longer quite so attractive as she was. She has to settle for smaller sums of money (she was not prepared to say what she charged) and is now prepared to do practically anything that is asked of her in order to live.

She had had a protector since shortly after she started operating from her own bedsitter. He's an Asian, too. They do not have sexual relations: she feels nothing for him but looks upon him as a friend. He in turn tries to get her some business but she feels that he is more interested in the younger girls. In the last 10 years, she has been cautioned twice and arrested three times. She herself is now forced to sit in the partially-illuminated window of her ground floor bedsit, trying to appear as enticing as possible.

From the moment she started a life of prostitution, she has had no men friends whatsoever. She formed a lesbian relationship with another Asian prostitute operating in the same area and that is continuing. They go out from time to time together and exchange experiences and reminiscences. Her friend is five years younger than she is but has retained a certain amount of her original freshness. As Jenny put it, 'when I am out with her sometimes they mistake me for her mother'. She is very philosophical about her life. She feels that her Asian background is ultimately to blame and that her family must bear some of the responsibility. Although her family still live in Birmingham, they are still not on speaking terms.

She tried to rationalize the attitude of society towards prostitutes. She has no particular view as to whether she is performing a useful service but she is angry that greater recognition is not given to prostitutes in terms of working conditions and pensions. Asked whether she had heard of the Kinsey Reports, she replied that she had although she had not read them, and had no incentive to read them for, as she claimed, there are too many people who talk about prostitution and have no real knowledge of 'what is involved'. She claims that even some of the leaders of prostitutes' associations like the English Collective of Prostitutes are not really prostitutes themselves and therefore cannot understand 'what is involved'.

Asked whether she would be in favour of the system suggested recently by the Birmingham City Council of tolerance areas similar to the Dutch model, she says that it would not really matter and it would not solve any problem. She was not quite sure whether she would feel happier operating from such areas or from her own bedsitter. She thinks she is just as likely to be assaulted by a psychopath in her own bedsitter as she would be in a controlled zone.

Asked whether she was in favour of the legalization of brothels, she said that it was too late for her to have any interest whatsoever in such a development. She would not go and work in one, even if she were asked (but she doubted that that would be so, because of her age). On balance, having thought about it, she added that it would be good for the younger girls, since they would have greater protection both from violence and from disease. Asked whether legalized brothels would reduce if not eliminate the number of pimps operating in any particular area, she thought that that would certainly be so and that it would be a good idea to give them a try. She had long become accustomed to the concept of sharing her earnings with her protector. As she said 'Brothels would make no difference to my life, but I am not against them'.

She does not drink and smokes about a packet of cigarettes a day. She has never gone to India, no longer speaks the language of her parents although she understands it, has a very marked Birmingham accent which contrasts oddly with her colour, but speaks quietly, sensibly and correctly. She claims that she finds it difficult to concentrate on watching television but enjoys reading a good book. Asked what sort of books interested her, she said that her tastes were quite extensive but she avoided reading anything to do with prostitution.

She expressed no preference whatsoever for one type of man over another. On the whole, she preferred white men as clients, because they were less exacting and because with them 'it was all over quickly'. She did not mind going with Asians or West Indians: in fact, she gave the impression that as things stood at the moment, she did not really care with whom she went or what she did; she was desperate to survive. She claimed that the recession was also affecting the business of prostitutes generally. Primarily, her business had fallen because, in a broad sense, she had become less attractive to men. But even the younger girls were making less money than previously.

She seemed bitter above all at her prospects as she was getting older. She felt that the State was letting prostitutes down. As she put it, 'I may be welcome in certain places as a lesbian but not as a prostitute; what's the difference?' Recently, she had started suffering from cystitis. She was not sure whether this was due to the life she had led or other factors which she could not or would not identify.

Asked whether she considered that she was at risk from violent men, psychopaths etc., she said that she never thought of that particular aspect of her life. She explained it away on the basis that she did not think of the possibility of having an accident when she drove in a car. She herself did not possess a car but her lesbian friend did. As she put it: 'What would I need a car for? I sit by my window and that's the way I pick up customers'. There was some sadness about the way in which she spoke; but above all, about her appearance.

Chapter Three

A short history of prostitution

This chapter offers a simple outline of the history of prostitution, in order to make three essential points. The first is that it was not always the case that a prostitute was considered to be part of the dregs of society. Secondly, whereas it might be possible to eliminate prostitution in a very small town or village where everybody knows everybody else and is, therefore, inevitably subject to certain strict social, if not economic sanctions, nowadays, given the largely urban structure of Western society, it is virtually impossible to get rid of the prostitute. Thirdly, contrary to what a number of psychologists and sociologists have maintained, prostitution has nothing whatsoever to do with sexual permissiveness. (Readers who are interested in its historical development are referred to Dr Fernando Henriques' study *Prostitution and Society*, Macgibbon & Kee, London, 1962.)

Our earliest records on prostitution go back around three thousand years to the times of the Pharoahs and the ancient Babylonians. Particularly in ancient Babylonia, as Herodotus recalls, a prostitute could be, and quite often was, a kind of priestess who had to offer her services only nominally for money (sometimes a silver coin). The so-called 'Myletta' rite (Myletta was the Babylonian Venus) required every female, at some time or other in her life, to sit in the temple of the local goddess and accept intercourse from the first stranger who tossed her a coin, as a form of worship of the goddess. The money could not be refused and, after intercourse, the women went back home and, possibly, lived chastely ever after. Similar odd (to modern eyes) rites prevailed in other parts of the Middle East, in India and in West Africa.

There was, in those days, a correlation between religion and prostitution which clearly no longer exists today. It had become tenuous by the time our best records start in classical Greece (around 1500 BC). The Greeks had a very high regard for certain kinds of prostitutes, what one might call the most exclusive, upper-class, learned prostitute of the kind that was to re-emerge in Renaissance Italy, or in Japan with the geisha who can play music, recite poetry, etc. This is understandable because it was said that Aphrodite, the goddess of love, extended her protection to those women who proffered sexual services coupled with aesthetic and artistic appreciation and literary knowledge.

To what extent Aphrodite may have similarly protected the cheaper kind of prostitute who worked in brothels must be a matter of conjecture. But we know that the man who did most to codify the laws of Greece, Solon, is also claimed to have been the founder of a system of brothels in Athens. The Greeks quite clearly made a distinction between what they called the 'hetaira' or upper-class prostitute, in the same way as present-day Japanese do with their 'geisha'; and the lower-class or 'common' prostitute, who was available to allcomers for a very small sum.

But then, the Greeks were exceptionally tolerant in sexual matters, as is demonstrated in their approach to homosexuality, which was not a cause for contempt but rather appreciation. For the Greeks, it was almost as if the perfect human being were the one who partook of both the male and the female and was bi-sexual in every respect.

Solon entertained no doubt that certain needs had to be catered for and he established State brothels staffed by a particular low-class prostitute, whose services were, initially, bought in by the State for the benefit of its citizens. As Dr Henriques has observed, these first Greek prostitutes were in a sense civil servants, for they had no say as to whom they should offer themselves and whatever they earned had to be paid over to the State. So, even in Greece, the State profited from the services of prostitutes.

With their great practical sense, the Romans went on to capitalize on prostitution's profit-making possibilities. It has to be said that what the Romans lacked in aesthetic sense and romantic appreciation for woman, they easily made up for by their ability to organize. The historian, Livy, records that as early as half a century before the birth of Christ, on the occasion of certain festivities, the Sabine youths forcibly abducted certain harlots.

The Sabines themselves were perhaps not unmindful of the fact that the foundation of Rome was based in essence on the rape committed by the Romans on the nearby Sabine women. Whilst the Romans were exceptionally concerned for the wellbeing of the family as a social, emotional and political unit, they realized from an early date that a structured environment for male sexuality had to be provided. No doubt this realization was reinforced by the fact that, as their armies spread through the then known world, they needed women to cater to the needs of the soldiers.

The Romans accepted that youngsters had to find an outlet for what filled their bodies and gain experience whilst they were young, and before they got married. In other words, their thinking proceeded along the lines that it was better for young men to visit a brothel than to go around pursuing other men's wives. Brothels were accordingly encouraged, but the Roman 'entered them with covered head and face concealed in his cloak'.

Against this background, it is hardly surprising that, from a very early date, the Romans endeavoured to control prostitutes by evolving a system of registration and licensing. What they licensed effectively were the lower-class prostitutes, in the main consisting of slaves. The better class, like dancers and musicians, although they might have been treated as prostitutes for all intents and purposes, were not required to register. Furthermore, as already noted, the Romans also accepted that prostitutes should be allowed, if not encouraged, to follow the army on its campaigns, a practice very much in vogue during the wars of the fifteenth and sixteenth centuries. In other words, they treated prostitution as a service.

The Romans, of course, were not the only ones in antiquity to take this view. Although Confucius had objected to prostitution, the Chinese seemed to have had little compunction about it, if Marco Polo is to be believed. In his book *Il Milione* he describes the prostitutes who occupied the streets of Hangchow.

The Romans maintained the same attitude when they came over to England and left their mark. It is a matter of record that, for centuries, prostitutes operated in many brothels adjacent to the River Tyburn. Henry II himself, at the beginning of the twelfth century, dealt with the legalization of the activities of prostitutes operating in English brothels, mainly in Southwark.

However, the spread of Christianity through Europe and Asia does seem to have brought about a significant reaction. The first recorded opposition by Christians to prostitution goes back to the year 350 A.D. But I have to say that this opposition was doomed to failure, as it always has been throughout the history of mankind; whatever the taboos on prostitution and however they were enforced, the system does not seem to have worked very well because we find in 532 A.D. that Theodora, who was a nude dancer as well as a prostitute and essentially a nymphomaniac, managed to climb the social ladder of the times by marrying the Emperor Constantine and making herself Empress of Byzantium. She then campaigned against prostitutes, unmindful perhaps of Christ's attitude to Mary Magdalen. Justinian, responsible for the codification of much law, also dealt with prostitution, making it theoretically punishable by death.

The fathers of the Christian Church condemned prostitution but at the same time had to acknowledge its usefulness. St Augustine of Hippo, one of the first Christian writers to look at prostitutes with an objective eye (but then, before being a great saint, he had been an extravagant sinner) says: 'Suppress prostitution, and capricious lusts will overthrow society', or perhaps more correctly: '(*De Ordine*, II, 12) 'If you abolish courtesans, everything will be upset.'

St Thomas Aquinas, who, as records go, was only a saint and had never been a sinner in the Augustinian sense, wrote in the same vein: 'Prostitution in the towns is like the cesspool in the palace: take away the cesspool and the palace will become an unclean and evil-smelling place.' These statements are harsh, but is it not conceivable that there is more than a grain of truth in them even today? In any event, throughout the Middle Ages, prostitutes continued to thrive.

At the time of the Renaissance, which heralded a period of unsurpassed activity in the sciences, arts and literature, we find a more refined prostitute, a woman who sold her body at the same time as she used her mind. Clearly, the Italian courtesans of the Renaissance were no mere harlots. They displayed wit and style and conversational skills and were received either at Court or in the house of the nobility as honoured guests. Indeed, some of them followed the Court around. It was almost as if, coincidentally, they also made themselves available for sexual pleasure. However, it would appear that the Renaissance ladies lacked one of the essential characters of the prostitute, namely they were not indiscriminate in their choice of sexual partners. True, they sold their bodies for money or money's worth, but were highly selective; that was probably the ennobling feature of these 'cortegiane'. It was much the same for the Venetian prostitutes of the sixteenth and seventeenth centuries.

Rome and Venice were particularly tolerant towards prostitutes, whether high or low class. For example, it is said that a Roman prostitute called Imperia was the first woman of her ilk to whom the term 'courtesan' was applied. She was so well known and liked by both the aristocracy and the humbler folk that when she died she was buried in the church of St Gregory on Mount Celio and the following inscription appeared on her tomb:

Imperia, cortesana Romana, quae digna tanto nomine
('Imperia, a Roman courtesan, well worthy of that title')

Another Roman prostitute, Faustina, was immortalized when Michelangelo wrote a verse epitaph for her: in it, he praised her beauty but thought she had not put it to good use.

Thus, from the onset of Christianity to about the seventeenth century, it can be said generally that throughout the period, prostitutes were alternately accepted and rejected. With the arrival of Luther, prostitutes once again came under attack. Luther himself launched the campaign against prostitutes in his 'Address to the German Nobility' of 1520 when he argued that just as villages managed to exist without houses of prostitution, so should the cities. Gradually, brothels were closed down throughout Germany (with some limited exceptions) and prostitutes, who were already liable to being whipped and imprisoned, found themselves also condemned to the pillory. Calvin himself was totally against any kind of sexual irregularity. Indeed, in 1556 he went so far as to propose that adultery should carry the death penalty, though it would appear that the city fathers in Geneva were not prepared to go quite so far. It was a thankless task. For a long time, the armies of the fifteenth and sixteenth centuries were allowed to take along women who, in addition to providing sex, cooked and laundered: a measure aimed both at satisfying the soldiers and at avoiding problems with the local populations through which the armies moved.

This see-saw approach to prostitutes is, it seems, one of the features of the human condition. Depending on the society and the religious beliefs prevailing at the time, a prostitute was either welcomed or shunned. This is exactly what we are doing in the 1990s, but we do not appear to have learned very much from history.

In 1469 Louis XI of France actually approved a brothel in

Montpellier; on the other hand, just over two hundred years later in 1687, Louis XIV of France tried unsuccessfully to get rid of harlots but did not make very much progress. And so, through a series of alternating luck and luckless phases (for the prostitute), we come to the nineteenth century. In 1843 in Paris we find the first compulsory registration of prostitutes, whereas at the same time across the border, in Prussia, there was considerable objection to them; so much so that, in 1846, those campaigning for reform managed to close all brothels in that particular country.

Progress towards abolition was also being made in England where the number of prostitutes had increased quite dramatically. This is understandable, because the Industrial Revolution had brought with it the kind of urbanization and exploitation which were ideal conditions for prostitutes. As G.M.Trevelyan puts it (*English Social History*, London, Pelican Books, 1967): 'The great army of prostitutes, which had existed in all ages, had swelled its ranks with the increase of wealth and population', since the growing respectability of the well-to-do classes made it more difficult to keep mistresses, who on the other hand had played such a major role in the previous century. The demand was thus increased for the prostitute who could be visited in secret, endorsing the double-edged, not to say hypocritical attitude towards her which marked the Victorian era and which is so well highlighted in Trollope's *The Vicar of Bullhampton*.

Trollope was not the only one to use an idea popular amongst reformers, namely that the prostitute was a victim of man's natural lusts. On the other hand, it should be said that whilst some looked upon her destitution pitifully, others (like a group of clergymen who wrote to *The Times* in 1858) objected violently to the 80,000 or so prostitutes who operated in London at the time '... with a disregard of public decency and to an extent tolerated in no other capital city of the civilized world'.

As usual, religious fervour and social reform with respect to prostitutes found its justification in considerations of public

health. Both in 1832 and in 1848, there were outbreaks of
cholera which were due to the inadequate sewage systems and
to the insanitary conditions in which people lived. The first
Public Health Act dates from 1848. The first Contagious
Diseases Act dates from 1846.

It is interesting to note, however, that, almost simulta-
neously, British society was also concerning itself with the state
of the institution of marriage and its possible dissolution. In
1850 a Royal Commission had been appointed to consider
matrimonial offences; it reported in 1853 and in 1857 the
Matrimonial Causes Act was passed. Since it was 'expedient to
amend the law relating to divorce', divorce law was reformed
substantially along the lines which lasted well over a century,
that is to say, until the Divorce Reform Act of 1969.

One of the features of the 1857 legislation was the
establishment of fault or guilt as the basis of divorce. It is
noteworthy that legislation liberalizing divorce, that is to say,
giving effect to the individual's freedom of choice and self-
determination which was and is part of the Protestant/
Calvinist tradition, was brought into being at the same time as
discriminatory legislation was passed equating some individuals
– prostitutes – with criminals. This attitude persisted. As late as
1871 a Royal Commission declared: 'We may at once dispose
of (any recommendation) founded on the principle of putting
both parties to the sin of fornication on the same footing by
the obvious but not less conclusive reply that there is no
comparison to be made between prostitutes, and men who
consort with them. With the one sex the offence is committed
as a matter of gain; with the other it is an irregular indulgence
of a natural impulse.'

Contagious diseases legislation continued to be passed,
although some of it was suspended as a result of the vigorous
anti-prostitute campaign by Josephine Elizabeth Butler, – the
first abolitionist legislation being passed in the United
Kingdom in 1886. Here it is worth remembering that
whereas in previous ages society had attempted to control the
activities of prostitutes if only geographically, in the second

half of the nineteenth century throughout the Western world the emphasis shifted from control to eradication. The successes of Josephine Butler were followed by abolitionist legislation in Norway in 1890, Switzerland in 1897 and Denmark in 1901.

But, as history continues to show us, it is easier to decree that the activities of prostitution are illegal than to cause them to disappear. It will come as no surprise, therefore, that at the turn of the century it is estimated that there were at least 60,000 prostitutes in London and the same number in Paris, 50,000 in Berlin, 30,000 in New York and 25,000 in Vienna. According to Tolstoy (*Resurrection*) the life of the Russian prostitute Katusha Maslova last century was 'led by hundreds of thousands of women'.

These figures are obviously estimates and I am bound to say that any such estimate of prostitute numbers is almost certainly meaningless. The figures that were obtained in the nineteenth century, as in the 1990s*, are derived from records kept by the police and the medical profession. That is to say, they identify those prostitutes who either have had problems with the law or who have themselves become infected. But for every prostitute who has a problem with the police, one would venture to suggest there are ten or more who manage to avoid trouble with the law. Similarly, (as my own case-studies suggest but one cannot be specific or certain about this aspect of the matter either), for every prostitute who is infected by disease, there must be at least another one who is not.

*   *   *

There is still the position of prostitutes in the twentieth century to consider. However, before doing so, I would like to pause for a moment and make the point (again) that it is only in more recent times that we have looked upon

---

* In 1993 prosecutions in England and Wales for brothel keeping totalled 96 and for prostitution/soliciting (females) 7904. Police cautions in the same period were 28 and 3616 respectively.

prostitutes as contemptible creatures. We have already considered the standing of the religious prostitutes of Babylonia and the courtesans of the Italian Renaissance. But both the Old and the New Testament have to be recalled in context to show how, throughout history, the prostitute has received varied degrees of recognition.

For some, it may perhaps not be very palatable to be reminded that David was descended from Rahab, a prostitute. But Ezekiel (23, 2-10) mentions two very sensual creatures, Aholah and Aholibah. Joshua (2 and 6) records how Rahab, a prostitute, was saved when Jericho was destroyed. As Stephen Charnock (in his *Mercy for the Chief of Sinners*) has observed: 'God often makes the chiefest sinner object of his choicest mercy. The stock whereof Christ came seems to suggest this; God might have ensured that the stock, from which Christ descended according to the flesh, was kept pure and free from being tainted with any notorious crimes: but even among Christ's forebears we find sins of a crimson dye.'

There are no women listed in Christ's genealogy but some of those in Scripture, who are noted for their looseness, are: Tamar, who played the harlot with Juda, her father-in-law; Rahab, the harlot of Jericho; Ruth, a gentile Moabitess, the root of whose generation was Lot's son, by incest with his own daughter; Bathsheba, David's adulteress. He chose these repenting sinners out of whose loins Christ was to come, 'that the greatest sinners might not be afraid to come to him'. And one may add to that, St Mary the Egyptian, a sinner who after her conversion lived a straight life of 47 years in the desert; and Mary of Magdala, who according to John Bunyan, 'was a loose and wanton creature', who would 'frequent the house of sports and the company of the vilest men for lust'. It is true that Tamar merely acted the part of a courtesan (when Juda saw her, he thought her to be an harlot because 'she had covered her face' – Genesis 38, 13); but that merely shows woman's versatility in matters sexual.

Nor should the biblical references be taken as marks of approval. Quite clearly, Solomon's woman was a danger. As

Proverbs puts it (Chapter 7): 'She has cast down many
wounded, yes, many strong men have been slain by her. Her
house is the way to hell going down to the chambers of death.'
Even Dante Alighieri, who was most respectful of women,
mentions a whore, Taide, in his *Inferno* (Canto XVIII). The
literary references, taken up by music composers, are just as
important. Dumas's celebrated *Dame aux Camelias* is one of the
best known novels and, apart from making Sara Bernhardt
famous, was ennobled by Verdi in *La Traviata*. Whilst
Rossetti's *Jenni* received no further ennoblement apart from
his verses, Manon Lescaut excited both Puccini and Massenet,
Moll Flanders inspired Defoe, a Japanese geisha girl is the
protagonist of Madame Butterfly, Delilah helped Saint Saens
along, as did Salome Strauss. Other female free spirits can be
found in Puccini's *Boheme* (Musetta), Verdi's *Rigoletto*
(Maddalena) and Ravel's *L'Heure Espagnole* (Conception). In
Mascagni's *Iris*, one of the characters is the keeper of a brothel.
Additional research will no doubt produce many more
examples.

But the biblical, evangelical, literary and musical references
seemed inadequate, or insufficient when we entered the
twentieth century for, in 1927, the German abolitionists
succeeded in having brothels closed in that country (echoes of
Luther and Calvin there, surely!) and, if we consider Western
Europe, the matter remained more or less fluid thereafter. By
this is meant that in most countries of Catholic or
Mediterranean tradition, brothels existed and were either
tolerated or treated as lawful and were controlled, or the
problem was ignored and prostitutes were, metaphorically,
swept under the carpet.

Soon after the Second World War, however, there was a
flurry of activity. It started in France, where Madame Marthe
Richard succeeded early in 1946 in having brothels closed
throughout the country. The State registration system was
ended and the so-called 'houses of tolerance' were closed,
whilst a little later in 1946 a card-index system was established
for contact tracing and the treatment of venereal disease. In

1948, further legislation tightened up the law and, whilst it was inspired by the desire to examine prostitutes on a more regular basis, it could be said to have been, in a strange sense, a return to the old system of registration.

Five years after her brilliant campaign to abolish brothels, however, Marthe Richard wrote her book *L'Appel des Sexes*. In it she acknowledged that she had been wrong, she accepted that brothels were necessary and pleaded that one should go back to the old system or, at least, that brothels should be allowed in the neighbourhood of army camps.

A courageous woman, Marthe Richard. If the reader is wondering what caused her to change her mind, then he/she should be told that it was the accelerating and extravagant spread of venereal disease after the 'maisons de tolerance' were closed that prompted the French national heroine of World Wars I and II to change her mind. Her crusading spirit, however, had been contagious. In Italy, for instance, a member of the Senate, Angelina Merlin, achieved equal success in trying to force the closing of brothels, although it should be recorded that it took some time to bring the law into full effect and the Italian brothels were not officially eliminated until 1958. (Law No. 95, 20 February 1958.) According to *Time* magazine (12.4.63) the number of reported cases of VD in Italy jumped from 1679 in 1958 to 16,395 in 1962, thus bearing out the worst fears of Mme Richard.

In the United States, houses of prostitution are illegal in most States but the activities of prostitutes are not pursued by the law unless minors are involved or a public decency offence occurs. (See Chapter 9.) The interesting thing about the situation in the United States is that state and inter-state legislation dating from the early years of the twentieth century seemed to be based on the concept that prostitutes were slaves and, as such, were moved from one State to the other. As will be seen, this view relies on a total misconception of the reasons why women turn to prostitution and in any event, in the United States, as in the UK, the result has been to drive prostitutes underground.

It is difficult to decide what moral weight can be attached to any statement made by the French writer, Baudelaire (the author, amongst others, of *Les Fleurs du Mal*) but he called prostitution 'the unavoidable vice'. On the basis that it occurs in every kind of society and age, as we have seen, I am rather inclined to believe that the description has considerable merit. At the beginning of this century it was thought that prostitutes would exist mainly in societies where early marriage was difficult and intercourse outside it socially disapproved. It was argued, therefore, that the moment we ceased to repress intimacies outside marriage, prostitutes would gradually disappear. This is a wholly erroneous and narrow approach which is typical of the Anglo-Saxon world. It was first propounded by Havelock Ellis in Volume 2 of his *Studies on the Psychology of Sex* (Heinemann, London, 1906) and it reflects what one may term the Protestant ethic regarding prostitution.

This is quite different from what could be called the continental Catholic view and not merely because, as has already been observed, in traditional Catholic countries brothels have always existed and have been tolerated, where they were not considered legal. I believe that there is something much more fundamental which accounts for the two very conflicting approaches: fundamentally, it is a totally different view of sexuality which, in turn, is a consequence of climate and diet.

Nevertheless, if we take the Western world as a whole, it is a fact that we have reached the point where we do not really know what to do about prostitutes. There is no obvious consensus emerging. As is shown in Chapter 10, which considers the response to prostitution in countries other than the UK, Holland and Germany have gone one way, while Britain and the USA have followed a different course – at least in the sense that officially we do not approve of prostitutes; whereas the Mediterranean countries have not really changed their attitude very much at all.

Chapter Four

The theoretical
causes of prostitution

According to Havelock Ellis, the principal causes of prostitution were detailed in his study published in 1906. These are: (1) economic necessity; (2) biological predisposition; (3) moral advantages; (4) 'civilizational' value. I would now like to set out my own views on each of these factors and attempt to bring the 1990s' reader fully up to date.

1. ECONOMIC NECESSITY

Ellis claimed that most prostitutes came from the lower ranks, such as factory girls, domestic servants, shop girls and waitresses. Certainly, as far as England in the eighteenth and nineteenth centuries was concerned, this was perfectly true. W. Acton, in his book *Prostitution* published in 1870, said that prostitution is 'a transitory stage through which an untold number of British women are ever on their passage' and this seemed to be the common practice not only for English but also for other European women.

That prostitution is an industry of sorts, cannot be denied, but the true value to be attached to economic necessity (as distinct from the profit motive) as a cause for prostitution has changed over the years. Modern theory attaches very little significance to it as a primary cause of prostitution.

2. BIOLOGICAL FACTORS IN PROSTITUTES

These were hotly advocated by the Italian school. Both Lombroso and Ferrero equated (in psychological and anatomical terms) the criminal and the prostitute. According to them, prostitution is only the feminine side of criminality (*La Donna Delinquente*, 1893).

There is certainly a biological component for what a prostitute does, but it is not necessarily a sexual component. Again, some modern studies point to the fact that most prostitutes have no great sexual drive and are probably either frigid or lesbians, or both. To the extent, however, that it is accepted that there exists a biological factor, it is quite clear that the behaviour of prostitutes, like that of criminals, can in fact be treated as a form of heredity affected by the environment.

The school of thought according to which there is a degenerative view of prostitution is contested by Morasso in *Archivio di Psichiatria* (composed in 1896) where he refers to the upper-class prostitutes ('Prostitute di Alto Bordo'), and claims that in them the signs of physical or moral degeneration are no more common than in ordinary women. Prostitutes are those women who have realized that, because of their physical attributes, they can make a success in life solely on the basis of providing sexual gratification. Morasso cannot, however, contradict entirely Lombroso's theory that there are some young girls for whom modesty has no existence and who experience no emotion in showing themselves undressed or abandoning themselves to any chance individual whom they might see or who sacrifice their virginity at the oddest opportunity; nevertheless, his comments have a modern ring about them.

Although denigrated for decades, the views of Lombroso could very well be proved much more correct than the 'economists' of criminal behaviour – and psychologists who follow them – may have thought. Recent studies (see *American Journal of Human Genetics*, June 1993) appear to indicate that there is a defective gene which is inherited and which results in aggressive and sometimes violent behaviour in criminals. In other words, there is a specific genetic mutation for some men which, by producing a build-up of natural chemical messengers in the brain, leads them to over-react in an aggressive way, coincidentally with a tendency to develop learning difficulties. The technical explanation is that '... the inherited predisposition to aggressiveness is the result of a mutation in the mono-amine oxidase A gene'. This results in a shortage of the enzyme that in turn causes a build-up of neurotransmitters and over-excitation of the nerves during stressful situations.

I would venture to suggest that it will not be long before scientists succeed in finding a similar defective gene in women who are prostitutes. But be that as it may.

Quite clearly, the observations of Lombroso and Morasso must be related to Western society. Modesty, or a sense of modesty is obviously dependent upon the cultural background to the society where it is considered. Totally different views of female modesty prevail, for example, amongst the Eskimos, the Afrikaans and, say, the Japanese, to choose three environments at random.

One of the principal criticisms that can be levelled against all nineteenth-century sociologists, sexologists or academic writers is that they relied upon a view of society which in itself is out-dated so that the results of their clinical investigations, often quite thorough, as is the case with Havelock Ellis and Lombroso, are not very relevant as we approach the year 2000. This is certainly not my view. The fact is, that there is a timelessness about sexual activity which ensures that judgements that could be supported 200 years ago still retain their validity, at least as a matter of principle. Obviously, details of sexual behaviour change with the passage of time. For example, in the 1930s Marie Stopes would have been extremely surprised to read in a fashionable magazine like *Cosmopolitan* that women should be educated in the meaning and the techniques of oral sex, both for them and for men. This is something which she would never have countenanced, in the same way as she did not endorse any form of sexual permissiveness (save possibly as regards male homosexuality).

However, this is a matter of detail in sexual behaviour, and interesting/significant though that detail may be, it does not of itself affect the fundamental conclusions that are reached as regards both male and female sexuality.

3. THE MORAL JUSTIFICATION OF PROSTITUTION

Here we go back both to Balzac and nineteenth-century France, according to whom prostitutes sacrificed themselves for the Republic and made of their bodies a rampart for the protection of respectable families. In the same way, Schopenhauer called prostitutes 'human sacrifices on the altar of monogamy'. Lecky called the prostitute '... the most efficient guardian of virtue, ... the eternal priestess of humanity, blasted for the sins of the people'.

There is nothing new in this. In his Satires, Book 1 (2), Horace, dealing with the Romans' attitude towards prostitutes, records Cato as having expressed satisfaction on seeing a man emerge from a brothel, on the basis that otherwise he might have gone to lie with his neighbour's wife.

4. THE 'CIVILIZING' VALUE OF PROSTITUTION

This is more debatable as a cause, though it may be an effect of what prostitution does. Havelock Ellis claims that, since modern urban life delays marriage, the substitutes for marriage become more important. Some prostitutes are inclined to the business, others love display, luxury and idleness, are bored with their work and are seeking amusement.

On page 295 of Part 2, Volume II, Havelock Ellis maintains that, according to connoisseurs, the English prostitute as compared with her Continental and especially French sisters, fails to show to advantage, being usually grasping as regards money and deficient in charm.

Interestingly enough, though of no great significance, little seems to have changed – even in the nineties. On the 14 August 1992, a Channel 4 television programme recorded the views of an Englishman who, having decided that he wanted to experience the differences between English and continental prostitutes, travelled to Hamburg where he had repeated intercourse with a German prostitute. He claims that he found her helpful, friendly, not concerned about how much time he spent with her, eager to please and, all in all, much more enjoyable than what he had found at home.

There is certainly a value for society in those situations where the wife is not really keen on becoming the complete sexual mate for the husband and the husband, without being carried away by any impulse of strong passion or any desire for infidelity, seeks in brothels what he cannot find at home. There is nothing new about this. It is part of what Ellis calls 'a mysterious craving for variety' and he quotes, as his best example, Samuel Pepys. He also considers the prostitute's 'civilizational' value in the case of what he calls 'sexually perverted men' on the basis that '... the conventionally bred woman often cannot bring herself to humour even some quite innocent fetishistic whim of her husband's, for it is too alien to her feelings and too incomprehensible to her ideas, or the husband himself may not wish to ask'. This point is considered in greater detail in Chapter 5.

According to Ellis, the Greek 'hetaira', the Italian courtesan, the Japanese geisha, the Chinese flowergirls and the Indian bayaderas all show some not unnoble features, namely the breadth of a free artistic existence. But that may be wishful thinking on Ellis's part. The difficulty is that what we call our sexual morality is the result of inherited traditions which have to be modified as the environment changes. Where tradition is strong, adaptability is lost and moral life tends to decay; we go to the other extreme nowadays, when adaptability is too easy, with the result that the moral life becomes meaningless and carries no weight. One ought to be able to synthesize the two approaches, but that is the problem of the late twentieth century. As Lecky puts it (W.E.M. Lecky, *The History of*

European Morals, New York, Longmans Green, 1911): 'Of all
the departments of ethics, the questions concerning the
relations of the sexes and the proper position of woman are
those upon the future of which there rests the greatest
uncertainty.'

Havelock Ellis claims that the arrangements whereby a
certain group of women should be set apart to minister
exclusively to men's sexual needs, whilst another group is
brought up in asceticism as candidates for the privilege of
ministering to the household and family necessities, has
worked very well until now; but this traditional order of
things, as it were, is not working at the moment because we
have reached a different type of social organization. Today we
are a democratic society with economic independence for
both men and women and similar sexual responsibility for
both men and women.

It is true that recent studies do appear to confirm some of
the points made by Havelock Ellis. For example, in 1963
Armand de Mergen published the results of his investigations
into prostitutes. He showed that out of the 500 whom he had
interviewed, 56 were found to be 'obviously feeble minded'
and 81% admitted frigidity. Other studies show that a good
60% of prostitutes are, in fact, lesbians. According to Armand
de Mergen, the prostitute knows perfectly well that 90% of
her clients require special treatment and that she does not
simply have to lie down; he claims that in the United States it
is a different scenario, namely that there it is the man who
wants to be told what to do.

With this kind of American approach to prostitution, we
should compare the flagellation culture in England and the
spread of brothels that specialized in flagellation. In fact, round
about 1800 the flagellation houses had become so famous that
this particular kind of sexual practice was termed 'the English
disease' and it is said that even George IV when Crown Prince
claimed that he had visited some of these places. According to
Armand de Mergen, this particular form of sado-masochism
resulted from the English educational system (involving

regular beatings by cane or birch) and possibly the harsh naval life (involving extensive use of the lash).

Whichever way we look at it, however, prostitutes continue to exist, despite the fact that promiscuity or abstention from sexual relations is only a custom. This point is made on pages 152 to 167 of *Sexual Behaviour in Society* by Alex Comfort (published in 1950 by Duckworth and republished in 1964 by Pelican under the title *Sex in Society*). Comfort accepts that the relationship with a prostitute is exploitive but has got the advantage that the client knows more or less what he will get, what it will cost, that there are no social preliminaries and waste of time and that there will be no social comeback either in terms of blackmail or in terms of attempts to transfer the relationship to another level. He also notes that prostitution is a way of life which is freely chosen in present-day England.

Nevertheless, the myth persists even with Comfort that the prostitute is either an idiot, a lesbian or she is frigid. In maintaining this, he goes along with the other authors who argue that the dichotomy of sexuality which is expressed by the terms sacred and profane is in effect the result of infantile sexual urges. There are, of course, persons whose sexuality is so twisted that they may express love for idealized objects, love which others would call sacred, but be incapable of profaning the same object so that no sexual gratification is forthcoming, other than with less idealized sexual objects whom one despises. But it is difficult to call such individuals, in any sense, balanced. Their sexuality is perverted. They are the type of husbands who may be quite impotent with their wives but otherwise capable of performing with tarts.

Other writers have underlined different possible causes to try and explain away why a woman becomes a prostitute. The German historian of prostitution, Iwan Bloch, considers that one of the many causes of prostitution, additional to those that have already been referred to above, is that it follows on from physiological male masochism; by which he means the impulse that man has 'from time to time to plunge into the depths of

coarse, brutal, sexual lust', the need for self-mortification and
self-abasement which can only be satisfied by going with a
prostitute because by definition she is a comparatively
worthless creature. What this means, according to Bloch, is
that some women have developed as prostitutes in order to
satisfy such a need.

The same point is made by another German authority,
Heinrich Schurtz, when he claims that visiting a prostitute is
for some men like a breath of fresh 'unrefinement and coarse
naturalism' which represents a safety valve for even the most
ideal man who is unable to free himself from his body. This is
a refinement of Havelock Ellis's concept of the civilizational
value of prostitution, for it considers the prostitute as a
therapist. Such a notion was popular in the nineteenth
century, especially in Victorian England; whether it represented a rationalization of Victorian prudery is debatable, but it
clearly looked upon lustful thoughts as having a cathartic
effect, at least for men.

The Victorians also endeavoured to explain prostitution by
describing it as the opposite of female chastity. Put differently,
prostitution was brought about because women whose
function was to procreate and look after the family as a unit,
emotional but above all, socio-political, needed the protection
afforded by the prostitute. Again, this alleged cause of
prostitution is no different from its moral justification as
identified in what has been said above.

When considering the various theories as to the causes of
prostitution one must always distinguish between the religious
prostitute of Judaea, Greece, and the East, and our own more
modern kind. The former did not always do it for money and
there is evidence to indicate that for them an element of sexual
enjoyment was usually present. In recent recessional times,
however, economic factors became more relevant, and the
concomitant, inevitable feature is the emotional indifference,
if not frigidity, of the whore.

The economic motive originating in poverty was
paramount in the theory of the French writer Parent-

Duchâtelet, but of lesser significance, as has been seen, for Havelock Ellis as well as for Woods Hutchinson, W.H. Sanger, and Hammer. But Parent-Duchâtelet was more conscious of poverty than the others, who looked at economic factors in the general sense.

It is not poverty that causes women to become prostitutes in the twentieth century, except in particular circumstances, e.g. in the Europe born of the 'liberation' by the Allies and more recently following the collapse of Communism. But it is money that motivates the modern prostitute, as will be seen in Chapter 6. Where women are better off financially, they will charge more for their services as prostitutes. In poorer areas, they will charge less. If, as is submitted, the demand is constant, the price of the offer will be ultimately irrelevant.

There is, of course, an element of truth in all the explanations of why prostitutes exist but no single theoretical cause appears adequate to explain the permanence of the phenomenon because what may appear as a valid explanation of the prostitute's trade in particular economic circumstances, ceases to make sense when the social and economic structure changes. For example, the argument that prostitutes are such because of economic necessity may have had some merit at the time of the Industrial Revolution when women, particularly of the lower ranks, were treated as sexual objects within the family where they were working; and then found it just as easy to carry on the trade of a prostitute outside that family. The argument that it is economic necessity that drives women to prostitution cannot possibly make any sense in the 1990s, except in cases (admittedly increasing), where teenage girls, for whatever reason, are living on the streets and have taken to prostitution in order to eat.

The contention that there is a civilizing value to what the prostitute does, or at least a moral one, namely that prostitutes save marriages, may have been valid for the Victorians, but is meaningless to us, correct though it may well be. It is meaningless, of course, because of the increase in the rate of divorce which, by denying marriage, consequently reduces the validity of the argument that prostitutes save marriages. If a husband feels the need for sexual variety in present-day Western society, there are plenty of women who cannot be labelled prostitutes – according to the definition that was adopted at the outset – who will be only too pleased to satisfy his whims.

With the passage of time, one is more and more forced to wonder about the validity of certain theories which, when they are first put forward together with statements that sound fairly absolute, appear convincing, but which, some years later, are found to be inaccurate. For instance, forecasts of the greater stability that would result in Western society from the use of contraception and abortion have not been borne out.

As a further example, in his book *Is Marriage Necessary?* (W.H. Allen, London 1974) Eustace Chesser – who, incidentally, was one of those who were heard by the Wolfenden Committee, was a psychiatrist, an abortionist and one of the few who, in his day, felt able to state openly that pornography is good for you, says at page 87: 'Contraception and legalized abortion will in time reduce the number of unwanted children to negligible proportions. They are unlikely to be so numerous that adoption presents a difficulty.' Anyone reading him at the time would have accepted the statement as reasonable and logical. The statistics analysed later on, concerning the increase in illegitimate children in the UK since 1974, would appear to cast some considerable doubt on the validity of Chesser's thinking.

I pause at this stage to observe that as a matter of principle the moral values and constraints to be attached to the marriage vows would, of themselves, be sufficient to make prostitution quite unnecessary. But it is a fact that these constraints and vows have largely ceased to have any real significance. The statistics quoted on divorce and adultery show that this is so beyond any shadow of doubt. The only relevance of divorce to the issue of prostitution is that it lends ammunition to the argument that it has rendered prostitutes surplus to require-ments. This ought to be so as a matter of theory and also as a matter of feminist beliefs. On the other hand, the fact remains that, despite the very high rates of divorce in Western society, particularly in the United Kingdom, prostitution still flourishes.

I think it fair to say, however, that our sexual customs and cultures are in a state of great flux, which makes consistent evidence and therefore accurate proof almost impossible to achieve. Statements, for example, which may have been valid 20 years or so ago have lost their significance today; similarly,anything that one says nowadays may equally be proved wrong and out of fashion in 20 years time or less. Thus, in my view, it is clear beyond a doubt that no single explanation or cause can be given of why some women are prostitutes. In a sense, the fact that none of the explanations as to the causes of prostitution has absolute value, points in the direction that it may well be, for reasons which so far nobody has succeeded in identifying but which are closer to the biological argument adopted by the so-called Italian school of criminology, that there are women who, if they will forgive the expression, *are actually born prostitutes.*

I should make it clear here that I am not considering for present purposes the question of male homosexuals. Whether catamites are born as such, or not, and whether the observations that follow could be equally applied to male prostitutes, is a matter which is, to some extent, outside the present terms of reference and about which much can be said.

Equally, I am discounting for present purposes any argument that may arise as to the consequences of the woman's defloration. Much greater significance was attached in the past than in the twentieth century to this very significant event in a woman's life. Perhaps 200 years ago it might have been relevant to consider who, when, at what age (for both parties), why and in what circumstances (whether by force or blandishments) brought about the loss of virginity. I personally do not think that this is such a relevant consideration today as far as prostitution is concerned.

This does not mean that all those women who, according to

such a definition, are born prostitutes, will actually ply their
trade as such. Whether they do or they do not will depend on
their individual circumstances, the society in which they live,
their cultural, religious and moral upbringing, their psychological heritage, and perhaps, on pure chance or luck. As I
have already observed, it may be that there is more to the
'biological' argument than even Lombroso realized, not in the
sense that a prostitute is a degenerate, for that argument cannot
stand, particularly in the 1990s, but at least to the extent that
there are some women whose inborn restraints as to behaviour
are, for one reason or the other, weak or almost non-existent.

It is difficult for those men who have studied prostitutes to
follow this argument through and insofar as, at least until the
early 1960s, the majority of those who analysed the sexual
behaviour of prostitutes were men rather than women, it can
be said that the feminine input into such studies is minimal. It
is only over the past 20 years or so that women themselves
have spent more time considering this phenomenon.

One can, however, ask a woman reader who is not or at
least does not consider herself to be a prostitute, whether she
attributes the fact that she is an 'honest' woman to chance, to
physical or psychological make-up, to moral upbringing, or to
her family environment or education, or to a combination of
all such factors, or to mere accident or luck.

I should point out here that the definition of prostitute
provided in the Introduction does not necessarily cover certain
situations where one may be entitled to question the 'moral'
integrity of the woman involved. Consider, for example, a
woman who has two or three or four lovers regularly, with
whom she enjoys a harmonious sexual relationship. Alternatively, what about a woman who marries several times.
Could she in any sense be termed a prostitute? An interesting
point. My own reaction rather favours the logic of the Latin
satirist, Martial, when he said: 'Who weds so often, does not
wed. She is a licensed adulteress. I am less offended by an open
wanton.' However, I readily accept the fact that in the closing

years of the twentieth century this may strike some as being a very parochial, if not naïve approach.

As regards the woman who has several lovers, in no sense could she be termed a prostitute, because she is not motivated by money and is not indiscriminate (according to our original definition). It is simply a fact that she sleeps with two, three or four men, with whom her relationship is particularly fortunate.

There appear to be no known studies that have been made to consider these questions. Criminologists, psychologists and doctors have asked prostitutes why they are what they are, and have come up with different answers at different times. It is almost impossible to ask honest women why they are not prostitutes and quite difficult to get a satisfactory answer once the question is put; but they are the ones who should be asked.

The matter is complicated by the fact that until recently men have under-estimated and misrepresented woman and her abilities. The misrepresentation is of long standing and was compounded by the Church and by psychologists generally. By the former, since woman was depicted either as virginal and angelic (hence the Mother of Christ) or as sensual and as a whore (hence the burning of witches and the treatment of prostitutes); psychologists, notably Freud, misrepresented woman when they focused on her inferior position arising out of her so-called penis envy. It is perhaps no coincidence that until very recent times all psychologists or psychiatrists of any notoriety have been men: from Freud and Jung to Adler, the list is fairly substantial and can be added to. The only female practitioner of any significance, apart from Anna Freud, is Melanie Klein. As a result, a wholly one-sided picture of woman has been projected.

It is easy to conclude that there have not been any female psychologists because woman is not fit for the job. It seems much more likely that it was lack of education or facilities in a particular kind of society that resulted in a paucity of women psychiatrists. Meanwhile, the picture that has so far been projected of woman in the psychiatric field is wholly mistaken, and, to a considerable extent, it has coloured the relationship between the sexes.

In deciding what causes a woman to be a prostitute no benefit can be derived by asking her client what his needs are. These are multifarious, as will be seen in the following chapter, but provide no guide whatsoever to a successful analysis of what makes a prostitute behave the way she does and of what deters the 'honest' woman from indulging in a certain kind of behaviour on a regular basis and for money.

We are left with the conclusion, therefore, that nobody knows and nobody has so far succeeded in providing an adequate explanation of why prostitutes exist. This is reassuring for the purposes of the present study, for it endorses the view that since we have always had prostitutes and we have never been able to determine conclusively why they are with us, it must be taken for granted that we shall continue to have them. It is almost a contradiction in terms, even a denial of our nature perhaps, to imagine that we would ever find a way of eliminating them. In fact, we never will have such means at our disposal because the prostitute, although sometimes stated to be a product of her environment or of bad social upbringing or conditions or poverty or unemployment or lack of equal rights etc. etc. (and the more reasons one can find for the prostitute's existence, the more permanent the imprint on society), is a natural manifestation of woman. Put differently, as stated earlier, it may well be a question of a simple, natural phenomenon – an essential component of the human condition – that some women are born prostitutes.

This may not be a very palatable conclusion to reach but it is probably an inevitable one, in view of how woman's twentieth-century life has so dramatically improved, at least in our Western world, including the social, psychological, legal and economic conditions of daily life to a point that could never have been envisaged even by the most ardent of the early feminist writers. Yet, we still find ourselves troubled by prostitutes.

It could be argued that it is the demand for the prostitute's services that creates the supply; equally, one could argue that because there are so many prostitutes offering their services they in turn are creating a demand. This is a 'chicken-and-egg' situation for which it is difficult, if not impossible, to provide a satisfactory explanation.

It used to be said that inasmuch as in Victorian England there was, because of economic pressure, a considerable number of women who were willing to sell their bodies, it was to be accepted that the Victorian male should indulge his sexual whims with such women. That was inevitable, but also convenient because he did not have to impose his possibly deviant sexual requirements on a wife considered, wrongly, to be devoid of libido. Sociologists then went on to argue that as women became emancipated, they would replace the prostitute because, at least within the same social class, men would prefer to have affairs with women of their own class rather than go to a prostitute.

This argument was clearly wrong because, far from ceasing to be fashionable, prostitutes are entirely in fashion. What has changed is the form in which the prostitutes ply their trade; but there seems to be no evidence to show that the number of prostitutes is reducing. In fact, if the World Health Organization is to be believed, the numbers of prostitutes are increasing dramatically in every country.

Before considering what prostitutes are like in the 1990s (Chapter 6), I think it makes sense to look briefly at the male client. (Heterosexual prostitution is considered the norm in this context simply because, numerically at least, this is the most important group. Later chapters will also deal with the female prostitute who provides lesbian services as well as with the male prostitute who provides both homosexual and heterosexual services.)

It is said by most writers on matters sexual that man is essentially polygamous and has a sexual craving for variety; that man is naturally promiscuous; and that the sexual act for man satisfies primarily a physical need and only secondarily a psychological one, so that in intercourse the sexual element can, for men, be divorced from the emotional. Broadly speaking, as I mentioned earlier, these statements are true. But it is not only the polygamous/promiscuous/sybarite male who needs the services of prostitutes.

Finally, it is also worth recording that there are some men who do not actually need prostitutes. As Lord Foppington put it, a long way back: 'I think no woman is worth money that will take money.' But such a high moral stance is lost on most.

Chapter Five

The prostitute's client

Those who require the services of prostitutes can be broadly classified as follows:

1. THE MALE WHO FOR ONE REASON OR THE OTHER IS DEPRIVED OF SEXUAL GRATIFICATION.

This is a broad category which includes not only those men whose wives, for example, may be temporarily or permanently incapacitated, or in prison, but also those whose professional or business activities make it difficult for them to have a regular sex life. One has in mind for example, commercial travellers, policemen, wagon-lit attendants, prisoners, soldiers. Another class to consider is the widower who may not wish to remarry or form a more-or-less permanent attachment and finally, the 'normal' man with a particularly strong sexual drive who cannot find satisfaction with one woman only. (Perhaps not so common a creature these days!).

2. THE 'SHY' YOUNG MAN

By this, is meant the youngster who is incapable or unwilling to experiment with girls of his own age group, perhaps because he is unsure of himself or because, before he does so, he wishes to acquire experience so as to emerge as a more satisfactory sexual partner, and who, accordingly, finds his sexual training with a whore.

Some people may think that the 'shy' young man is rarely to be found in the 1990s. Not so. Many of the prostitutes who were interviewed for the purposes of this study have mentioned that quite a number of their clients fall within this category. It is fair to say, therefore, that this type of client is by no means unusual. He was an exceptionally common client in times past, particularly in Victorian England, though mainly for the upper classes (the lower classes had always adopted a more sanguine approach to matters sexual).

It was a very normal occurrence, even in the twentieth century, in those Mediterranean countries where wives were expected to reach the marital chamber inviolate or in those countries where the virginity of the bride was considered to be of value. In theory, the number of such youngsters should be reducing because, in our society, accommodation can be found with girls of the same age group without recourse to prostitutes.

3. LONELY MEN

Their numbers are increasing. Every man who has found himself alone in a large city knows how unwanted one feels at times. As Dr Henriques (op.cit. volume 3 page 266) has so aptly put it: 'Not enough attention has been paid in the literature to the component of loneliness in the motivation of the client. It is a component which has become more significant as urban life has increased with its inevitable emphasis on the anonymous and the impersonal. The therapeutic aspect of the prostitute's role in Western society has been overshadowed by the more sexually obvious characteristics of that role. The failure to recognize this is a reflection of the general disrepute in which the harlot is regarded.'

4. UNLUCKY MEN

By this expression we mean the crippled, the hospitalized, the malformed, the blind, the ugly, the diseased and, to an extent, the old who are still sexually active but without a partner. Where do all these classes of people find outlets for their sexuality? And what about the unloved or unwanted, for whatever reason?

Under this category must also be included those men who are impotent in the functional though not in the emotional sense, on the one hand, and those who, though not functionally impotent, cannot really be considered adequately potent; and finally, the psychologically disturbed who may need sexual therapy.

5. THE 'OCCUPATIONAL' CLIENT

The classic example here is the sailor; but we now have workers who operate on oil rigs and perhaps, in the not too distant future, men who will be based in space.

The practical needs of such men are self-evident and quite obviously they most certainly will have recourse to prostitutes, if they are given the opportunity. (This is an alternative category to 1 above.)

6. THE DEVIANT CLIENT

This is probably the broadest category, for it includes most men whose sexual needs are not satisfied by normal intercourse with a woman.

Under this heading are to be included all those with impersonal sexual fantasies: namely, all exhibitionists, sadists, masochists, sado-masochists, the sexually perverted, those who feel the need to humble themselves before woman, those who enjoy odd or unusual or perverse sexual practices which do not include genital contact, those who are stimulated only by impersonal relations, those who have to degrade themselves before woman and those who can only find an outlet in sado-masochistic activities like active or passive birching; and lastly, the voyeurs.

In other words, the category embraces all those people who have problems with their erectile tissues or, as doctors put it, suffering from erectile dysfunction or malfunction, whose number, according to medical practitioners, is increasing at an incredible pace, and whose performance has been assessed by Kinsey.

7. THE 'MENOPAUSAL' MALE

Amongst the men who could be said to fall within the first category we have mentioned earlier on, namely those who for one reason or another are deprived of sexual gratification, particular attention must be given to those husbands whose wives of menopausal age may be less inclined to sexual intercourse than they perhaps were a few years earlier.

The attempts that have been made over the past 20 years or so to demonstrate that a woman passing through her menopausal phase need not feel in any sense disadvantaged are, in themselves, commendable as a psychological aid to those women who feel, in one shape or other, the beginnings of the onset of old age; but the women are not the only ones who may welcome reassurance at this particular moment in time, since many men are equally affected.

The trouble is that all too often these attempts to 'normalize' the female menopause are dictated by the same feminist foibles that, mainly as a result of American influences, aim at making another fairly typical manifestation of femininity, namely menstruation, more acceptable.

When I was young, the monthly female cycle was commonly referred to as 'the curse'. It is interesting to note that nowadays this expression is seldom used since much is said to show that such a cycle is no more than a very temporary embarrassment for woman, something almost like a recurring cold, and the more we talk about it, the lesser its impact and trouble, and the more woman can, in the words of Professor Higgins of *My Fair Lady*, be 'more like a man'. Hence the freedom, unless we dare call it psychological need, freely and loudly to advertise sanitary protection no longer solely in women's magazines but much more vividly on television for all, young and old, male and female, to see and, hopefully, understand.

Apart from what appears to me to be evidence of a conspicuous lack of good taste, such advertisements cannot change the troublesome nature of that important female manifestation. In like manner, to brainwash women over 45 by telling them that the menopause is nothing at all to worry about, cannot change its reality and impact for some women.

May I say immediately that I readily accept that there are women – but I do not believe there are many – who hardly notice that they are passing through a menopausal phase, just as I accept that simply because a woman is over the age of 45, she does not cease to be as capable, charming, attractive and sexually interested and interesting as she was before her menopause started. However, for most women in the age group 45-55, the menopause is a particularly difficult period in may ways, and more especially in terms of their marital relationships, since the number of more or less obvious symptoms of this phase is such that it cannot easily be ignored.

According to those in the know, such symptoms include nervousness, headaches, instability, insomnia, poor memory, moodiness, feelings of inadequacy, tiredness, lack of concentration, palpitations, backache and aching joints. These occurrences would in themselves be such as to have an effect on the woman's interest in matters sexual but, more particularly at this time in life, unless I read the relevant literature incorrectly and my personal observations are to be discounted, the loss of oestrogen causes some atrophy of the genital tract with a possibility of resultant vaginal irritation and discomfort, as well as reduced sensitivity of the vaginal walls and greater lack of response, which, combined with the other manifestations that have already been mentioned, makes a loss of libido quite likely; and even when intercourse is actually wanted, it can prove either less satisfying than usual or less acceptable, or, in a number of cases, even quite painful.

The literature does not go so far as to tell us what is to be done with the husband in such situations. The forms of relief alternative to sexual intercourse, which are obviously still available to him within the framework of the marital relationship, may not always be adequate for a full-blooded man, especially if his wife had been a willing, satisfying and satisfied partner until the onset of the menopause.

What will he do? Abstain? That of course could be said to be highly commendable; but it may not be too likely. Force himself on his wife? Possible, but not something which a sensitive and loving man would wish to do.

If recent novels and, above all, scandals are any guide, a man who by then could be said to be at the peak of his business life, may find it quite easy to get himself a young girl or a mistress, or go to bed with someone else' wife. 'What bastards men are', modern women might say at this stage, (though not entirely accurately in the context, but that is part of a much broader question). Many men, in the situation that I am considering, turn to street-walkers or other types of prostitutes, at great risk to themselves and ultimately, to their spouses. But I suggest that this is not the best way of solving the practical problem which will remain, despite the occasional fling, possibly for the duration of the wife's menopause.

I subscribe to the view that it is infinitely to be preferred for a man in such a situation to pay a more or less occasional visit to a sanitized sexual establishment, rather than to take a mistress or pick up a tart in the street. The latter is by definition physically unclean and the former, by tendency, morally corrupt.

That the man who is tempted to stray whilst his wife feels less inclined to intercourse because of menopausal and related difficulties, is likely to get himself into trouble, is borne out by official statistics. Presumably, at about the same time the man may be having problems with his own 'menopause' (clinically, 'climacteric') because he may be losing confidence in his own youthfulness and sexual prowess and accordingly would wish to find reassurance outside the marital relationship. It is easy in these situations for the man to turn to younger women. It is significant that the rate of divorce is fairly high in this group. If we consider the government's own statistical service publication, Series FM2, No. 19, by the title *1991 Marriage and Divorce Statistics*, page 50, Table 4.1, 'Age at Divorce', we find that of the 158,745 divorces which took place in 1991, a fairly high number (13,607) occurred when the woman was aged between 45 and 50. Within the same age group, 16,896 men divorced. It is often said that this fairly high rate of divorce is due to the fact that the children have left the home. But this is a fallacy because the highest rates of divorce occur in the age group 30-34 years of age where the figures are 33,532 for men and 33,195 for women. The presence of children does not seem to have any deterrent effect on whether the parents divorce. Indeed, at the age group of 25-29, in 1991, a peak occurred for women divorcing with a total of 35,582. It appears that the modern trend is for the spouses to ignore their children when they divorce. If one looks at the same publication, pages 62-67, it is quite clear that in 1991, of the 158,745 couples who divorced, 110,630 couples had children of any age, and of these, 88,346 couples had children under 16.

8. THE 'CASTRATED' MALE

The men who belong to this category, which I have created, have not been analysed in any great detail, if at all, by modern sociologists and psychiatrists. The category embraces all those men who, whether as fathers, lovers, or partners, find themselves under psychological pressure because of the fact that modern woman is a) freely available and b) in the ascendant.

To understand this category it is necessary to make a slight digression. Giving the fullest possible justification to Darwin's theory of the survival of the fittest, man has developed over millennia as the hunter and the fighter of the species, whereas woman has been concerned primarily with procreation. Man has developed bigger muscles and a much more violent fighting instinct to enable him to assert himself and provide the food for which his mate was grateful and for which she may even have forgiven him being dragged by her hair into the cave.

I have never quite believed these fairly primitive representations of primitive man and woman. But the physical and psychological truth is that man throughout history has had to hunt, both for food and for sex.

Accordingly, man has developed as the head of the family because he was the breadwinner, as the father, the protector of the family, the hunter of food and women, the lord and master of the universe.

Look around. For whatever reason – and it would take far too long to investigate this aspect of the matter – very often woman is the principal, if not the real breadwinner. The primary function of man with a family, that of maintaining and supporting them, has gone.

Man then settled down to being a mere father and for quite a long time, despite the difficulties of proof, he managed to get away with it. Nowadays, however, man has brought about his own demise since we can so easily provide woman with a child not only without the physical presence of the father but even without either not knowing who the father is or was, or selecting as father of her child a person of the male sex who has bequeathed his seed to posterity. So much for the sexual aspect of being a father. Furthermore, the State is replacing him in all his functions; gradually, it is true, but inevitably. More and more people, especially women, are relying upon the State rather than upon a man to support them and their children, as statistics clearly show.

By the same token, man can no longer be looked upon as the protector of his woman and his family. We now have the national health service, the social services, the local authorities, the police. Furthermore, any father is at serious risk of breaking the law if he even spanks his children, let alone caresses his daughter. And if we consider cynically any possible financial benefit accruing to his family from his presence, it is probably true to say that in most middle-class families in the Western world, mother and children would be infinitely better off if the father were dead rather than alive either because of the payments to be made by his employers under pension schemes, or through individually maintained insurance.

I suppose it is also true to say that if a father does earn a good income, then, particularly in certain strata of Western society, he may be able to provide his children with special advantages, like private education, or equivalent benefits; but it is difficult to see where his present-day economic utility lies. The correctness of this analysis is endorsed by the number of women who have children as a matter of choice without either marrying or co-habiting with man, which number is increasing all the time, as the statistics also show.

On top of all this, man's hunting instinct has practically disappeared. True, he has to struggle to assert and prove himself *vis-à-vis* his colleagues in business, in the professions or on the factory floor. But by hunting instinct I mean the basic need to kill or use violence in order to survive and to use force in order to obtain sexual satisfaction. That instinct has been dulled almost into insensitivity by the fact that man no longer needs to hunt in order to satisfy his sexual proclivities since women are exceptionally ready and willing, through their emancipation but, above all, through reliable contraception controlled by them, to offer their sexual partnership, whether on a casual or on a more permanent basis.

Clearly, recent social and scientific developments have resulted in the emasculation of man. For present purposes I am not concerned with the effect that the disappearance of the concept of man as a father will have upon woman. I have always thought that there is an intimacy in the relationship between mother and father, stemming from the cooperation needed in rearing the children and totally unrelated to sexual relations *per se*, which is incapable of being replaced by any other sort of set-up, and which ensures the psychological stability of the children brought up in a nuclear family as traditionally understood. But this point is not relevant, save indirectly, to the present discussion. What is relevant, is the lesser status of men being established in unison with the emancipation of woman.

Man has handed over to the State absolute control over those who threaten his family; he had renounced his privilege of feeding and clothing them when welfare services were established ready to take over at any time that he might fail; he abdicated from his position of master when he invented the contraceptive pill, which enabled woman alone to control her reproductive function; he converted himself into a nonentity as far as procreation is concerned at the stage when his own scientific advantages enabled sperm to be preserved for posterity; he surrendered his pride, his prestige and his inheritance at the same time as he began to find his fellow men more interesting and acceptable than his women.

A combination of these three factors, namely contraception, man's greed to profit from new inventions and his ever-decreasing masculinity, all occurred in effect within the last hundred years but at an ever-accelerating speed over the past twenty years or so.

It is hardly surprising, therefore, that nowadays man sits back and watches pornographic violent films where he sees displayed the kind of violence that he finds more and more difficult officially and lawfully to indulge in himself. He thus gets frustrated, because disorder is established in his mind and his frustration very often turns to violence, when he finds sufficient strength left to overcome his passivity.

People react in surprise and despair when they hear of manifestations of inexplicable and totally unwarranted violence, particularly of a sexual kind. Some even turn round and determine that it is only man – as opposed to woman – who is capable of being a criminal; others argue that in a world run by women, such violence would not exist;

there may be some who feel that perhaps all men should be castrated (but preserving a few grams of seed for use, if required).

This may sound like an exaggeration, which of course it is, but it is no more than an attempt to focus the reader's attention on a category of men who need prostitutes as much as those who were earlier classified under various headings. The group I refer to now consists of those men who want to use an element of force and violence within a sexual context, remnants perhaps of a more basic and all pervasive hunting instinct which can no longer find a natural outlet. Such men may find it safer to vent their anger, frustration, annoyance, call it what you will, upon a willing prostitute in a properly supervised environment than either by sublimating such frustration through constant viewing of pictures depicting woman as the object of lust and violence or by taking it out at random on wholly innocent passers-by.

The reader who feels that this analysis is extreme is reminded of the painful and apparently inexplicable manifestations of sexual violence on women and children. Some of it is clearly attributable to perversion; but a part of it is the frustration of the hunting instinct and for that, brothels would provide some kind of outlet.

Finally, a great advantage that a number of them would derive from more regular, socially tolerated access to prostitutes, would be the ability to recognize the type in other women. Experienced philanderers never cease to marvel at how actors, newspaper editors, Members of Parliament, ministers, leaders of the armed forces, and so on, are taken in, with extremely grave consequences for their career and their families, by all sorts of actresses, starlets and sometimes even wives, who could quite easily be recognized as whores by their shape, posture, features or behaviour, and, as such, would need to have been approached with a great deal of care. There is a naïveté in some of these public figures or high-ranking personages who are caught out, which would, in all likelihood, not be displayed by much younger men.

Chapter Six

Present-day prostitutes

The French have a saying: *plus ça change, plus c'est la même chose.* Which is another way of expressing the concept that the more we appear to embrace change either within our society or ourselves, the more things remain exactly the same.

This is, of course, a Gallic exaggeration which, like many things the French say, is not to be taken too literally. However, it is meant to reflect a basic truth, namely that human beings are the same no matter where they are, what they are or in which century they exist, in the sense that they have to satisfy some common needs which have universal application throughout the globe and which remain on the whole unchanged, despite the passage of time.

The validity of the basic belief that human beings are the same and that there is nothing new under the sun cannot easily be challenged. Let me explain what I mean by this statement. There are obvious differences between various races and nationalities: these are the result of varying social backgrounds, climates, diets, etc. The sanitary requirements of a Tartar, for example, may not be quite the same as those of a Frenchman; a Mexican may well look upon women differently from a Dane. But, on the whole, the same basic requirements have to be satisfied wherever men and women live together and they have resulted in certain traits which are common throughout the world.

Whilst one is generalizing, one may also observe that it is a regrettable fact of life that human beings, apart from their sameness, are weak, unreasonable and unreasoning. There will always be a minority of individuals who are strong, reasonable and reasoning but it is probably fair to say that, if left to his own devices, man is essentially an easy prey to his basic instincts. Recent political and social history provides us with many examples to support this statement. Hitler considered that Nazism would provide a panacea for the world's, or at least for Europe's evils, and would establish a state of healthy and fit supermen: the millions who died in the Second World War and the Jews who were exterminated bear witness to the absurdity of such contention, as well as to the evil inherent in one man. Human beings continue to slaughter one another: one need only mention Korea, Vietnam, Cambodia, Northern Ireland, the Jews and the Palestinians, the Serbs, Bosnians and the Croats, the Hutu and the Tutsi of Rwanda: human folly continues unabated.

If man were strong, reasonable and reasoning, there would be no need for violence, and no drug-taking, smoking or alcoholism; the rain forests would not be destroyed and the centres of our cities would not be clogged and choked to a halt by unnecessary traffic, But man *is* inconsistent, and often unreasonable and irrational. Hence, if left to his own devices, he will drug himself insensitive, nowadays abuse his sexuality to a degree such as history has never witnessed before, and smoke or drink himself to death.

Every now and then, some individuals prod the State to wake up. Whether, when so awakened, the State acts out of genuine concern for society as a whole or out of fear that the very same people who represent it in power might be affected by the very problems that one is trying to cure, is a topic not relevant to this discussion. But usually, as we all know, a crisis is needed. I say usually because there are exceptions: Wilberforce's campaign to abolish slavery was not the result of any pressure by the State, any more than the reforming spirit of Shaftesbury for factories and child labour. But the benevolence in the social sphere which, from time to time, prevailed in nineteenth-century society, is not always reflected in the activity or the inactivity of twentieth-century man.

Banning smoking on the London Underground, as I mentioned earlier, could have been decreed at least twenty or more years earlier: the plain fact is, it needed the King's Cross disaster for those who govern us to come to their senses as regards smoking in public places. Pulling down large tracts of virgin forests in South America for profit was obviously wrong when it first started; it needed a hole in the ozone layer for the world to begin to understand that it cannot with impunity tamper with nature. Nor is it enough to argue that once upon a time most of Europe was forested and it is not now because, meanwhile, we have acquired the means of knowledge to determine the environmental damage that the depletion of forest causes to the world as a whole.

It has been well known for decades that an abnormal intake of alcohol damages the liver of most people: it has taken a few more dramatic instances of cirrhosis to bring the medical profession to the view that up to 28 units per week are the maximum we are sensibly, or at least safely, allowed to drink. (I am aware that there is a continuing argument regarding the amount of alcohol consumed, the value of wine etc etc.) The relevance of these observations in this present context is that it may well require the crisis brought about by the spread of AIDS for the world to dedicate some of its time to more detailed analysis of how to deal with lust.

Whilst one must, of course, be somewhat cautious about generalizations, especially in matters sexual, it seems possible, nevertheless, to identify three broad sexual trends in what one may term Western society. (Eastern society is not considered here, because of its different social requirements, and an analysis of what happens in countries that are not governed by the Western-style of thinking seems unnecessary for present purposes.)

The American, the Anglo-Saxon and the Latin show different trends in their approach to women and to prostitutes and there are clear sexual differences that can be highlighted within these trends. For example, as we have seen, it is well established that the American male, on the whole, prefers to submit to woman rather than to control her. Accordingly, American men must be responsible for the way in which American women rule the roost. There must be an element of submission to the female (psychological submission in the first place and, secondarily, physical subjection) which causes this result. Studies of American prostitutes have shown beyond any doubt that the American customer will be inclined to ask the woman what she wants to do rather than tell her what she is expected to do for the money.

The Anglo-Saxon traits have been different. Flagellation has been prominent in England (as opposed to Scotland or Wales) and one need only spare a few minutes looking at some of the 'advertisement' cards that litter our principal cities (in telephone kiosks, newsagents etc etc) to see that the majority of prostitutes still offer this kind of service to an increasing extent. Services are not offered unless there is a demand for them. On the other hand, the Latin man goes out of his way to assert his power over woman. He believes that he can tell her what to do to fulfil his particular desires.

In Great Britain, the largest impact of the various ethnic groups on prostitution should not be under-estimated. There are no reliable statistics available, so that any quantitative comment is inappropriate; qualitatively, however, there is a clear difference between prostitutes of different ethnic groups and their 'British' white counterparts. Apart from the fact that it has been common experience in the United States of America that many whites prefer 'coloured' partners, it seem to be almost universally accepted that prostitutes from different ethnic groups other than the white are generally friendlier, more smiling, and more willing to indulge the client. They are submissive when submission is required, and masterful when they feel that that is what the client wants. They do seem to have a better understanding of sexuality than their white counterparts and, so far as the client is concerned, it is almost universally accepted that they give better value for money.

This is a constitutional trait and a question of make-up of both coloured women (that they should be able to give better service than white) and of white women (who are very often incapable of providing the same service). Indeed, as has already been remarked, the English prostitute comes out very poorly in comparison. To quote but one learned author in this field, Dr Harold Cross in *The Lust Market* (Citadel Press, New York, 1956 pp 63 & 64): '...the performance of the English professionals is in accord with their dull appearance and the dinginess of their surroundings. It is rated far below that of other countries, including the USA' The same is said by Benjamin and Masters. (See below p.96.)

But clearly, the impact of such prostitutes on the UK scene is not yet great, although the availability of prostitutes of all ethnic backgrounds has continued to change over the years. There is no doubt that, in sexual terms, men divide into active and passive groups as regards their relationships with women. Sometimes, the two alternate but, generally speaking, certain traits can be easily identified. (One is ignoring for present purposes homosexual relations, where the distinction is even more clear cut.)

The different streams that have been identified are not so far fetched as the reader might first imagine. For example, one need only consider the depiction of the sexual act on British television. Apart from its ever-increasing appearance, which is presumably dictated by the need to titillate and therefore attract audiences, it is interesting to note that it is frequently the woman who is shown above the man rather than below him. One must assume that titillation is the principal objection of juxtaposition. However, one cannot ignore the fact that, if challenged, the very director who has chosen to represent intercourse in this fashion may reply that he/she is only depicting what happens in life.

Well, we all know that, generally speaking, that is not true.

Certainly, the first time a British woman has intercourse with
any man (unless she is a prostitute) she is unlikely to have
intercourse in that position (the situation may not necessarily
be the same in other countries, i.e. India): surely, the variation
comes later, when the partners get to know each other better.

The reasons why these representations occur are symptomatic of a new-found sexual and psychological need. Woman
is exercising her power in that manner, woman wishes to be
on top and to be in charge. We are not concerned with
whether it could be argued that the particular posture provides
greater satisfaction for either man or woman or both. It is not
the private exercise that concerns us at present, but its public
representation.

After all, let us consider whether the director/scriptwriter
who determined that intercourse should be represented that
way, was a male or a female. If he was a male, then it is clear
beyond doubt that he is the kind of male who is naturally
submissive to woman, otherwise he would not have indulged
in that kind of representation; if she was a female, then it is
equally clear that woman was showing, in this context as well,
her assertiveness over man. Either way, the practice may well
be a recipe for disaster in personal relations if that kind of
sexual activity is not only maintained, but reflects a
psychological rather than a physical need. Indeed, it is hardly
a coincidence that these representations should occur at the
same time as one repeatedly hears the expression 'non-
penetrative sex' being used: that expression is almost
meaningless where man is to indulge in coitus in the way in
which a man normally does.

These differing trends are reflected in the activities of the
modern whore who is more apt, and better equipped, in some
respects, than her predecessor for the satisfaction of various
needs and has a supply of modern technological equipment
that caters for deviant or obsessive tendencies (whips, chains,
leather costumes, boots, dildos, vibrators, etc.); the proof of
the changed needs can easily be found in the increasing
number of sex shops found throughout the country and now

open to the general public. The reader who is interested in learning more about contemporary deviancy needs is referred to pages 63 to 77 of Lindi St Clair's *The Autobiography of Miss Whiplash* (Piatkus, London, 1992).

If we apply the same basic criteria to what prostitutes are and do, we then find that the changes that have taken place in the last 100 years or so are, in a sense, largely cosmetic.

Here, it is worth remembering the various efforts made in this period to try to identify the causes for the behaviour of prostitutes have been prompted in the main by two desires: namely the thirst for knowledge and understanding as well as the search for a remedy.

Those who have sought knowledge may not always have been motivated by altruism. For example, it is my firm belief that in the case of Havelock Ellis, his obsession with sexuality was the result of a particular need for excitement, resulting from a dissatisfaction with his own experience as a male. Havelock Ellis was a doctor and a scientist who took a particular interest in sexual matters and who, after very many difficulties, succeeded in having his *Studies on the Psychology of Sex* published in London by Heinemann in 1906. In the six volumes that record his professional experience, he collates most of the notions that existed before him and is, on many issues, quite modern in outlook. His classification of the causes of prostitution has already been mentioned.

The difficulty about the credibility of Havelock Ellis's work, however, is that he was impotent, even though he endeavoured to find reassurance. The whole of Chapter 2 in volume I is headed 'The Art of Love'. It runs from page 507 to page 575 and considers the physical aspects of lovemaking by identifying the different numbers of methods of intercourse selected by writers before him (such as Aretino, Veniero and Forberg). Pages 376 to 476 from Volume II are dedicated to what he calls 'undinism'. A further 30 pages or thereabouts are included on the same subject and this time he uses a different word, 'urolagnia', in the previous chapter headed 'Mechanism of Sexual Deviation'. The reader will be hard put to find the two nouns 'undinism' and 'urolagnia' in the dictionary since they were coined by Havelock Ellis and are not officially recognized in the English language. They are meant to represent the causes and benefits of sexual enjoyment of watching women urinating. (Nor is this a neglected idea: in the 1990s we have seen at least one well-known Hollywood film portrayal of a popular actress urinating.)

Reassurance of his masculinity he found not only in writing his book but also by displaying his sperm to Olive Shreiber under the microscope, pointing out the motility of the cells. (See *The New Women and the Old Men* by Ruth Brandon, Secker & Warburg, London, 1989 p.37). One is bound to wonder, in fact, whether Havelock Ellis was really qualified at all to teach anybody anything about sex. Nevertheless, Chapter 2 (Vol. I) does contain some enjoyable passages like the comparison that Balzac made when he equated the husband making love to his wife to an orang-utan trying to play the violin.

The historians and psychologists of the Italian school, on the other hand, studied prostitutes within the framework of criminology, starting from the theoretical premise that the errant behaviour of the prostitute was an aspect of criminality, the prostitute being unstable and alcoholic, and effectively reaching exactly that conclusion at the end of their life-long studies. The students of the German school may have reacted to prostitution in line with their own Teutonic temperament, more akin to the Anglo-Saxon in matters sexual than to the Mediterranean.

Finally, those who studied the causes of prostitution in order to derive either political conclusions from their findings (the workers were exploited and so was woman) or because they felt the need to emancipate woman from her slavery to men (women were slaves, manipulated by men to their evil desires) had the crusading spirit, but may have lacked the objectivity necessary to come to terms with the fundamental problem caused by prostitutes. Meanwhile, no remedy has been found to cure, reduce or eliminate prostitution, probably because there is no single cause that can be identified for it.

The truth seems to be that the prostitutes themselves have never given any real thought to their own motivations, save where the prevailing reason for their behaviour is the economic one. This is quite easy to identify regardless of education, culture or objectivity. Everyone understands money and the profit motive, and, by and large, it is money that qualifies modern prostitutes.

Linked to the pursuit of money, however, is quite another amazing and different phenomenon which has also been observed and recorded in the past. Writers of such varying backgrounds as Alexander Kouprine (in *La Fosse Aux Filles*), Pietro Aretino, Middleton and Dekker, all make the point that no man will walk past a prostitute without turning round two or three times to look at her. He is bound to detect at once a certain peculiarity about her. Clearly, there is something that distinguishes the prostitute and she could be said to suffer, as C. Hayward has so aptly put it in his book *The Courtesan* (London, The Cazenove Society, 1926) '. . . from the peculiar disability of being unable to look modest' so that even when she does not particularly wish to be the centre of attraction, she finds it difficult not to look bold. 'The resemblance between this and looking modest is sufficiently close for the two expressions to be puzzlingly alike, yet not close enough for the one to be decidedly mistaken for the other. The passer-by looks once at the courtesan, because she is attractive, as a modest woman may be, he looks twice because he sees that there is something peculiar about her, and that it has to do with sex.'

I do not think we need to labour this point. It is clearly self-evident, and so-called men of the world, womanizers and philanderers know only too well how easy it is to identify the woman who, for one reason or the other, whether for money or for pleasure or for glory, will not be ungenerous in granting her sexual favours.

*   *   *

Leaving on one side women who are by nature promiscuous and who, from a high moral standpoint, cannot be differentiated from prostitutes, but who for practical purposes do not fall within the scope of the definition that has been adopted, one finds that the present-day prostitutes can be divided broadly into three classes: (1) The lower-class prostitutes. (2) The call-girl. (3) The 'pleasure-girl'.

The lower-class prostitute is the English street-walker, the American hooker, the prostitute that does not necessarily operate from a fixed place of abode and who relies on what one might term passing trade. She is by definition the kind of prostitute towards whom the efforts of the police authorities are almost exclusively directed because she presents a greater threat to public order and decency and, in most cases, could be termed a public nuisance. She is the 'criminal' of the female class, the poor relation, the lowest of the low. Her monetary requirements may not be very great and her activities vary, as do those of all prostitutes. We do not need to concern ourselves here with the detail of the services usually available from any prostitute. Suffice it to say that, for practical purposes, prostitutes can be termed as one-way, two-way, three-way and sado-masochistic girls. Little imagination is needed to understand these terms.

The call-girl is the better type of prostitute. Her services are no different from those rendered by her sisters in the lower class, but they are inevitably more expensive because the cost of the accommodation, which is often of a high standard, and a telephone, have to be defrayed. She can also afford to be somewhat selective both in the choice of customer and in the services she is willing to perform. She is the sexual entrepreneur of the modern age.

Then there is the pleasure-girl. This term has been adopted as a generalization to cover beauty queens, 'hackettes', social climbers, cover-girls, models etc. In a word, the term refers to all those women who use their bodies and female allure, not merely in return for money but in consideration of obtaining contacts with famous or powerful men, and to achieve social advancement. Also under this heading are to be included all those women who use their allure to marry aristocrats or millionaires, or to sleep with public figures so that they can make money by writing about their encounters at a later date.

In the same way, over the past decade or so, there has been a polarization, in the United Kingdom of political tendencies and of social status, so that the middle class has been weakened and there are more people with less money at the bottom of the scale and fewer people with more money at the top end of the scale. By the same token, we have achieved a polarization even among prostitutes. There are plenty of street-walkers in London, Glasgow, Manchester, Birmingham, Liverpool, Edinburgh, Sheffield and other principal cities. There are also many more call-girls. The call-girls are doing much better than the street-walkers. If they do not have their own flats, they operate from hotel lounges or bars, have contacts with hotel porters and with massage parlours or escort agencies.

Interestingly enough, the present-day distinction between the different classes of prostitutes has existed throughout history, in the sense that there have always been clients prepared to pay more money for a better kind of service. And human nature being what it is, it is not surprising that in the superior types of brothels, prostitutes are paid to affect the style of the 'gutter' (street-walker) girls, whereas in the cheaper establishments prostitutes take on the airs of ladies from the upper echelons of society. As has been observed, the soldier who frequents a low-class brothel expects to meet a representation of the kind of upper-class woman whom he would not, in the normal course of events, be able to approach. In the more expensive establishments, customers prefer the style of the gutter: this is a point which reflects human nature and is made by Zola's 'Nana' when she says: 'The most gentlemanly-looking men were generally the most filthily-minded. All the polish vanished and the brute appeared beneath, exacting in his monstrous tastes and refined in his perversions.'

The distinction between high- and low-class types of prostitutes also struck Tolstoy. In *Resurrection*, when comparing a street-walker with a 'well-shaped and aggressively finely-dressed woman', he says: 'This woman of the street is like stagnant smelling water offered to those whose thirst is greater than their disgust; the other one in the theatre is like the poison which, unnoticed, corrupts everything it gets into.'

Furthermore, women themselves like to be treated in a manner which is the reverse of their true nature. According to most experienced philanderers, one should treat a prostitute as though she were a lady and a lady as though she were a tart, thus emphasizing, I suppose, the contrast between reality and fantasy. Nowadays, in a strange sense, we take less exception to the 'call-girls' who operate in this manner; we accept them in the same way as the courtesan-type prostitute of the Renaissance was accepted. Yet we reject the street-walker. Clearly, the recommendations of the Wolfenden Report were the result of a class effort based on the principle 'Out of sight, out of mind'; despite or perhaps because of the absence of adequate representation by women on the Wolfenden Committee, the result is not only sexist but snobbish. This matter is considered further below.

The same thing has occurred in the United States. Prostitutes exist in all the major centres, from New York and Chicago to Los Angeles and New Orleans. But the street-walker type is gradually disappearing, replaced by semi-professionals and amateurs and, more particularly, the call-girl. The major difference between the UK and the USA as regards the operations of call-girls, however, seems to lie in the fact that in America, vice syndicates have largely taken over the activities of the call-girl, which they supervise and organize, and from which a great deal of money is made.

The distinction between these three types of woman, however, is only a temporary one, for the lines of definition are breaking down. Just as modern woman is distinguishable from her predecessor of a hundred years ago, so the modern prostitute is developing in different directions.

The intellectual and physical emancipation of woman from man has given her the initiative. By ceasing to be a mother, she is no longer house-bound. Her virginity is no longer so prizeworthy as it was and therefore she has intercourse at a much earlier age. In her relationship with man, she does not have to stop and consider whether of the two persons who have to ride a horse, one would have to ride in front. She is riding the horse on her own.

By this I do not mean that a prostitute is motivated solely by economic necessity: in the last decade of the twentieth century no Western woman is forced to become a prostitute. I mean simply that woman is spurred into adopting the way of life of a prostitute by realizing that through selling sexual favours, she will earn more than by being a receptionist-telephonist, or whatever, or will be able to supplement whatever other income she has for whatever reasons.

This is not a popular approach to modern prostitutes. It would be so convenient to say that modern woman is forced into prostitution by unemployment, poverty, the slave-trade, the lack of social services, unwanted pregnancy, ill-treatment by men; in other words, by all those factors which, from Mary Astell through Mary Wollstonecraft and on to Josephine Butler, caused feminism to campaign with violence and ample justification against the way in which the men of past centuries treated woman. Those feminists were quite right in what they said: times continue to change. The modern prostitute knows exactly what she is doing and her degradation, if that is what it is, occurs no more as a result of social circumstances than smoking as a result of misinformation. Like Cynthia, the celebrated mistress of Propertius, she keenly '. . . looks at the gold and not the hand that gives it'. She is fully aware that for some men she provides compensation for what Flaubert termed 'boredom, that silent spider'.

Furthermore, it should not be forgotten that there is definitely a prostitute type, as we have already seen – not in the sense in which Lombroso understood the matter, since he looked upon prostitutes as biologically degenerate, the criminals of the female sex, but more along the lines laid down by the so-called psychological theory, formulated quite clearly in *Sex and Character* by Otto Weininger. Weininger maintains that the mother and the prostitute (the 'matron' and the whore) are the two poles of femininity. Obviously, for the purposes of his theory, the word 'prostitute' is not confined to street-walkers but includes large numbers of respectable or married women: the distinguishing feature seems to be their attitude and behaviour in relation to the male.

The predisposition in some women towards prostitute-like behaviour cannot be doubted. Most teachers of young girls will tell you that in each class, even in the 11-to-14-year-old groups, there are always one or perhaps two girls who exhibit precocious traits of sexuality. This is not to say that they will become prostitutes; of course, that would be absurd: there are virtuous women who are highly sexed. Equally, as my own case-studies show, in a number of prostitutes, both love and sexuality are much less marked than the man in the street would believe. As Nanna puts it in Aretino's *The Education of Pippa* but much more pointedly in his *The Life of Courtesans*: '*A woman who submits to all men cannot love one*'. In the same vein, '. . . a whore is not a woman. She is a whore'.

Elsewhere, when asked by her friend, Antonia, to whom she was explaining the attitude of prostitutes, where she had left the lust of a whore, Nanna replies: 'Antonia: he who keeps on drinking never feels thirsty and he who is always at table rarely feels hungry and if a whore ever feels inclined for a man, it is because of a certain craving like that of a pregnant woman who eats raw garlic and green prunes. And I swear to you, by the happy fate I am seeking for Pippa, that lust is the least longing harlots have, for they are always thinking how to tear the heart and liver out of others.'

The statement that some women are born prostitutes is often vigorously challenged by psychologists, sociologists and feminists, each having their own particular axe to grind or their own theory to defend. But apart from being of venerable antiquity, it is capable of being defended on the facts. In the days when parents had the willingness and, above all, the power to influence their children's choice of spouse, the sons were urged to look at the prospective wife's mother and project the prospective wife's image further in time by some 20/30 years, on the basis that the girl would end up by being the same as the mother and the pretty teenager would become the possibly worn, more mature woman.

This approach reflected all three of the reasons why the statement that, if the mother is a whore it is more likely that the daughter will be one too, can be supported. Firstly, there is the natural mimicry, the imprint deriving from child-rearing and cohabitation, which makes the young girl copy what her mother does. From the painting of nails and the application of lipstick at an early age to other more sophisticated techniques and mannerisms, any daughter is, in most cases, almost a carbon copy of the mother who has reared her.

The second reason is a variation of the first and arises from environmental considerations. A girl brought up in a household where the mother is known to have lovers or 'customers' or generally is promiscuous, will herself find a promiscuous way of life much easier, much more normal, if not inevitable, to adopt. It is not only a question of a less censorious attitude on the part of the mother or, indeed, the parents generally; it is rather the fact that the air the girl breathes is permeated with a 'moral' looseness which cannot fail to leave its mark from a very early age. In the same way, the daughter of a sluttish woman will, herself, be sluttish; whereas a child brought up to adopt certain standards of personal cleanliness will probably never forget them.

Similarly, it has been proved statistically that children brought up in families where one or even two of the parents smoke, will almost inevitably be smokers themselves. The reverse is also true, namely that it is much less likely, statistically, that the children of non-smoking parents are smokers.

The third reason, however, is much more fundamental and at the risk of being criticized for repetition, it is that there is something in the make-up of certain women that predisposes them to being prostitutes: at least in the sense that it makes it easier for them to adopt a life of prostitution, if the other factors, whether of an attraction or predisposition, are relevant. This is not to say that all prostitutes are born such but merely to restate unequivocally the concept that, quite simply, some women are, in fact, born prostitutes. This, more than any other consideration explains why we have so far been unable to eradicate prostitution, and are unlikely ever to do so.

To return to Weininger, it is quite clear that he is not interested in the theory that prostitutes are made by social conditions and, although Helene Deutch has severely criticized, if not derided, Weininger's hypothesis ['This complete unmotherly type is possibly a fantasy product in a certain type of men who have in their own imaginations established a sharp division between sexuality (prostitutes) and motherliness (unsexual mothers)'], one is left with the sneaking suspicion that this typecasting of some women has more to be said for it than modern contemporary psychiatric research would like to believe.

The reader's initial reaction to this proposition may well be sceptical, to say the least, either because it challenges basic notions of common sense allied to free will, or because of conditioning in the context of a Calvinist/Protestant ethic. The reader might feel that self-determination would ensure that no one was compelled to follow any particular path, that man being master (or woman being mistress) of human destinies, it should be inconceivable that there were any element of 'pre-determination' about one's sexual inclinations.

The proposition, however, that some women are actually born prostitutes is more readily acceptable on closer examination. After all, we do have human beings who are affected by satyriasis, nymphomania, priapism and recurring or even constant hyper-sexuality. There are some who maintain that nymphomania is essentially a state of mind, but it cannot be denied that the other 'pathological' states which have just been mentioned are of a physical nature and result either from hormonal imbalances or other causes which originate in the physical/chemical side of the body first and then transfer to the psyche.

I am not a doctor and cannot give a full medical explanation. But it is within my experience that although some prostitutes are nymphomaniacs, and some may even be hyper-sexed, most of them are neither. And yet, they embark on a life of prostitution. Here, I am reassured to read in Lindi St Clair's *The Autobiography of Miss Whiplash* (Piatkus 1992, page 166) that the view that I hold is shared by her. She says:

> Having busily researched prostitution at first hand since I was 13 years old, I have proved that only certain types of girls *with a particular chemical make-up* enter the trade.

The emphasis is mine. She goes on to say:

> I can accept the argument that some no-hopers drift into prostitution through poverty and desperation, but these girls are not virgins and are sexually permissive to begin with. I back up my findings by comparing these girls to others who are in the same situation, but have a different chemical make-up. They are the ones who say 'I would rather die than sell my body' and they get by through doing menial jobs or begging or stealing. They would never prostitute themselves because they are 'not that type'.

Lindi St Clair ought to know, for she earned a living and acquired notoriety through prostitution. I would attach greater weight to what she says than to what is stated in a dozen text books by sociologists and psychologists who, in reality, have no first-hand experience.

It has always seemed eminently sensible to me that in order to achieve results and to understand how things work, one should seek the views of those who earn a living successfully out of what they are doing, rather than listening to what theoreticians have to say. For example, if I want to know how to make money, I seek the advice of a Rothschild or, indeed, of anyone else who has proved how to make money, because he has got it: I do not listen to so-called 'good ideas' I may hear in the pub. If I want to know what is wrong with my cow, I listen to an experienced stock-man or to a vet, but I do not go and consult any budding Oscar Wilde. If I need advice on the law, I go to an experienced solicitor, but I certainly do not listen to what a musician in a jazz band tells me. For these reasons, I believe what Linda St Clair has stated about the inherent pre-disposition of some women to live as prostitutes. And I am reassured that quite independently of her, I reached the same conclusion.

*   *   *

Every writer who has endeavoured to identify one or more causes for the activities of prostitutes – with a notable exception to which reference will shortly be made – has concentrated on one or two characteristics in an attempt to distinguish the prostitute from other women. Accordingly, findings of fact have been exhibited, usually as a result of studies and interviews, and case histories meant to be more or less titillating, have been appended, to show that the normal prostitute is either: frigid, lesbian, criminal, of below average intelligence, greedy, insensitive, sadistic, infertile, unloved, a neglected or abused child, an anti-social being, the daughter of a whore, a drug addict, lazy, a thief, a nymphomaniac, a witch, or comes from immigrant families, is apathetic, a man-hater, incapable of orgasm, mentally ill, oversexed, immoral, amoral, alcoholic, spendthrift, an idiot, fond of living dangerously, easily bored; or has become a whore as a result of: seduction, abandonment, ill-treatment by parents, relatives or husbands, idleness, drunkenness, alcoholism, pregnancy, (either unwitting or unwanted), loss of virginity, drunkenness of one or both parents, or an unstable personality or of inferior homelife generally.

It was left to Harry Benjamin and R.E.L. Masters in *Prostitution and Morality* (Souvenir Press, London, 1962) to set the record straight and try to explain that no single cause or event provides a satisfactory explanation of why some modern women are prostitutes and others are not. In their work (pages 90 to 100), they accept that each prostitute has '. . . her own

peculiar constellation of motives and formative experiences
relative to her adoption of a career'. They themselves
subdivide prostitutes into two groups, namely the group of
women '. . . who may be said to have voluntarily entered into
"the life" on a more or less rational basis and mainly as the
result of a free choice'; and the second group, made up of
women '. . . who engage in prostitution mainly because they
are compelled to do so by their own psycho-neurotic needs'.
The former, they term voluntary prostitutes; the latter,
compulsive prostitutes.

They further analyse the problem by determining that with
regard to the latter type of prostitute, namely the one who
does not exercise a free choice as to her profession, there are
three factors that influence the 'decision', namely (1) predisposing (2) attracting and (3) precipitating. Predisposing
factors are, for example, a broken home or parental
promiscuity; attracting factors are the larger earnings or a
more exciting life and precipitating factors may be an unhappy
love affair, enticement, etc.

One cannot quarrel with Benjamin and Masters but the
feeling one gets when considering the prostitutes of the
nineteen eighties and nineties is that they are motivated
primarily by the profit motive. As has been said more than
once, men want sex and girls want money. It could almost be
said that, for some girls, the search to improve their lot,
provided by life as a prostitute, through greater earnings for
less work, is no more than the extension (in a time where
money seems to be the only god) of woman's innate feeling
for security. Of course, there are prostitutes who display some
or all or a combination of the characteristics that have been
listed above. But in the majority of cases it is the attracting
factors, as identified by Benjamin and Masters, which
determine whether a woman becomes a prostitute and of
these attracting factors, money is the principal, if not the only
factor.

There is one final consideration peculiarly relevant to greed.
In Britain, in the 1990s, the recession is affecting the type of

woman who becomes a whore. There are now very young girls, hardly out of school, who are willing to perform sexual services of most kinds, often in underground car parks, usually in motor cars; the locality seems unimportant. There are many wives, whose husbands are out of work, who take advantage of their spouse's absence at the pub or the employment exchange, or elsewhere, to earn sufficient money to keep the family together by offering their sexual services to motorists or others; some of them even take part in lesbian activities, usually well remunerated by their much better off and socially elevated sisters.

According to J. Haskey (1989 Population Trends N.55 HMSO), one half of the single mothers with children who are now classed as 'lone parents' are under 25. In 1986 there were about 1.3 one-parent families caring for two million children, nine out of ten of such parents were women and nearly two-thirds of them were living in poverty, i.e. either receiving Income Support (formerly Supplementary Benefit) or having an income below subsistence level. Of these, it is estimated that women were less likely to work than men (four out of ten only). Estimates are not available, but it is commonly believed by social workers and researchers that a percentage of these 'lone parent' women have turned to prostitution for survival. One of the case-histories referred o earlier (Lyn) clearly falls into this category.

Prostitution is spreading at most levels of Western society generally. But this is not a truth that we wish to face; much better to wallow in titivating news and pornography than to acknowledge that our next-door neighbour may be, if not by leaning, then out of necessity, a tart. It is these changed social conditions that make the assessment of present-day prostitutes very difficult. Gone are the days when the noun 'prostitute' identified a particular kind of woman well known to be operating on the fringes of society, whether working in brothels or independently, on a full-time basis. These were the prostitutes that became known to the police, to the medical profession and sometimes to psychologists. It was from them that numbers were derived that gave some indication of how many prostitutes there were, and what their leanings might have been.

However, it must not be forgotten that, even in times past, it was difficult to be precise, because prostitutes did not broadcast their activities or their numbers. Even the most recent statistical information obtained on prostitutes in the UK, that collated by Kinnell as a result of a study carried out in Birmingham in 1988, which gave a figure of 2,000 prostitutes as working there, had to rely mainly upon information obtained from street prostitutes themselves. Furthermore, another important factor to be borne in mind is that many investigations into the causes of prostitution are made of those women who have been caught by the police and are actually in prison or before the courts, or, in a few cases, in hospital.

At the outset I remarked on how regrettable it is that no large-scale enquiry of prostitutes along similar lines of the Kinsey Reports has ever been carried out. (You may recall that Dr Kinsey and his colleagues interviewed 12,00 males and 8,000 females.) Conclusions continue to be drawn, therefore, from inadequate and incomplete studies and very often, it is easy to base them particularly upon the so-called abnormality or abnormal personality of the prostitute in question. It has been remarked quite accurately that '. . . if similar investigations were made regarding secretaries or night club performers, similar results would be shown' (Dr Fernando Henriques in *The Sociology of Prostitution*, page 311).

That there is a 'neurotic' component in a particular type of woman who decides to be prostitute cannot be disputed; equally, it is so easy to make much more money as a prostitute than as a clerical worker. And one thing is certain: the rewards are much more immediate and can come at a much earlier age. How many girls in their late teens or early 20s have the opportunity of meeting such interesting and important men as some of the more select band of prostitutes do nowadays? Politicians, judges, journalists, doctors, spies. Benjamin and

Masters (page 110) argue that this particular 'glorification' of
the work of the prostitute resulting from her mixing with the
kind of people that she would never come across in her
ordinary life, is one of the principal reasons why it is almost
impossible to rehabilitate a certain type of prostitute.
Ultimately, though, whatever other factors may be
significant, money overtakes them all. The French used to
say that it is money that makes wars. We could paraphrase that
to say that it is money that makes whores. It is certainly not
lust, if Pietro Aretino is to be believed, whom we have already
quoted; and it is not as though Aretino was a misogynist. What
he says echoes Plautus and is picked up, albeit in different
style, by all those who wrote about prostitutes, from Lucian,
Bandello and Brantôme to Villon and Baudelaire.

One final observation, which is valid for prostitutes of all
times and all needs. It is a common criticism of them that
prostitutes degrade love. This objection to their activities is
clearly the result of a misapprehension. Love is no more
degraded by prostitution than human dignity is by sewage. A
prostitute does not provide love but merely gratification.
Whether the *quid pro quo* for sexual services is the jar of wine
to which Martial refers in one of his epigrams or the bag 'from
Ancre's in the Rue de la Paix worth 4,500 francs' which Cora
Pearl received from the Duke of Nabaud, only in the most
exceptional circumstances does the prostitute provide love to a
customer. On the emotional plane, one must never overlook
what C. Haywood in *The Courtesan* (page 489) terms '. . . the
difference between the apparent eagerness and the real
insensibility of the courtesan'. As Oscar Wilde put it in the
Harlot's House, although one could hear inside 'that house' the
sound of music and dancing, according to him 'the dead are
dancing with the dead'.

If I may be forgiven for quoting him again, Wilde sums up
admirably the moral insensitivity of the prostitute when in his
other poem, 'Impressions du Matin', he finds himself along the
Thames Embankment at dawn. Day has come, one trace of
the night remains:

'But one pale woman all alone
The Daylight kissing her wan hair,
Loitered beneath the gas lamp's flare
With lips of flame and heart of stone.'

Chapter Seven

Arguments against decriminalization & legal brothels

A rguments against decriminalization of the activities of prostitutes and the establishment of licensed brothels are put forward mainly by three categories of people: (a) moralists in the general sense; (b) those concerned with religious considerations; (c) feminists.

Summary

The arguments can be summarized as follows: THE MORALIST ARGUMENTS: (i) To give official recognition to what prostitutes do would amount to the codification of a double standard in human relations and would encourage promiscuity. More particularly, if a prostitute and/or a brothel were to be taxed, the State would be deriving income from an immoral activity. THE RELIGIOUS ARGUMENTS: There is a sanctity in human sexual relations which is perverted by sexual activity with prostitutes; promiscuity is sin. THE FEMINIST ARGUMENTS: It is beneath the dignity of woman to be treated as a chattel that can be bought and sold; woman should not be a slave to man. When examined in some depth, however, all these objections appear to be hypocritical as well as logically and practically deficient.

The so-called moralist objections

The difficulty of applying so-called moral criteria to sexual behaviour is well known. Equally known is the fact that the course of history has often been altered by man's sexual whims. Indeed, in some Mediterranean countries, there are old proverbs to the effect that the pulling power of a single pubic hair is greater than that of a fully masted brigantine or, as D.H. Lawrence put it, that the woman of today is the captain of the hymenal barque.

It is of course theoretically possible to legislate against sexual drive, but extremely difficult to be successful. In fact, the history of our Western society shows beyond a shadow of a doubt that the tendency is towards liberalization of sexual conduct rather than towards any further control by way of the criminal law. It is true that certain constraints still exist; for example, we legislate against rape, incest and indecent assaults. But the legislation is aimed at protecting the unwilling party and certainly does not apply to consenting adults. In fact, we have now liberalized almost completely, save for minors, the laws against homosexual males; consenting lesbians were never subject to the criminal law, save insofar as their conduct may have been treated as indecent and as a public nuisance.

Clearly, by providing a service, the prostitute consents. It could be argued that by giving official sanction to the activities of prostitutes, the State is, in a sense, elevating the sexual urge to a higher plane than maybe it deserves. There is force in this argument, but the truth is that if the premise is correct, that order has to be restored to sexual relations, then the liberalization of certain activities by prostitutes, must be less objectionable from the moral standpoint.

The moralist objection, it must be admitted, is a respectable one. Despite the strong temptations of the flesh by which Dr Johnson was often vexed, he and Boswell could quite happily agree '. . . that much more misery than happiness, upon the whole, is produced by illicit commerce between the sexes' (*Boswell's Life of Johnson*, Saturday, 30 July 1783). One wonders, therefore, whether both of them might have been applying double standards in so agreeing: Boswell's own inclinations are well known.

As for the famous Doctor, much respected in most fields, one must be somewhat wary of adopting his judgements in the sexual sphere for, it should be recalled, he would 'steadily' enforce more severe laws against fornication, 'and would promote marriage' (ibid., Friday, 5 April 1776). Highly commendable, but quite unrealistic in the world of the 1990s, where fornication and divorce are the order of the day. Not that the good Doctor had anything against prostitutes, for his charitable spirit caused him to take good care of one of them whom he found '. . . coming home late one night, . . . lying in the street, so much exhausted that she could not walk'; he took her home and took care of her '. . . with all tenderness for a long time, at considerable expense, till she was restored to health'. Indeed, he even endeavoured to put her 'into a virtuous way of living', though Boswell does not relate (June 1784) how successful he was.

As to the argument that if the activities of prostitutes were legalized, taxes would have to be levied on the consequent profits and in this way the State would truly be committing an immoral deed because it would be profiting from depraved activity, it hardly bears scrutiny. Most modern States already profit from taxes on immorality. The problem starts when you endeavour to define what morality and immorality mean.

To some people, gambling is clearly immoral; and yet, profits from gambling are taxed, bingo and lotteries are booming. To others, contraception is objectionable; and yet, contraceptives are sold quite openly and there is a very rich trade in them at present. There are people who would argue that the health hazards consequent upon smoking make taxes on cigarettes highly immoral. There are others who believe that doctors should not earn a living performing abortions, that pornography is regrettable and that the sale of armaments is a disgrace. And yet, all these activities are perfectly lawful in most countries of the world and all attract taxes. Why is it that when it comes to sexual activity with prostitutes, the 'morality' flag is run up the mast with breakneck speed? What has happened to legitimize all the other activities that have just been referred to?

The vagaries of our tax laws are historic and quite numerous. Illegality and immorality have already created their own problems. But there is no need to carry principle too far, any more than was done in the Middle Ages when not only local authorities but also some popes taxed prostitutes and brothels. It is a matter of record that Pope Clement II (Pontif 1046–47) decreed that anyone engaged in prostitution should leave their property to the Church; prostitution itself was taxed also in France, Germany, Portugal and Spain. For modern purposes, we might also take some comfort from the dictum of Holmes J. in the 'United States v Sullivan 274 US p259' who, in the USA Supreme Court, gave short shrift to the argument of a bootlegger who contended that the Fifth Amendment, directed against self-incrimination, entitled him to refrain from making an income tax return.

Closer to the matter in hand, Canadian law has decided favourably the question whether a prostitute's professional earnings are subject to income tax, arguing that the source of monies did not matter and it was taxable. This decision occurred in 1955 but there are subsequent decisions in 1960, 1964 and 1965 to the effect that the expenses of running a call-girl business in Vancouver, for instance, were deductible from the gross income for the purposes of income tax, if they could be proved. Nor is this a novel concept, since it is recorded that at Nuremburg, in the Middle Ages, money spent visiting prostitutes was tax deductible.

A further point made by those who argue that the State should not profit from illegal or immoral conduct is that, once you have established the principle that the relevant profits should be taxed, you cannot help investigating the detail of conduct which is sinful. On the other hand, there are some people who genuinely believe that it is iniquitous that the earnings of a prostitute should be tax free.

In English law it would appear that, either as a result of a dilution in moral principles or because of real need on the part of the Revenue or, hopefully, because of greater logical consistency, it has now been decided that, although a trade or a contract may in themselves be illegal in the sense that the law would refuse to enforce them, the resultant profits are nonetheless taxable (IRC v Aken 1988 STC69), it being left to the Commissioners to decide as a matter of fact whether a particular tax-payer carried on a trade, (trade being defined by the law as 'every trade, manufacture, adventure, or concern in the nature of a trade').

It is clear that prostitution *per se* is not illegal in the UK and therefore the profits acquired thereby are taxable as the profits of any trade would be, under Case I of Schedule D. To that extent, moralists have failed. The State is already reaping a profit in the form of taxes, from the 'immoral' activities of prostitutes. Economic force has prevailed over morality. The trouble is that human beings are contradictory creatures and there will always exist a difference between officially stated aims, whether governmental or personal, and resultant conduct.

Many of those moralists who object to prostitutes on the ground that they encourage and endorse immoral behaviour would not lift a finger to stop tobacco companies flooding Third World countries with life-threatening cigarettes, or to prevent the sale of armaments. One wonders how many more people are killed by lung cancer, heart attacks or strokes as a result of smoking, and by the manufacture and use of armaments, than by a life of whoring. True, lechers might catch VD in some form or the other; but even that can be avoided by taking suitable precautions.

As for encouraging promiscuity, the reader is referred to the pages which follow and deal with the rate of adultery by spouses. We have enough promiscuity at present in our society to which neither prostitutes nor brothels contribute one iota. (This particular objection is considered at greater length in Chapter 8.)

Apart from Holland, Germany and Denmark, countries

which have accepted the fact that prostitution cannot be eradicated and have allowed brothels, the response of the remaining Western countries to prostitutes and brothels is like that of the ostrich. It is often said that, as a society develops, social projects will be embarked upon which will result in the rehabilitation of the street-walker. There does not seem to be any real sign of such projects on the horizon in any European country. Whether any exist in the USA I have been unable to ascertain. In any event, when the expression 'social project' is used by well-meaning people, it seems to revolve around the notion of sex education in schools. Whatever their merits, sex education programmes have had absolutely no impact on the existence of prostitutes of all kinds throughout the Western world, save that it just might have encouraged more (and younger) girls to wider sexual experimentation and 'profiteering'.

It would be much more profitable to accept that prostitutes are socially, if not morally, necessary and that any pangs of conscience we may suffer as a result of accepting that argument, ought to be weighed against the benefit that would derive not only to society as a whole, but in particular to the prostitutes themselves, if we ceased to treat them as evil.

There are many fields where strongly-held beliefs clash violently with each other on specific issues: for example, what to do with the motor car, with cigarette advertising, abortion, the sale of arms, the protection of the environment and so on. The very same broadminded and so-called democratic society which allows different opinions to be canvassed on any one of the above issues finds it difficult to digest the argument that what a prostitute does is no more unconscionable than what an adulterous spouse does.

The moralists who maintain that to recognize a prostitute is to codify a double standard, ignore completely, it seems to me, the difference between love and lust for which human beings have found it very difficult, throughout recorded history, to find any kind of reconciliation. This is the nub of the problem. It can be said that for some men sex is no different from a good massage: it is all a physical sensation with no emotional ties.

Equally, there are women – and now that reliable contraception has eliminated the risk of pregnancy, their number is increasing – for whom the distinction between love and lust is at least as clear as it is for some men. To acknowledge that prostitutes, whether male or female, may perform a useful service for these people, is not to codify a double standard but merely to recognize that, in matters sexual, certain human beings can be almost schizophrenic.

It is understandable that, from a high moral standpoint, one would not wish to aggravate the lot of those women who, by adopting a life of prostitution, have in a sense let the side down. If the number of such women were reducing, then the nature of the moral objection would be more cogent; but against an increasing number of prostitutes, it amounts to burying one's head in the sand.

The religious objection

Since we are concerned mainly with Western society, the religion which is to be considered is the Christian one. On this occasion, too, one is entitled to complain of a great deal of hypocrisy in tackling the problem. This hypocrisy is only marginally less objectionable than that adopted by the Christian religions when dealing with divorce. (I exclude Roman Catholics from this stricture.)

The association of ideas between divorce and prostitution is not so remote as may first appear and is considered in greater detail elsewhere. Adultery is immoral according to Christian values, but Western society has embraced divorce warmly. Both when dealing with divorce and when dealing with prostitutes, the Christian religions seem to find it difficult to make up their minds. A few examples will illustrate the point. In the first instance, one should underline the concept that when it comes to divorce, both the Old and the New Testament take fairly opposite views. Under Jewish law, a man was quite free to write out divorce papers and send his wife away from her home (*Deuteronomy* 24). A wife was to be respected but did not obviously have the same rights as a man. In addition, it was fatal to marry foreign women. When Ezra learned of the inter-marriage with non-Jews, he knelt in prayer to the Lord and asked forgiveness for this disgrace (*Ezra* 8) and arrangements were made for the foreign women to be sent away (*Ezra* 9 and 10).

This approach to divorce no doubt reflects the general approach to woman by the Bible which, again, seems inconsistent. The rather cavalier fashion in which these 'foreign' wives were dealt with does seem to contrast with the passionate feeling for woman contained in the 'Song of Songs'. And yet, when Zachariah's angel saw the lid of the basket being raised and a woman appear, he said '. . . this woman represents wickedness' and pushed her down into the basket and put the lid back on (*Zachariah* 5). One pauses to observe that this is often the way in which the churches would wish to treat prostitutes. Let us hide them in the wicker basket and forget about them.

One does not know, of course, how far those who recorded the words of the Lord are to be trusted, for it is unlikely that a Supreme Being would be inconsistent in matters of such importance as the relationship between man and woman. If we are to believe Malachi (*Malachi* 2), the Lord God of Israel is recorded as saying: 'I hate divorce. I hate it when one of you does such a cruel thing to his wife. Make sure that you do not break a promise to be faithful to your wife.' Which goes perhaps some way to redress the balance between Ezra's and Zachariah's statements and to anticipate the New Testament, but is of little comfort to those who seek consistency.

Both the Bible and the New Testament appear to strike discordant notes also when it comes to the relationships between man and woman. This is hardly surprising, for they are both concerned in different ways with the status of marriage which, by definition, differs according to whatever century or culture one is considering. It is exceptionally difficult to draw a general principle which will cover every marriage situation or even to find the principle which will embrace a concept which some people consider practically the *opposite* of marriage, namely prostitution.

Others might say that divorce is the opposite of marriage and yet we have been quite content to acknowledge divorce as a fairly normal event, as statistics show. It does seem a little odd that we find prostitution objectionable whilst embracing divorce. But back to the Old Testament, where there are concepts which, by modern standards, appear somewhat repugnant. One instance will suffice, namely the destruction of Jericho: the city and everything in it was destroyed by being burnt to the ground, saving only things made of gold, silver, bronze and iron, a useful booty. Only one person was spared together with her household because she had provided help to Joshua's spies. She was Rahab. It may be a coincidence, of course, that Rahab was a prostitute (*Joshua* 6).

The New Testament at least is more consistent since Matthew, Mark and Luke are unanimous in stating and supporting the sanctity and indissolubility of marriage (*Matthew* 5.31 and 19.3, *Mark* 10.2 and *Luke* 16.18) and it is no doubt true to say that the Catholic Church rigidly maintains the indissoluble nature of marriage, certainly in theory (we are ignoring the vagaries of Canon Law) and mainly in fact (notwithstanding the reservation 'for the sake of fornication' made by Matthew in 5:17:37).

The Protestant Church, on the other hand, recognizes divorce but strongly opposes prostitution and State brothels, as evidenced by its representations to the Wolfenden Committee, as do the Methodists, despite the words they use in their marriage service. The least hypocritical seems to be the Jewish religion, at least in the sense that in the marriage service the spouses do not bind themselves for life. Jews, Moslems, Hindus, Protestants, Baptists and Catholics, to choose but a few, all seem to have different views about divorce in the same way as they have different views about prostitution. One is tempted to remark in passing that if there is only one God, as most people would suppose, His spokesmen have been taking liberties with His doctrine.

The same kind of hypocrisy applies to prostitution and in this case it is just as marked in Catholic as in non-Catholic countries. Brothels were legal for decades, for example, in France, Italy and Spain. The Church did not lift a finger to ensure their abolition; but then, it is my belief that the Church of Rome has always adopted a more tolerant and understanding attitude to certain aspects of sexuality, despite its theoretical abhorrence of adultery, promiscuity and all kinds of deviant conduct.

It is accepted that there is a clear-cut difference between love and lust. The fathers of the Church set the tone: the views of St Augustine and St Thomas Aquinas have already been noted: women were regarded as producers of the next generation and the sexual act was intended exclusively for procreation. This, of course, is technically quite true. The two essential natural functions are survival and the perpetuation of the species. The former is catered for by food and the latter by intercourse. In order to ensure such aims, marriage and the family unit are necessary; the marriage should be indissoluble ('What God has joined together let no man put asunder') and the family bond should be strengthened. And that is why the Catholic Church has always maintained that the primary purpose of the contract of marriage is the generation and education of offspring; it is only as a secondary purpose that we find references to mutual help and the allaying of concupiscence.

The view of the Catholic Church, however, is not universally true. Whereas it cannot be denied that marriage and the family unit are vital to the stability of society, the fact is that procreation and the continuation of the species can be ensured also by polygyny and polyandry. For the Church of Rome, sexual gratification is an incident of the marriage relationship, the procreative function being paramount. Gratification of erotism is to be found elsewhere.

However, as has been seen, the fathers of the Church did acknowledge that gratification was needed and would have to be found with prostitutes. St Thomas Aquinas provides a healthy dose of cynicism by saying that this mentality explains why the Catholic Church has always tolerated the existence of legalized prostitution. Its primary aims, namely procreation and the strengthening of the marital bond, took precedence over any theoretical, moral judgement. The Catholic Church, whilst preaching restraint and respect for the marital bond, has accepted the realities of life.

One would venture to suggest that adopting the same approach that the end justifies the means, if confronted with evidence that showed conclusively that the activities of prostitutes should be decriminalized, the Catholic Church at least would not be too violently opposed, since early on the Church accepted that prostitution was, in fact, a profession of sexual activity. But it is true that ambivalence has always prevailed. For example, in the year 305 A.D. a Council of the Church excommunicated whores, except those who had married Christians. The theory was that by marrying and receiving Communion, they had left their previous life behind. Even a Christian Emperor like Theodosius continued the Roman practice of levying taxes on prostitutes.

It was left to Justinian, who did so much to codify the laws of the Roman Empire, to increase penalties on prostitution. But then, whatever he did in this context must, in retrospect, be suspect since he married a notorious woman, Theodora, and, as has been recorded, one of his generals, Belisarius, appears to have been himself the son of a prostitute.. His wife apparently was only marginally better than Theodora.

The contention that the official recognition of prostitutes and brothels represents a safety valve and helps to preserve the marital relationship is of venerable antiquity. Even leaving aside the 'capricious lusts' referred to by St Augustine, and the view of prostitutes adopted by the Christian Church throughout the intervening centuries, it was felt safer for a married man to indulge in extra-conjugal activity with a prostitute than with a mistress. These days, prostitutes who agree to be interviewed by the media, in general claim that they do indeed perform a useful function and that many a marriage, according to them, has been saved by the service that they offer to errant husbands.

Feminists and most moralists decry this approach, as they reject prostitutes and what they have to offer. And so do the Churches. The usual criticism of the activities of prostitutes levelled by the Christian churches is that fornication is a sin and should not be encouraged. This, of course, is logically unexceptional and sounds admirable in theory. In practice, the position is otherwise.

Murder is a sin, as is theft. It is not suggested that the State should do nothing about such acts that are contrary to the moral law. To protect society, we have to lock up murderers and thieves. The greatest commandment of the Christian faith is love for one's neighbour. It is not suggested that consequently wars should not exist. The State has to cater for the consequences of murder and theft by punishing the offenders; and States make war. Why should the State not cater for the consequences of fornication by dealing with prostitutes?

The counter to that is that by confining murderers and thieves to prison, one is reducing the incidence of those crimes, whereas by confining prostitutes to brothels, one is encouraging fornication. But despite the apparent attractiveness of this argument, it, too, is not well-founded. It is not by failing to provide properly supervised and maintained State-controlled brothels that one eliminates fornication. The statistics that will shortly be quoted, concerning the number of divorce petitions on the grounds of adultery, show that fornication will occur. The demand for extra-marital sexual activity is there and if it is not satisfied by prostitutes of either sex, it will be satisfied by men and women who do not fall within the definition of prostitute which has already been provided.

It is wrong to maintain that because brothels do not exist, fornication is eliminated or at least reduced. The reverse seems to be the case and in practice society has always endeavoured to protect itself from activities which are either criminal in the social sense or immoral in the strict sense, or otherwise unpleasant. Sewage is no longer thrown out of the windows as it used to be in the Middle Ages and even later, but suitably disposed of from the household and sometimes even turned to good use in the form of fertilizers. Our Western society seems to be perfectly happy to deal with human excrement, but not with lust. One wonders why the higher standards of hygiene and medicine that have been attained over the past 100 years cannot also extend to a better appreciation of the services provided by prostitutes.

After all, and this is a point to which we shall return in the next chapter, when taking any kind of religious view of life, one has to balance it against the practical necessities of modern society. The scale is tipping in favour of recognition of the services rendered by prostitutes. Also, though not necessarily only, because the value of religion seems to be reducing. One can no longer convince spouses to be faithful to each other. The evidence points clearly and unequivocally in the opposite direction. For example, in the United Kingdom in 1987, of 150,557 divorce petitions which ended in divorce, 42,568 were granted to the husband and of theses, 18,989 were on the grounds of the wife's adultery.

The figures for 1988 are comparable. Out of 152,633 divorce petitions which ended in divorce, 42,977 were granted to the husband and of these 18,719 were on the grounds of the wife's adultery. In 1989, the equivalent figures are 150,113 divorce petitions, of which 42,350 were granted to the husband; and of these 18,143 were on the grounds of the wife's adultery. In 1990, we reached a peak in the number of divorce petitions of 152,523. Of these, 42,958 were granted to the husband, 18,143 on the grounds of the wife's adultery. (One should observe in passing, at this stage, that of the total number of divorce petitions in 1990, 109,565 were granted to the wife (two-and-a-half times the number of divorce petitions granted to husbands) but of these only 25,893 alleged adultery by the husband. In other words, more

husbands accused women of adultery than wives husbands.)
(H.M.S.O. Publications Series FM2 Nos. 14, 16, 17 & 18,
pages 89 and 90.)

The later set of statistics is found in the Office of Population
Censuses and Surveys Publication Series FM2 No. 19 of 1993,
which contains the figures for 1991. Summarized, these show
that of 158,745 divorces which took place in that year, 44,160
were granted to,the husband and 114,192 were granted to the
wife.

Of those granted to the husband, 18,356 were in respect of
the wife's adultery and of those granted to the wife, 26,381
were in respect of the husband's. Put differently, just under
50% of the husbands who got divorced in 1991 alleged
adultery by the wife, whereas in the case of the wife who was
divorcing the husband, just over 20% of them complained
about the husband's adultery.

Cynics might be tempted to remark in passing that these
figures may mean that the premise for about 40% of all
divorces in England and Wales was that the wife was not
satisfied with the husband's behaviour generally. So far so
obvious: but I would go further and say that in all likelihood,
she was not satisfied with his sexual performance. Given the
inherent stability of woman, it seems a little far-fetched to
believe that 40% of divorcing spouses were, in fact, satisfied
with the sexual prowess of their partners. It seems to me that
if their husband had performed well in bed, they would not
(a) have committed adultery themselves and (b) divorced
him.

Finally, one has to record with considerable regret the fact
that the impact of religion, in the broadest possible sense,
whether Protestant, Catholic, Methodist or whatever, in
Western society, is reducing. The tenets of the Christian
Churches as regards pre-marital abstinence, chastity (if not
virginity) and fidelity in marriage are heeded by fewer and
fewer people.

The feminist objection

Caution would appear to be recommended when using any derivative from the noun 'feminism' since it conveys different meanings to different people and, indeed, has different meanings in varying contexts. Even to try and define it is not easy, because any definition automatically amounts to a restriction and that in itself would not be acceptable to a true feminist.

Feminists themselves are a little uncertain about what they are supposed to be. It is a little trite, for example, to say as Dale Spender does (*Women of Ideas*, Pandora, 1982, page 8) that 'A feminist is a woman who does not accept man's socially-sanctioned view of himself. . . '. That is an unhelpful statement since there are millions of women who do not sing men's praises, either discordantly or in unison, but nevertheless do not go and burn their bras.

Another way to define feminism – an a definition is required in order to understand the nature of the feminist objection to prostitution – is to describe it as a view of nature and of life which argues that men and women are exactly the same, not only by reference to their equality before the law, but also in the physical sense. Unfortunately, there are certain feminists who maintain that not only are they are entitled to equal rights or job opportunities but who decry their physical and psychological traits, tendencies and peculiarities and equate themselves to man. Having gone that far, some feminists also argue that women are in fact far better than men. It is hardly a coincidence that Lady Mary Wortley Montague in her work *Woman Not Inferior to Man* claimed that the female sex was the better on the basis that '. . . no-one will deny but that at least upon the most modest computation there are a thousand bad men to one bad woman'.

This reminds me of how pithily Bertrand Russell put it in his *Marriage and Morals* (Unwin Paperbacks, London 1976, page 59): 'The rights of women did not of course depend upon any belief that women were morally or in any other way superior to men; they depended solely on their rights as

human beings or rather upon the general argument in favour
of democracy. But as always happens when an oppressed class
or nation is claiming its rights, advocates sought to strengthen
the general argument by their contention that woman had
peculiar merits and these merits were generally represented as
belonging to the moral order.'

There is no logical inconsistency here. No-one can dispute
the claims by women to equal treatment with men in society
and in the market-place. By the end of the present century,
observers of society will look back with astonishment to
women's battles for the vote, equal pay, better career
prospects, maternity leave etc. and wonder how primitive
and selfish our society was in the bad old days when women's
right to equal treatment was not recognized. It is perfectly
proper and useful that woman should be allowed and entitled
to do the same jobs as men, since there seems to be no sphere
of remunerated work where women should not be allowed to
prove that they can perform as well as men.

The difficulty, however, is that no matter how vigorously
women's rights to equality are pursued, both by the individual
and by the State, it is not easy to overcome the basic physical
and psychological differences between men and women that
have evolved over thousands of years. No matter how much
feminists and the Advertising Standards Authority may
complain, woman is physically, biologically and emotionally
different to man and that is the natural order of things. On the
one hand, we have attempts to defeminize woman by allowing
her a suitable place in business or on the career ladder; and on
the other hand, we have sexist descriptions of her. The
Advertising Standards Authority on the 28 February 1990
published a report where it considered the views of the public
on the way in which women are treated in advertising. In
1963 Betty Friedan had published *The Feminine Mystique*, a
book which sparked off a long debate on whether advertisers
were doing women an injustice when they created models
that women aspired to attain, whether it be in clothing or
body smells or otherwise, which were in fact overflattering to

women simply because they showed her principally as a sex object. It is not quite clear what the net result of the campaign and the findings of the A.S.A. is. From the nude women to Pirelli-type calendars, the choice is great but it is difficult to draw firm conclusions as to the effect on the relationship between the sexes of depicting women as objects of lust, since this is really a matter of taste and representation.

Advertising and the depiction of women is one thing, the existence of prostitutes is a totally different issue. They are the bad sheep of the family and they interfere with what feminism is trying to achieve. One of the most important things which women have achieved, thanks to reliable contraception which is controlled by women, is the same freedom as men in matters sexual.

The almost obsessive desire for official recognition of equal treatment of woman with man coincides with woman's present intention, if not ambition, to be allowed to perform all the jobs normally done by her male counterpart. Such intention and ambition are part and parcel of the otherwise wholly laudable striving for a full, legally-acknowledged recognition of equality which is irreproachable, and indeed inevitable as a matter of principle. Its execution in matters of detail and practice, however, is a different thing entirely.

There are side-effects to the new feminists' order. Of these, the most typical and aesthetically repugnant is woman's increased vulgarity, whether she be English, French, Italian: it matters not. In modern times, her speech has become interspersed with words and expletives, imported in the main from the United States, which are unbecoming, if not demeaning. At the same time, and almost as an inevitable concomitant, there is her dissent when she is referred to as a lady, rather than as a woman; as though, by choosing for her a more dignified form of address, man was distracting from the validity of her newly-acquired position as his equal.

Similarly, I notice that the pitch of her voice has become more shrill; and her tendency to raise its level beyond any reasonable and acceptable degree of intensity, if not to shout when speaking, appears to be a form of protest which follows from a psychological imbalance of one kind or the other. It is clear that woman's delicacy has gone at the same time as her assertiveness has increased. In this context, it is hardly surprising that many men now shun the opposite sex, and prefer either other males, or prostitutes whose vulgarity is, in a manner of speaking, constitutional.

There have obviously always existed rough and vulgar females, but they were not in a majority: nowadays, they appear to have taken over. Equally, it is hardly surprising to be told by our psychologists that women's thoughts are becoming increasingly obscene. Obscenity is, in part, lack of style: and extremist modern woman certainly lacks that. Her clothes and her perfume may come from Balenciaga but they are not sufficient to cover up either these inelegancies or the smell engendered by her vulgarity of manner and, above all, of thought.

It is interesting to note that the spread of reliable contraception, which coincided with the assertion of women's rights, has also had the effect of achieving a change in the role of woman from her predestined one of perpetuator of the species to that of provider of pleasure. Put differently, women no longer wish to indulge in sexual intercourse in order solely to give birth to children. If this be correct, it is difficult to see why, just as woman freely gives her body for reasons other than procreation, some women should not be allowed to sell their bodies. It is, of course, true that prostitution antedates reliable contraception. But for one reason or the other, intercourse with prostitutes does no on the whole give rise to too many births. Put differently, a man does not visit a prostitute in order to give birth to children but purely to satisfy his lust. Equally, a woman would not frequent a male prostitute for the purposes of procreation but solely for enjoyment; and by definition, homosexual relations do not give rise to children.

In other words, any kind of intercourse which is prompted by lust and not love is of a kind that falls outside the primary

121

function of woman.. Of course, this is not to say that there is anything wrong about a healthy sex life whether within or outside marriage, such as some couples enjoy. But the point that is being made is that, once there is a divorce between the function of procreation and that of pleasure, the act of intercourse itself loses some of its importance and by eliminating the risk of pregnancy, woman is more likely to be looked upon as a receptacle of enjoyment. If this is true, then her role has changed dramatically and the implications as far as man is concerned can be quite serious because at the moment that he ceases to consider woman as the potential mother of his children, and looks upon her in the same way as he would an object or tool by which he can more efficiently pander to his pleasures, he may find it easier to accept that the same pleasure can be obtained by going with a prostitute.

It is hardly a coincidence that the divorcing of the function of woman from that of procreation initially assigned to her by nature, coincides with her claim to be free to do as she pleases. It seems inconsistent that in this free-for-all egalitarian environment, resistance should still be shown to allowing prostitutes to ply their trade, to form themselves into trade unions and to be allowed to operate from properly supervised establishments.

There is clearly a contradiction in the approach by feminists of both sexes to sexual matters. It was, of course, perfectly proper that Josephine Butler should campaign, for well over a decade, for the repeal of the 1846 Contagious Diseases Act and attendant legislation. Feminists, however, go on to argue that these Acts really represent the high watermark of the Englishman's inhumanity to prostitutes, for under them prostitutes could be forced to undergo a medical examination on penalty of imprisonment, on mere suspicion of having infected a man with disease, the diseases themselves not being even specified. The possibilities of abuse were infinite and obvious, when the Acts represented such an extreme violation of civil liberties. The protection afforded to man, as distinct from the whore, was wholly disproportionate and, in most cases, also unjustified.

It is a little difficult to follow the feminist argument in all its implications, for it could be said that the Acts were useful, inasmuch as whoever was found to be infected, could be sent away to be cured. The difficulty is, however, that there is no evidence whatsoever that the Acts were ever applied to men, as distinct from women; and feminists are quite right when they criticize the man-inspired legislation and compare it to the more recent 1913 Mental Deficiency Act (which came into force on 1 April 1914 and was not repealed until 1959) under which women who behaved in a manner which was considered immoral, more particularly by having intercourse at a fairly early age outside marriage, were treated as feeble-minded and were hospitalized in institutions.

It is a pity that feminist campaigners approached the matter from the starting-point of the violation of their civil liberties, for the Acts also applied to a number of other infections (meningitis, cholera and TB). But broadly, their attack was justified. Where, however, it became logically questionable, was when feminists went on to assert that prostitution made woman a slave to man's lusts. I shall revert to this point shortly.

I subscribe to the theory that procreation is sacred. From this, I argue that what feminists then and now fail to see is that the moment one argues that the function of sexual love is not limited to procreation but extended to self-satisfaction and pleasure also outside marriage, a differentiation is created between sacred and profane love which makes it very difficult to refuse recognition to outlets for the latter.

The reluctance to take the next step and legalize brothels is not so easy to explain logically, for it stems from an inability to consider practicalities. If what a prostitute does ceases to be criminal in every respect, an association of prostitutes to improve their efficiency and working conditions cannot possibly be criminal. Indeed, it ought to be welcomed. In the United Kingdom, from a very early date, we have recognized the legality and usefulness of political parties, trade unions and trade associations; why should not the same protection be extended to prostitutes? After all, women and men dispose of their bodies almost daily in any sexual manner they consider fit; it seems lacking in coherence to attempt to differentiate in those cases where the consideration is expressed in purely monetary terms, since there is always some consideration for sexual relations, be it love (which can include the notion of 'reward'), lust or the search for advancement or favour. Why such reluctance to put matters on a formal footing?

It is often said that to license brothels would be to set the clock back a hundred years. This is not only mistaken but is clearly impossible. Sexual permissiveness is rather like freedom; once conferred, it can no longer easily be revoked. The provision of licensed brothels would be a step forward, for it would be the logical outcome of the application of principles of sexual freedom which, in theory at least, prevail in our society.

Another argument that is put forward from time to time revolves around the prostitutes themselves, some of whom are said not to be in favour of brothels. There is no evidence available to support such a contention. Indeed, it is difficult to believe that any street-walker, if offered the alternative of steady working hours and wages in a sanitized environment, subject to medical supervision, with safety from violence and abuse, would prefer to ply her trade in the same manner as at present. It is true that those prostitutes who are addicted to drugs will object because, by definition, drug-addiction would not be tolerated in licensed brothels. But they are surely the only ones who could possibly object; and by being kept outside brothels, they would be more easily differentiated and controlled.

Nor should there be too much concern about the concept of medical supervision. In the first place, those who feel that they have any 'libertarian' concern about interference with the rights of prostitutes, would be well advised to read the comments of Dr Harold Cross in *The Lust Market* (Citadel Press, New York, 1956, republished in London in 1959 by

Torchstream Brooks; the pagination is the same, 7 photos and
1 drawing have been added). He there refers to his experience
as a doctor specializing in VD and visiting brothels, and
records that in Paris earlier this century, prostitutes were issued
with an identity card incorporating a photo and a record of
their last medical examination. As he puts it, known 'bad'
women can be kept clean; it is the 'good' women who do the
damage.

Secondly, no one would be forced to become a prostitute.
A medical for a prostitute would be no different from a driving
test for a driver. If I wish to drive my car, I have to satisfy the
authorities as to my fitness; no reason why a woman who
wished to sell her sexual favours from a brothel should not do
likewise. As to the argument that some prostitutes might still
operate outside brothels, one would expect the significance in
the numbers of such prostitutes to reduce as they gradually
became aware of the benefits of operating from within an
established system.

A final objection (which has been included under this
heading, for it was initially supported by the most ardent
feminists of the eighteenth and nineteenth centuries) is that
prostitution should not be recognized and should be
eliminated because women who become prostitutes are
really the slaves of men. Perhaps there are echoes in this
argument of the successful campaign of William Wilberforce
to free the African slaves, in the sense that no right-thinking
member of the community would wish to support an activity
which originated in coercion and slavery. That argument was
never true of prostitutes and is even less true today.

There are, of course, instances of women who do become
slaves and are turned into prostitutes. They occur throughout
the world, particularly in certain African, Middle-Eastern, Far-
Eastern and South-American countries. But it cannot be
realistically argued that the call-girl of the Western world who
has a smart flat in any of its major cities, is a slave to anyone
but herself. Nowadays, the profession of prostitute is in most
cases freely taken up. By legalizing prostitution, one would

also reduce, if not eliminate entirely, the kind of criminal connotation which was particularly noticeable in the 1960s (e.g. the 'Maltese Connection').

The truth seems to be that when it comes to the availability of sexual favours, women can be divided into three categories.:

THOSE LOYAL TO ONE MAN

1. To the first category belong those women who are only loyal to one man and who would prefer death to 'forced' intercourse. There are examples of this type of character in history and in literature. One can think of the Roman matron, Cornelia, the mother of the Gracchi brothers; and there are many others who would rather sacrifice their life than their chastity.

Women in this group, who obviously share the same moral values of like-minded men, are quite praiseworthy but, in my opinion at least, they are rare. A love of religion, higher moral values, a strong family tradition, cultural background, and self-respect, are but some of the reasons why this type of women can still be found, but in ever diminishing numbers.

THE NOT-SO-HIGH-MINDED

2. To the second category belong the majority of women. They are perhaps not quite so high-minded that they would rather die than dishonour themselves, but are not really willing to sell themselves. They might sacrifice their honour on the odd occasion for the advancement of their husbands, themselves or their children, but on the whole they do not give themselves, save possibly for love. To this category belong most of the heroines of literature, at least those who do not commit suicide rather than suffer the ignominious fate of unwanted intercourse, and most average wives and mothers.

THE SALESWOMAN

3. To the third category belong those women who, whether as a result of a failure in moral upbringing or in the environment or because of their hormonal development or

their psychological heritage, attach no great significance to that very significant part of the female anatomy and are perfectly content to sell it.

If this analysis is correct – and nobody really knows either whether it is, or if it is, why it is so – no amount of moralizing, religious thundering or feminist campaigning will stop prostitutes from plying their trade. It is true to say that, generally speaking, most modern feminists would prefer that prostitutes were not treated as criminals, but do not themselves approve of brothels.

As mentioned above, it was left to Harry Benjamin and R.E.L. Masters in *Prostitution and Morality* (Souvenir Press, London 1962) to set the record straight and to try and explain that no single cause or event provides a satisfactory explanation of why some women are prostitutes and others are not.

I believe that few feminists have given Benjamin and Masters's work the attention it deserves. Ultimately, however, in this sphere women, whether feminists or not, are troubled by one fundamental consideration, namely that deep down they are aware that no amount of wishful thinking will cause prostitutes to disappear: women know very well that it is not unusual for a man to marry a woman whom he honours and values, but to whom he may not feel so strongly attracted in the physical sense. They know it because it is one of the features that differentiate man from woman who, in general, is most unlikely to suffer from this kind of dissociation.

The point is admirably made by J.C. Flugel in his book *The Psycho-Analytic Study of a Family* (pages 112, 113 and 114) and it is common experience that the sexual elements of love are more frequently aroused in a woman, together with elements of tenderness and esteem, whereas in man they can be so easily divorced from one another. Equally, woman well understands, and some men do as well, that she is very often only capable of experiencing sexual desire or gratification in relation to men for whom she feels affection, admiration or respect, whereas man can, without too much compunction, perform more or less satisfactorily with a slut. When, earlier in this chapter, I equated sexual intercourse to a massage, I was not exaggerating.

One may readily admit that some part of this difference between man and woman is due to environmental and, above all, educational factors, as Flugel himself correctly observes. But the two functions of woman, namely the sexual and the sympathetic, are undoubtedly aroused by different types of men.

A further consideration, which I advanced earlier, is that some women realize, although they may be reluctant to acknowledge it, that there is an element of the prostitute in all women in the sense that women have from time to time made use of their bodies to obtain favours or advancement from men. This, however, is less significant than even women themselves believe because it could just as easily be argued that some men – albeit if present statistics are to be heeded, an ever-decreasing number of men – use their sexual prowess or appeal to obtain favours. What I term psychological and social inter-relationships of this kind I discount completely for present purposes, since I am only concerned with the prostitute who plies her trade and not with whatever occasional lapses a woman may indulge in for the sake of advancement or even for some form of financial benefit, whether for herself, her husband or her children. There is a final point. Whatever may have been woman's position in the past, modern female emancipation is adding to the difficulties that women experience in acknowledging the existence of prostitutes. In fact, the more progressive, emancipated, self-confident and powerful a woman is, the more she finds it difficult to accept what are the inherent weaknesses of her own sex.

But woman's reluctance to acknowledge the existence within herself of these very characteristics which, when thwarted, mis-directed or corrupted, actually contribute to the make-up of the prostitute, prevents her from accepting the hygienic and almost cathartic role of prostitution. At all times, but particularly in the twentieth century, progressive woman only sees that she is offended by the prostitute. The offence is compounded by the knowledge, deep down, that the prostitute merely does what every woman in every age, albeit in a different fashion, on a lesser scale, and for more limited purposes, and perhaps not even for economic reward, has done and continues to do. Prostitutes sell their bodies for money; women do likewise for love. Prostitutes tempt men with their scantily clad bodies; women do the same fully dressed. Over tens of thousands of years woman has developed the technique of surviving and of being beautiful for the sake of her partner and her children; a prostitute does the same for herself and (often enough) her pimp.

Chapter Eight

Arguments in favour of decriminalization and legal brothels

The arguments will be treated under the following three headings: Personal, Social and Environmental.

Summary

The above classification does not establish exclusive categories, in the sense that each argument propounds an advantage to be derived from making the activities of prostitutes, and brothels, legal, from the standpoint of the individual, society and the environment. It is obvious, however, that they all straddle one another. For example, if one argues that prostitutes provide essential services for the sick, the deformed, the invalid, the ugly etc. and this is a personal benefit for those people, one must at the same time concede that the benefit also accrues to society as a whole. There is, therefore, an intimate connection between each of the points that are made in favour of decriminalization: the classification has been adopted purely as a matter of convenience.

a) PERSONAL ADVANTAGES

(i) Decriminalizing prostitution will result in a reduction in the number of teenage pregnancies [see also b(iv) below].

(ii) The sick, the ugly, the deformed, the invalids, the old, the lonely etc. will all benefit from a more open provision of the services of prostitutes.

(iii) Legalized access to prostitutes will reduce the number of homosexuals in society.

b) SOCIAL

(i) To decriminalize such conduct will not only make the traditional hypocrisy and double standards unnecessary but may also reduce crimes generally. There will be less blackmail, less violence, less need for pimps and touts and less criminal activity generally connected with what prostitutes do, e.g. drug trafficking.

(ii) There will be a substantial reduction in crimes of violence against women and children.

(iii) The legalization of brothels or equivalent establishments will contribute to strengthening the marriage bond and will reduce the number of divorces.

(iv) It will also reduce the rate of abortion and illegitimacy in women and in teenage girls.

(v) It will produce a substantial reduction in venereal and related diseases generally and also contribute to limit the spread of AIDS.

(vi) By reducing the number of divorces, it will contribute to strengthening the presently crumbling family unit, and thus reduce juvenile crime.

c) ENVIRONMENTAL ADVANTAGES

(i) Decriminalization will substantially reduce the trade in pornography and the proliferation of writing by dirty little boys and girls masquerading as 'literature'.

(ii) The containment of prostitutes in brothels will have environmental advantages by confining their activities to special districts. [see also b(v) above].

*   *   *

Personal Advantages

(i) DECRIMINALIZING PROSTITUTION WILL RESULT IN A REDUCTION IN
THE NUMBER OF TEENAGE PREGNANCIES

As everybody knows, the pressures that our Western society exerts upon youngsters in matters of sex are enormous; at times, one could be forgiven for thinking that it is almost as though nothing else but sexuality mattered and that a hedonistic life was the norm. The sad truth, however, is that these pressures are generated through greed, for there is much money to be made in exploiting the youngsters' sexual interests. There can be no doubt that some sexual activity by teenagers is at least in part due to natural curiosity, in the same way as some youngsters are tempted to experiment with cigarettes, drugs and alcohol. But the adults are there to exploit these natural weaknesses, for profit.

All this is happening in the late twentieth century against the background of a society which is clearly obsessed by things sexual. This generalization may trouble some readers but it can be borne out in fact; nor should it be thought that such obsession is confined to Britain and America. Even in countries like France, Italy and Spain, where one would expect a more pragmatic approach to matters sexual, the obsession exists and it stems from the fact that our Western society has not been too successful in dealing with such matters on the physical plane.

There is some evidence that northern societies, as distinct from Mediterranean, Asian or African, are psychologically troubled nowadays by sexual instincts that fail to find a satisfactory physical outlet. But it would appear that this ever-increasing concern, if not dedication, is ultimately not so much sapping our energies, because in sexual terms there do not appear to be many of them left, but clouding our vision.

It is true that youngsters are maturing at much earlier ages. The onset of menstruation in girls, for example, is now occurring in some parts of the Western world as early as the age of 12. Boys also appear to be maturing sexually at earlier ages. In Africa, sexual maturity for both sexes is even earlier.

The pressure on young girls, therefore, as far as sexual relations are concerned, arises much earlier in their development than it did for their grandmothers and this earlier maturity may account in part for the fact that youngsters are getting married or start cohabiting at earlier ages. It seems doubtful, however, whether this precocity is matched by a similar emotional and intellectual maturity. The evidence seems to point to the contrary.

The Family Planning Association has maintained throughout its history that this situation can be catered for by the provision of contraceptive advice and aids. Certainly, the philosopher, William James, who woke up in the middle of the night to write down the great discovery he had made in a dream with the resulting verse 'Hogamus, higamus, men are polygamus; higamus, hogamus, women are monogamus' was not thinking of prostitutes when he confused polygamy with promiscuity.

I have no doubt that what James meant was that men do not necessarily enjoy having several wives but they do enjoy promiscuity. On this particular point, I prefer the view of Edward Westermark (*The History of Human Marriage*, 5th Edition 1921. London, Macmillan, page 459) to the effect that '. . . although polygamy occurs among most existing peoples and polyandry amongst some, monogamy is by far the most common form of human marriage'. Recent zoological studies have endorsed this view, particularly amongst monkeys.

But James was clearly highlighting the concept, for which there is abundant evidence throughout history, that men like variety and therefore can have, sleep with, and love more than, one woman at the same time. This is a concept that must not be lost sight of when we consider the sacredness and the profanity of intercourse. Whichever way one wishes to look at it, however, and ignoring completely any moral or religious considerations, the earlier age at which intercourse starts has resulted in greater pressure being put on younger girls to entertain sexual relations at an earlier age than previously. At the same time, whether as a failing of the educational system or because of an in-built psychological deficiency, the number of teenage pregnancies has risen consistently through the years, and this clearly without reference to any earlier date of marriage. In fact, in a sense, the earlier date of marriage (or cohabitation) is not related to the sexual needs of either or both the spouses, since these have already been catered for outside marriage.

It is common knowledge that throughout the Western world today both boys and girls appear to have extensive pre-marital sexual experience. A recent survey undertaken by Bristol University amongst 11,000 children born in one week of 1970, found that 1 in 2 girls aged 16 and 1 in 3 boys of the same age had experienced sexual intercourse. Apart from the interesting difference in the percentage between boys and girls, the survey provides scientific proof – assuming any were needed – of the fact that pre-marital sex in most Western societies is the norm rather than the exception.

From 1980 to 1988 the number of children born in the UK outside marriage has more than doubled, going from 77,000 to 177,000. At the same time, the number of illegitimate live births also doubled in the same period from 12% to 25%, the majority of these illegitimate births occurring to women under the age of 25 (2 out of 3 in 1988). In 1987, 14% of all 'families' with dependent children were families where there was a single parent. This compares with 8% for 1971 and 6% for 1961. In these 'families', the mother was the lone parent in 90% of the cases. Nor should it be thought that this is a typically British problem. In Australia, in the United States and in other European countries as well, the number of lone parent families has been increasing, but the UK still has the highest rates of teenage pregnancies in Europe. The recent (March '94) campaign by the Family Planning Association, sponsored by the Government, aimed at cutting teenage pregnancies through improved sexual education is evidence of increasing social concern about this almost inexplicable phenomenon.

The most up-to-date figures for the United Kingdom are now available in Population Trends No. 65 (J. Haskey) and show that for 1989 the total number of 'lone parents' was 1.15 million, of which single mothers accounted for 360,000. In 1991/92, as we have already mentioned, there were 1.37 million lone-parent families receiving either Income Support or One-Parent Benefit or both, lone-parent families having increased as a proportion of all families with dependent children from 8% in 1971 to 19% in 1991. The Family Policy Studies Centre Report of February 1993 states unequivocally that single (never married) mothers '. . . are the most likely of all lone parents to suffer economic hardship'.

If there were officially recognized outlets to the sexual needs of our youngsters, it would inevitably follow that pressure would be shifted, from girls in their teens to prostitutes; and those young girls – and there are many – who prefer chocolates to boys could more easily choose sweets in preference to sex.

It appears to be probably true that very young girls are less fertile than girls in their early 20s. At the same time, however, if they were the subject of fewer sexual attentions, it would have to follow that there would be fewer teenage pregnancies.

(ii) THE SICK, THE UGLY, THE DEFORMED, THE OLD AND THE INVALIDS.

A local newspaper in the south-east of England published recently an news item in the following terms:

RANDY-CAPPED

Officials are paying for a disabled man to have sex once a month – at the taxpayers' expense. It transpired that the 31-year-old Dutch man is unable to have a normal relationship with women so the local authority has stepped in to pay a woman who specializes in servicing the disabled. A government official in Noordoostpolder, Holland, said: 'It's all part of the civic services.'

There is clearly a lack of compassion in the text that has been quoted. The play on the word 'handicapped' (or maybe on the cartoon character 'Andy Capp') seems to manifest both crudity and surprise at the fact that a local authority should step in to assist the sexual life of a disabled man.

When one talks of the services provided by prostitutes, one is inclined to relate them to the promiscuous and the deviant. But frustration of normal physical desires can occur for many other people who may be neither. From the provision of conjugal visits for prisoners, to services rendered by prostitutes under the supervision of trained psychiatrists, the range is much wider than the general public is led to believe.

Take prisons. No study appears to have been made into the effect of sexual frustration on prisoners, particularly the long-term ones. This frustration in most cases turns to homo-sexuality which may or may not persist after the prisoner's release; but it may well be that it is a powerful contributory cause of many prison problems and possibly even of riots.

An American writer, Dr Louis Berg, (*Revelations of a Prison Doctor* Minton Balch & Co., New York, 1934, page 139 and 140) has written: 'Sex starvation is more serious in prison and among convicts than upon any other group who are denied or deny themselves the expression of this most vital urge. The religious – monks, priests, nuns and other ascetics – are able for the most part to sublimate or transform their procreative energy into devotional worship or into good works. In the end, they achieve a serenity possible only in those in whom the wells of passion have run dry.' He goes on to remark that, for the greater number of men in prison, the sexual urge can find no satisfactory outlet except in homosexuality.

He also makes the point that, after their release, many prisoners turn into sadists who may commit assaults and rapes because, having been deprived of woman's companionship and sympathy, they find it difficult to look upon woman in the same way as they did before they went into prison. How can the sexual urge of prisoners be catered for, therefore, save through prostitutes? Some prisoners may have wives or girlfriends who may be allowed to visit and stay on: but what about the others?

Anyone who has been in or associated with the Army knows how often prostitution thrives in the vicinity of camps and barracks. To expect a soldier to live a life of restraint is wishful thinking: are the options that remain open to him (masturbation and/or homosexuality) preferable to intercourse with prostitutes? The high moralist will no doubt contend that, as part of his training and in application of certain high concepts of discipline and self-restraint, the soldier should abstain from both types of sexual activity. But the man with a practical view of life knows full well that the position is different.

And what about men who, for one reason or another, are lonely, or deformed or old? One is entitled to ask, far from rhetorically, why it is that our society is quite happy rightly to condemn cruelty to animals, but is wholly unmindful of the cruelty that results to certain categories of human beings by denying them *official* access to prostitutes? Of course, it could be argued that at the moment no one is denying anybody access to prostitutes: technically, that is true. But such access is, first of all, circumscribed because of the particular manner in which prostitutes have to operate and, secondly, frowned upon, as witness recent scandals in the UK, for example, when the Director of Public Prosecutions had to resign because he was spotted trying to accost a prostitute, his wife not long after committing suicide.

There are, of course, a number of other reasons why men visit prostitutes, and some have already been mentioned. These have been analysed in great detail by very many writers and in particular, as noted earlier, by Benjamin and Masters, Albert Ellis ('Why Married Men visit Prostitutes' in *Sexology*, January 1959), Havelock Ellis, Leicester Kirkendall (*Premarital Intercourse and Interpersonal Relationships*, Julian Press, New York, 1961) and Phyllis and Eberhard Kronhausen (*Sexists of American College Men*, Valentine, New York, 1960). These reasons are listed below without comment, simply for the sake of completeness, and I am bound to add that I find it difficult to disagree with any of them:

1. Young men who wish to enhance their status or look upon a visit to prostitutes as a social activity.

2. Shy or insecure men or men too old to compete with others in winning sex partners.

3. Those with little time to court a girl – to conclusion.

4. Those who wish to avoid either obligations or emotional entanglements, or those who may be drunk at the time.

5. Those with a deep sense of inferiority.

6. Those who basically feel certain sexual activities are dirty and not to be imposed upon wives.

7. Those who may be manifesting hostility to their wives by going with a prostitute.

8. Those who wish to acquire expertise without experimenting with ordinary girls, perhaps because they are afraid of failure.

(iii) LEGALIZED ACCESS TO PROSTITUTES WILL REDUCE THE NUMBER OF HOMOSEXUALS IN SOCIETY

The first Kinsey Report concluded that in the United States four per cent of the adult white population were exclusively homosexual throughout their lives after the onset of adolescence, 10% of the white male population were more or less exclusively homosexual for at least three years between the ages of 16 and 65 and 37% of the total male population of the USA had had at least some overt homosexual experience to the point of orgasm between adolescence and old age.

The equivalent Kinsey figures for females are as follows: around half of college-educated women and approximately 20% of non-college-educated women had at least one same-sex erotic contact past puberty; only two or three per cent of these were exclusively homosexual during their entire lives. Of course, nobody knows for certain how many homosexuals, male or female, there are at present in the United Kingdom, or anywhere else in the world. Statistics of this nature are

exceedingly difficult to come by, but the recent campaign on
the vote to reduce the 'homosexual' age of consent did display
great numbers and belligerency.

But four facts cannot be disputed:

1. It is within the observation of most writers and scientists
that even mature males, with an established heterosexual track
record, may turn to homosexual contacts when women are
not available. The classic examples are prisoners and sailors and
all men who congregate in remote areas. The Germans have
referred to this change in sexual direction as 'homosexuality
for want'. When the contingent situation ceases, if women are
then again available, the homosexual tendency ceases too; but
in some cases it may persist.

2. There are some men who are theoretically capable of
responding to both sexes but on the whole prefer the opposite
sex. Very often this type of man prefers a prostitute to an
'honest' woman.

3. There comes a time, in the lives of all youngsters, when a
definite orientation has to be found to sexual activity. In many
cases, the orientation is dictated by one's genes. In many
others, however, it is not entirely clearcut. The existence of
prostitutes may shift the emphasis from homosexuality to
heterosexuality. But even in those cases where the orientation
is heterosexual, there is no officially recognized way of
satisfying it, other than by abstaining or going with girls of
one's own age and sex group.

4. The number of homosexuals in our society, male and
female, is increasing. Whatever may be the other causes that
have contributed to such an increase, one certainly is relevant
and it is the absence of officially recognized prostitutes. One
may ask whether the reduction in the number of homosexuals
in society is of itself an argument in favour of decriminalization. In other words, why should it be a good thing to reduce
the number of homosexuals in any given society?

This in turn raises fundamental issues of social policy, where
views become polarized. Ultimately, one answer seems to be
that heterosexual behaviour is to be preferred to homosexual

on the basis that the former is, at least in theory, aimed at procreation and therefore at the perpetuation of the species; whereas the latter is self-defeating, because no continuity of the species follows from the homosexual act. But whatever may be the social and moral implications of the question, the evidence seems to be that prostitutes may help in directing instinct towards heterosexual channels. In my view, there is a clear connection between the increase in the number of homosexuals in society, and divorce.

The causative element is not immediately apparent, but is there. It is common knowledge that whenever parents with young children (let us say, up to 16/18 years of age) decide on divorce, it is probable and sensible, in any legal system, that the youngsters be, as a general rule, entrusted to the care and control and/or custody of the mother. This principle is amply proved by statistical data and needs no restatement.

Despite the fact that the father in most cases is likely to be given certain rights of access, it has been shown, that, over the years, the degree of access by the father whilst the child is a minor, reduces, and his impact as a parent becomes less and less. The belief is becoming widespread that a father is only needed, if at all, to support the child financially and the psychological, let alone blood, bond between the two is discounted. This is utterly wrong: all children need a close relationship with two parents rather than one and it is easy to underestimate the psychological benefits of a loving father for children of either sex.

In normal circumstances, after divorce, the mother then has the choice of either bringing up the male child as a single parent herself, or of remarrying. If she remarries, the role of the stepfather is seldom the same as that of natural father and can be discounted for present purposes. But there are many divorced mothers who do not remarry, either because they do not wish to, or very often because they feel that it may not be a good idea to provide their children with a stepfather.

Where a boy is brought up solely by the mother, he finds it

difficult to identify with a masculine role. Indeed, one can go
so far as to say that it is almost impossible for the male child
who is brought up by a mother who does not have a strong
man by her side, to identify with the male role unless the
'mores' of the society in which he grows up incline strongly
towards a heterosexual trend. Here, we have to consider the
objection to this suggestion that could be raised as concerns
widows. In other words, does it follow from what has just
been stated that the child brought up by a widow stands a
good chance of becoming homosexual? The answer is in the
negative and the reason is this: where the father dies, the child
knows full well that he was removed from the scene, so to say,
by accident and not by the will of the spouses themselves. It
may be that the marriage was a reasonably happy one; in
which case, it is conceivable that the mother keeps photos of
the father around the home, she has memories of him, she may
mention him from time to time, she may compare features of
her young son with those of her dead partner. The memories,
if the marriage was a happy one, are usually loving ones and
the picture that the child builds for himself of his father is
almost an idealized one. Where there has been a divorce,
however, if the father is mentioned at all, it is usually in the
context of his having been useless, or violent, or a failure, a
spendthrift, a bad provider, an adulterer, or someone who fails
to pay the maintenance on the due date. There is no
comparison between the two situations from the psychological
point of view.

On the other hand, it is an undeniable psychological fact
that the children of either sex need both male and female
traits around them so that they may relate to the different
personalities: these find their logical and natural manifestation in their parents, and both of them. From the mother the
male child derives warmth, affection, sensitivity and a
tenderness which will enable him ultimately to make a
successful partner. From the father he derives the sense of
discipline, the masculinity and those 'manly' qualities which,
though badly devalued and debased in present-day society,

are representative of the features which woman naturally looks for in a man.

The male child, even more than the female, certainly needs both. Where the masculine traits are lacking, he becomes either too closely associated with the mother or finds himself in a position of conflict with her. In either event, his familiarity with and understanding of persons of the opposite sex – other than his mother – is badly affected. And this is one of the reasons why so many men are nowadays terrified by the women they see around them.

The ever-increasing assertion by woman of her rights, her sexuality and her 'feminism' are anathema to certain males. They run away, as far as they can, from such a package: they cannot understand it and inevitably they do not know how to cope with it. It is so much easier to find refuge in the bosom of one's sporting friends, or drinking or club pals.

It can hardly be an accident that the increase in the rate of spread of homosexual behaviour, let alone its consequences, has coincided with the upsurge in the claims of women openly to rule the world. The Amazon-like, athletic, strong-willed woman riding astride the horse of social impact and assertion spreads fear amongst the weaker males, in the same way as the Mongol hordes must have done to the local populations when they first invaded Europe.

A final consideration is that where a child is brought up with two parents, there may be a balancing of each parent's faults with those of the other; but where there is only one parent, if there are faults, as inevitably there will be, these strike the child with greater force. If the mother remarries, there is the possibility of conflict with the stepfather; if she does not remarry, she will have to harden herself to the realities of life and it is likely that in that process she may become less feminine. This lack of femininity will rub off on the male children.

The effects of brothels on the rate of divorce are considered in greater detail below.

*   *   *

Social advantages

(i) TO DECRIMINALIZE THE CONDUCT OF PROSTITUTES WILL NOT
ONLY MAKE THE TRADITIONAL HYPOCRISY AND DOUBLE STANDARDS
UNNECESSARY BUT MAY ALSO REDUCE CRIME GENERALLY.

May I immediately define what I mean by hypocrisy (double standards). I mean lack of clarity and understanding when dealing with sexual matters. I mean the frustration of the sexual instinct which leads people to vicarious enjoyment, through pornography and scandal, of other peoples' sexual weakness when they are caught out. I mean the inability to call things by their proper names and the retreat into a pseudo-moral stance when confronted by unpalatable sexual facts. I mean the very frame of mind that is making it difficult for us to come to grips with the problems posed by our own sexuality.

This is not put forward as a dictionary definition. It is a very personal, possibly idiosyncratic analysis: but it may enable the reader to follow the way the argument is put.

We need to understand at the outset that the association of prostitutes with criminals should no longer be taken for granted in the last decade of the twentieth century, to the extent that it was even before the outbreak of the Second World War. The reason is quite simply because of the increase in the number of call-girls or, at least, in the number of prostitutes who operate independently from premises which they themselves either own or have let in their own name. This better class of prostitute has fewer requirements for protection and is less likely to have a pimp. As an independent contractor, she is probably unwilling to share her earnings and be part of an organization. If she does take on, or associate with a pimp or protector, it is more likely to be because she herself is in need of some kind of attention, whether affective or otherwise, on the part of a male, and not because she needs protection against her clients.

In the lower classes, however, prostitutes are invariably

associated with criminals. Street-walkers in all the major cities naturally tend to get involved with pimps and touts and, almost inevitably, with drugs. If, as the present law allows, they are arrested and fined for public nuisance or soliciting offences, they may need the help of their protector to pay the fine off. Indeed, this approach creates and perpetuates a vicious circle, for greater sexual activity is needed of the prostitute who has been fined. She has to earn not only to keep herself and her pimp, but also to satisfy the fine that the Court has imposed.

Statistics will be referred to later which show that street-walkers who, for example, are on drugs, work much longer hours than those who are not. By parity of reasoning, those who have to pay off fines will have to work harder than those who do not get caught. The more frequent, and often repeated, contacts are more likely to result in the spread of disease, whether the normally sexually-transmitted diseases (STDs) or HIV.

Nevertheless, to decriminalize the activities of prostitutes would of itself reduce the street-walkers dependence on criminals. To the extent that brothels were legalized, there would be practically immediate reduction in crime and especially in drug use for, by definition, no prostitute who was on drugs would be employed in a licensed brothel. By the same token, the prostitute who operates from a brothel would not need protection of the kind offered by pimps or other criminal organizations, because the legal system itself, and the set-up of the brothel, would be sufficient to safeguard her from most types of unwanted interference.

It is common knowledge, derived from those countries that either still maintain legalized brothels or from the days when brothels were either legal there or, if technically illegal, tolerated, that attempts to clean up brothels have resulted in major increases in crime. At the very outset of their work (see *Prostitution and Morality* page 6), Benjamin and Masters highlight the consequences that followed from the campaign to clean up San Francisco. Benjamin states:

'San Francisco in the early 1930s was a truly cosmopolitan city, although it was even then no longer an "open town". The old, rather wild Barbary Coast had been considerably tamed, but the general atmosphere of San Francisco still contained traces of the freedom of the "Gold Rush Days" which gave it its indefinable charm and flavor. All this has now completely disappeared, together with the last remnants of the Barbary Coast. Fanatical suppression has taken the place of the earlier spirit of tolerance.

'In the early 1930s, when I went to San Francisco for the first time, a doctor attached to the Health Department conducted me through a number of brothels, from cheap ($3.00) to expensive ($15.00) ones, to show me how the different madams cooperated with his department, and how rarely a case of venereal disease occurred in these houses. Sailors were the most frequent customers of the cheaper houses, where they felt safe and where robberies hardly ever occurred. Quite naturally, all these houses, or at least the majority, had to "pay off" to the police, prostitution being an illegal profession. However, everything went smoothly and everybody seemed fairly well satisfied, except the reformers and the crusaders, some of them ambitious politicians.

'Gradually, especially during and after the war, attempts to "clean up the town" increased. About five years ago, a sailor said to me in a bar: "This has become the lousiest town for liberty. All you can do here is get drunk". Once, another sailor did just that, but then, his libido hardly appeased, he accosted a girl in the street, having been unable to find one anywhere else. The girl happened to be the wrong kind. She refused the sailor's advances in no uncertain terms, whereupon he got mad and "pushed" her. She fell so unfortunately that she fractured her skull on the sidewalk and the boy was arrested and charged with murder. Undoubtedly he paid for his [was it his alone?] crime with years in prison.

'San Francisco is now a thoroughly purified town. A few years ago it received a citation to this effect from the American Social Health Association, a principal guardian of public morals. A new administration, with the help of certain newspapers, had come to power. The new Mayor had appointed the most fanatical police chief he could find anywhere. When this Chief took office, he declared: "In all vice cases I shall take personal charge". [I am sure he never realised how much he betrayed with this remark.] Consequently, all known brothels were closed, madams were entrapped and jailed, individual girls were arrested or harassed until they left town. Some went underground, joining the city's criminal elements. Crimes of violence increased, as statistics clearly showed.'

Today, it has to be said, San Francisco has become almost synonymous with AIDS and homosexuality.

It is, however, rather difficult to relate an increase in crimes of violence directly to the closure of brothels, although there is no doubt as to the extraordinary increase in crime, especially sexual crime, in the UK from the years before the Second World War to date. To find a direct causal link is much more difficult and no such study has, as yet, been carried out in the UK. I have also been unable to obtain any information from countries like Holland, Germany and Denmark to see whether there has been any reduction in crime generally – as distinct from sexual crime which is dealt with in the next section – either because the experiment of the legalization of brothels is too recent, or because no data exist.

Nevertheless, it is worth reminding ourselves here that all feminist writers and most sociologists who have considered the plight of the prostitute are unanimous in maintaining that her conduct should cease to be subject to the criminal law. There is a single chord appeal for decriminalization, either on the basis that woman is being discriminated against by man, or because all human beings have their own essential rights and liberties into which, generally speaking, the law must not intrude or because,as has already been observed, woman is mistress of her body and if she wishes to sell it, society should not object.

Feminists and sociologists go on to argue, quite correctly,

that to fine a prostitute because of her behaviour insofar as the law considers it offensive to public morality, is, on the one hand, in contradiction of the basic principle of English law that prostitution of itself is not illegal; but on the other hand, the basic law creates a catch 22 situation in the sense that once the prostitute is fined, she has to go back to the very trade that caused her to become a criminal, in order to earn the money that will enable her either to pay the fine or to survive or both.

These arguments are unexceptionable, as we observed only a short while back. (I accept that the prostitute is not fined for prostituting herself, but for the public nuisance offence of soliciting. But this is really an example of the double standards which I have tried to define above. Soliciting is not an end in itself but a means to an end and the end product is the sale of sexual activity. Although we are claiming that we are punishing the public order offence, we are in effect stultifying the provision of sexual service. If that is not the application of a double standard, I do not know what is.)

Yet, as soon as it is suggested that prostitutes should be organized, either as a trade union or as a professional body, which the reader will recall is central to my argument, the very same supporters of decriminalization are up in arms and refuse to accept that brothels are as necessary an evil as the prostitutes themselves. It is as though both feminists and sociologists, of the one part, and society of the other, were prepared to go a little way along a certain road but reluctant to reach the destination. For example, in England it is still maintained that prostitution of itself is not a criminal offence; what is criminal is the conduct insofar as it offends public decency. But the reason street-walkers offend public decency is because they have nowhere else to go. If they had respectable premises from which to operate, it is less likely that they would wish to suffer the inconvenience of soliciting in the open air, particularly in northern climes. Loitering to attract trade in adverse weather conditions in some of the principal cities of the United Kingdom cannot be quite so enjoyable, perhaps, as a stroll down the Bois de Bologne: neither, however, is comparable to the 'quality of life' afforded by brothels.

We may not like it, but it seems probable that benefits would accrue to prostitutes as human beings as well as providers of services, if they were allowed to operate from licensed premises. There seems to be greater concern for society than for the individual; a more charitable view of prostitutes is sacrificed on the altar of a spurious morality.

As we have already seen, the counter to this approach is to maintain that many prostitutes would prefer to remain on the streets. But there really is no proof to support this argument whereas the evidence obtained in those countries, especially European, Mediterranean and Latin American countries, where houses of tolerance were, and in some cases still are, legal and supervized by the State, is clearly to the contrary. Once a prostitute knows the benefits of operating within a framework of protection and supervision, she will go for it in the same way as workers sought to shelter behind the shield of their trade unions.

Inevitably, there would be some prostitutes, especially those on drugs, who would prefer not to work in a controlled environment. But the majority would surely prefer better working conditions: and by reducing the number of those who do not wish to be controlled, especially because they are on drugs, the police and social workers would find it much easier to do their job and, in the long term, it would become accepted by the community generally that for most types of prostitution, the only proper way to operate is from licensed premises. The 'courtesan' type of whore, the better-class call-girl who owns her own flat or house, has never represented a serious threat to public decency and by definition would never wish to be regimented. But she is also much less of a social problem.

If brothels – whether of the hetero- or the homosexual type – were legalized, there would be less stigma attached to frequenting them, once the public got used to them. A person seen visiting one would be no more subject to blackmail than if he/she were seen entering a physiotherapist's premises. A minister, a public official or any other public figure, even a private individual, who chose to use a prostitute would have much less need for secret assignations or complicated cover-ups of the kind which, when unmasked, provide good opportunities and means for blackmail. One wonders how many decisions are taken, or refused, how many individuals promoted or demoted, what projects advanced or shelved in wholly undeserving circumstances simply because someone in a position of power is blackmailed over his sexually indiscreet, improper, irregular, deviant or adulterous conduct.

The possibilities for blackmail in relation to sexual indiscretions will lessen as the general public accepts that frequenting a brothel is no more socially blameworthy than entering a public house or a gambling casino; that a visit to such an establishment does not turn a caring husband, a good father, a competent minister of state, a capable public servant, a compassionate minister of religion, a dutiful royal personage, or whatever, man or woman, into someone contemptible and incapable of performing his duties. In short, it will become much more difficult for public opinion or the press to destroy a person's private life solely on the ground of sexual indiscretions.

(ii) THERE WOULD BE A REDUCTION IN CRIMES OF VIOLENCE AGAINST WOMEN AND CHILDREN

There is no doubt that the Second World War was a watershed both in social and in sexual terms. For example, in 1938 the total number of people who were found guilty of sexual offences was 2,321. By 1948 this figure had shown a first marked increase to 3,818. In 1949 it rose to 4,092 and in 1950 to 4,308. Of course, it was not only sexual offences that increased in the same way. The equivalent figures for violence against the person are:

1938	1,583
1948	3,183
1949	3,303
1950	3,839

A comparison may be made with the total number of persons
guilty of indictable offences in the same years:

1938	Males	68,679
	Females	9,784
1948	Males	112,181
	Females	17,203
1949	Males	99,054
	Females	15,240
1950	Males	100,948
	Females	15,075

It is interesting to observe at this stage that between 1938 and
1950 the increase in the criminality of males was about 32%
whilst that for women was 66.6%. There seems to be little
doubt that females over the relevant period have become more
inclined to crime. The explanations for this phenomenon are
not exclusively sexual and are not *per se* related to prostitution.
They may be accounted for in terms of social change
generally. Ten years later, the numbers had risen dramatically.
The total number of persons found guilty of all kinds of
offences in 1960 was 1,035,212. The number of people
convicted of sexual offences also rose quite steadily; in 1958 to
5,423, in 1959 to 6,161 with a slight drop in 1960 to 5,959.

Ten years later, in 1970, the figures had again increased
dramatically. The number of indictable sexual offences known
to the police in 1970 was 24,163. In comparative terms, the
total number of persons found guilty of offences of all kinds in
1969 had also risen to 1,606,728. Throughout the eighties,
too, the figures continued to rise. In 1980 the total notifiable
offences recorded by the police was 2,688,200 rising at a
steady pace to 2,963,800 in 1981, 3,262,400 in 1982,
3,247,000 in 1983, 3,499,100 in 1984, 3,611,900 in 1985,
3,847,400 in 1986, 3,892,200 in 1987, 3,715,800 in 1988 and

3,870,700 in 1989. The all-time high occurred in 1991 when the number of notifiable offences reached 5.1 million. One could be forgiven for feeling a little nostalgic regarding the figures for the early 1940s.

These figures cover all sexual offences and do not distinguish between offences against women or boys or against public decency. More specifically, offences of rape numbered about 460 in 1980, a 17% increase over 1979 and a third more than in 1978, but reached 3,400 in 1990, an increase of 3% from 1989. By comparison, fifty years earlier, in 1938, the number of persons found guilty of *any* kind of sexual offences was 2,321. In simple terms, the offences of rape alone in 1990 represent nearly a third more than the total of all kinds of sexual offences in 1938. ('Criminal Statistics – England & Wales', 1990). In the same year we also find that indecent assaults on females amounted to a record 15,300.

It is often said that the marked increases may be due to the growing willingness on the part of victims to report offences such as rape to the police. About this, two points should be made immediately. Point one, the 1976 Sexual Offences (Amendment) Act which enabled the victims of sexual offences to remain anonymous in respect of Court proceedings, came into force on 22 November of that year. By then, the number of sexual offences had already risen quite dramatically. Point two, it is difficult in any event to prove that this is so and probably the percentage increase which is due to a growing willingness on the part of victims to report the offence should be offset against the increase in crime generally. The Sexual Offences (Amendment) Act of 1976 gives protection to the victims of sexual crime but does not apply to ordinary crime. And yet, ordinary crime now stands at an all-time high of 5.1 million which is practically double the 1976 figure.

The graph that follows which plots these increases is extracted from Command 1935.

Crime (all kinds of offence)

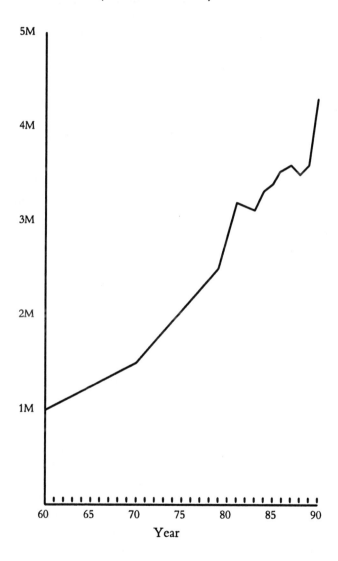

Year

Given the increase over the same period in the number of homosexuals in England and Wales, which flows inevitably from the present trends, discussed earlier, we have a reducing number of heterosexual males committing about three times as many sexual assaults on women in 1990 compared with 1980. Indeed, the phenomenal rise in the number of crimes of violence against women and children should be carefully noted. What the statistics do not reveal, however, is the frightening escalation in the degree of brutality of the crimes that are committed. These are reported almost daily in the press and on television and every now and then a politician, a doctor, a psychologist, a priest or a social worker, endeavours to explain why this is happening.

They may say that it is the result of the poverty in our society, or drug taking, or unbalanced minds, or a falling away of religious beliefs, and so on. There are as many opinions as there are voices. What is not often said or, if it is said, it happens almost casually, as an aside, as though the speaker is afraid of sticking his neck out too far and of having it chopped off as a sacrifice on the altar of feminist values, is that the recent horrifying increase in violence on women and children of all ages is the result of the picture that modern woman is projecting of herself. One of the most important components of that picture is the depiction of woman in all shapes and forms, but not as a professional whore. It should not be thought for one moment that this ostrich-like attitude to the problems created by prostitutes is confined to the United Kingdom. On the contrary, it applies throughout the Western world.

For example, there is no statistical information available for practically any European country, as to how many prostitutes exist there. No study has been made in any of these countries as to the consequences of the closure of brothels in the 1940s and 1950s. No statistical information is available as to the effect of such closure over the incidence of venereal disease. I have personally contacted the Law Enforcement Agencies and Health Departments or Ministries of Justice (different countries use different terminology) in the following countries: Belgium, Denmark, France, Germany, Greece, Ireland, Italy, Luxembourg, Netherlands, Portugal, Spain, Venezuela.

Much to my surprise, I received replies from all the bodies concerned and I am grateful for the trouble that was taken. However, those replies were of no real use to my thesis because either one department referred me to another, who then referred me back, merely to find out that the information was not available or, if it was, it was in a form that could not be either understood or used. Above all, there was the fundamental difficulty that nobody knew, or would even venture a guess, as to how many prostitutes were operating. This is a problem with which the World Health Organization is also grappling since no statistical information is available as to the activities of prostitutes. In the absence of that kind of up-to-date statistical information, the argument can be put somewhat differently. No one can dispute, at least for the United Kingdom, the increase in crimes of violence against women and children. The figures just speak for themselves and, as figures, cannot be challenged. Any more than it can be disputed that sexual morals are far laxer in the early 1990s than they were, say, in the 1950s.

The advent of AIDS has caused some interest in the problem but the World Health Organization is no better informed now than it was in the 1940s and 1950s as to what the numbers actually involved really are. There are occasional studies, run on a shoestring, and specialist projects are embarked on from time to time. For example, there was a 1993 project in Edinburgh which showed that there were at least between 500 and 700 female prostitutes and 100 to 200 male prostitutes who were active in that city. Another project for Glasgow claimed that in 1992 there were 200 full-time and part-time prostitutes. The figures for 1991 seem to be double that number, but are still less than in Edinburgh, which is odd, to say the least, given that Glasgow is a port where, by definition, one would expect a greater number of prostitutes.

But perhaps, Edinburgh prostitutes are better paid: Glasgow
prostitutes have always been poorly paid.

And yet, as noted already more than once, there is *no* study
of national significance in any of the countries we have
mentioned. It is often said, particularly by officials of the
World Health Organization, that the reason why no such
study exists is that governments do not regard the problem as
sufficiently important to allow it to jump the queue of other
more significant requirements. I do not accept this argument
either.

I think the reason why no studies of national significance
are available is because we would prefer not to know that the
problem exists. We hope it will go away. The trouble is that it
has never gone away throughout our history and is even less
likely to disappear now. As Tolstoy so aptly put it: 'Man
survives earthquakes, epidemics, the horrors of disease and all
agonies of the soul but, for all time, his most tormenting
tragedy has been, and is, and will be, the tragedy of the
bedroom.'

*   *   *

In the 'good old days', when men and women were brought
up to realize that there were women whom one married,
and prostitutes, the problems of the bedroom still existed, but
the repercussions on youngsters and on society were fewer
because of the clarity in the distinction between the sacred and
the profane.

Nowadays, however, this distinction has ceased to be clear-
cut, the picture has become blurred, the white and the black
have shifted in position and intensity and have turned to grey.
The mentally sick male, the violent, the psychotic, the
schizophrenic, find that, against this unclear background, any
woman is a prey. The loss of respect for woman carries with it
ineluctably a loss of respect for children and the elderly: hence
the apparently inexplicable nature of crimes of violence and
sexual assaults committed on elderly women or very young
children. I accept that not all attacks of this kind are sexually

motivated; the majority may well be the result of a warped and perverted expression of power and dominance. But even in those cases, there is a sexual component.

Against this background, would it not be reassuring to know that whenever one felt inclined to ill-treat or molest or use violence against a woman or child, one could do so without any fear of reprisal or retribution of any kind by frequenting premises licensed and supervised by the State, where certain women would be perfectly capable, by definition, of coping with most kinds of behaviour, odd, or violent, or otherwise?

I have already observed how we have downgraded the procreative function and endeavoured to eliminate the acceptability of the differences between men and women. It seems to me that, as a result, tension has been engendered between men and women, particularly in the workplace. The more acceptable woman has become in the market-place and in the workforce, the greater the number of crimes of violence against her which have taken place, regardless of age, and the more she is perceived and depicted as an object of exploitation.

The fact is that woman has gained her freedom. Perhaps, though, at the same time she has lost her respectability. It is no coincidence that more than one modern psychiatrist has remarked that nowadays women's subconscious thoughts are much more lascivious than they were some 30 years ago. This newly-manifested but long-standing lasciviousness of woman is reflected in the ever-increasing amount of women's writings on erotic matters which disguise a trend to female-generated and oriented pornography which is no different, and indeed in many respects, is also worse, than *Playboy* magazine. If one superimposes pornographic writing of the sexually explicit type upon works of 'romance' of the Barbara Cartland style, it is easy to see how the tendencies, the needs and the fantasies of woman herself can become confused.

Women's magazines, as I mentioned earlier, are not of any help. In the February 1993 edition of *Cosmopolitan* the

pleasures and techniques of oral sex are considered in some
detail, starkly, with nothing left to the imagination. One is
reminded of Maupassant: '. . . according to the measure in
which the veils of the unknown are lifted, so is the
imagination of man depopulated'. And, one may add, also
that of woman.

This misunderstanding of the nature of woman's emotions,
coupled with the failure to identify a correct modern role for
her, creates problems for men, because despite the great strides
taken by woman towards sexual emancipation, it still remains
biologically true – and the findings of both Kinsey Reports
endorse this – that the sexual urge is greater in the male than in
the female of the species. It must be accepted that, apart from
cases of nymphomania, the female urge to sexual behaviour is
at present less marked than in man.

If this analysis is broadly correct, one begins to understand
some of the causes for the increase in crimes of violence.
Where brothels do not exist, women find themselves under
pressure to give more than just the little they were giving
before; and nowadays, they are in a position to go 'all the way'
thanks to reliable contraception. This tendency, together with
the belief that most women hold that they are equal to men
and therefore are just as free to indulge in sexual intercourse at
any time they choose, produces images which are not only
confusing from the psychological angle but are spatially
problematical. As Lujo Bassermann has observed (*The Oldest
Profession – A History of Prostitution*, Arthur Barker Ltd., 1967),
in earlier times, bawdy houses had been erected beyond the
city boundaries or outside the city walls. The analogy with a
cesspit, which was kept away from the community and from
everyday life, is quite clear.

Within our present system, however, there is a kind of
'corruption' that permeates the whole community so that,
even though we have abolished brothels, we have not
abolished the prostitute. This spread of whoredom not only
makes for greater sexual promiscuity in the general sense, and
for a marked inability to distinguish between the professional

prostitute and girls who frequently change their partners, but makes it more difficult to distinguish between what is normal and what is definitely perverse sexual behaviour.

One does not wish to go all the way with Demosthenes when he said in his speech in defence of the prostitute, Neaera: '. . . we keep mistresses for pleasure, concubines for daily attendance upon our persons, wives to bear us legitimate children and be our faithful housekeepers'. Those days will not recur but, given a greater clarity in the role of woman and, above all, the availability of brothels, it is conceivable that women and children might find it easier to walk the streets of most cities in the Western world without having to worry too much about their safety.

*   *   *

I attach very great importance indeed to the lack of respect for women that is, it seems to me, increasingly manifested by Western men today. I can understand how it has come about; and some of the tensions which have arisen as a result of woman's determination to 'do her own thing' have already been referred to. But it is odd that at the very same time that a practically all-male Parliament in the United Kingdom has decided, over a period of years, to give increasing recognition and to enforce the strictest possible respect for women's rights, there has been an almost proportionate and parallel increase in the disrespect shown to woman as a human being. In my view, this is due almost exclusively to the fact that the images which modern Western woman, very often influenced by her American counterpart, wishes to project are not the hallowed ones of woman as a mother, as a queen in the kingdom of the family, as the doting grandmother for her grandchildren; in other words, as someone for whom respect was due simply because of the function which she performed.

I find it sadly ironic that I should remember quite clearly that when as a child I was taught the Ten Commandments, the second one was to the effect that we should honour our parents. This Commandment was thrown out of the window not too long ago; with it, we have also thrown out respect for either parent. I have already explained how in my view modern man has ceased to deserve any respect; but the effects of the lack of respect for modern woman are even more far-reaching than the ever-increasing homosexuality of modern man.

I think the recent article by Linda Grant (*The Independent on Sunday*, 23 January 1994) entitled 'Why do young men rape elderly women?' ought to be compulsory reading for all who take an interest in social affairs. The quotation that follows is abstracted from that article:

> Late last November, an 84-year-old widow was asleep in her house in Camden, north London, when a man broke in. He threatened her with a carving knife, then beat and raped her. He left her trapped in a wardrobe which he turned door-side down on the floor, piling furniture on top of it; she was only freed when a neighbour became suspicious about a smashed window and called the police. A 17-year-old has been charged and will be tried in the summer,
>
> Exactly a week later, a 71-year-old woman in Daventry, Northamptonshire, was woken up and raped at knifepoint by an intruder. Two weeks after that, on Christmas Eve, a man visiting his 83-year-old spinster aunt on a council estate in Southwark, south London, became concerned when there was no reply to his knock on the door. He called the police who broke in and found the woman also trapped in a wardrobe having been sexually assaulted.
>
> There are no figures for the numbers of sexual attacks on the elderly because the Home Office does not categorize its rape statistics by age. We may imagine that the rape of elderly women is a rare, horrible and peculiarly unnatural crime, but it is not. Looking at newspaper cuttings covering the past two or three years, it becomes clear that the rape of older women is not only commonplace but that the number of reported incidents are increasing.
>
> On Christmas Day 1991 a severely disabled 70-year-old woman was raped in Sussex. In January 1992 a man was jailed for nine years for raping the 66-year-old housekeeper of a Catholic priest. The following month a Worcester man was jailed for life after sexually assaulting an 88-year-old, punching her in the eye and mouth and slitting her clothes from the chest down. He had already served an eight-year sentence for raping a 50-year-old woman.
>
> In April 1992, Manchester Police investigated what the police

authority's chairman called 'the worst case of its kind I have ever
heard of'. An 88-year-old widow was left with a fractured skull, two
broken ribs and other injuries after a four-hour attack in which she
was kicked, battered and bitten by two men who raped her three
times, forcing her to carry out what newspapers called 'a series of
perverted sex acts'. In June of that year, a 16-year-old was convicted
at Norwich Crown Court of the rape of a woman aged 100.

The author, to whom I am grateful, can reach no
conclusion. She quotes Dr Jill Mezey, Susan Brownmiller
(the author of *Against our Will*) and Malcolm Holt, who each
in a different way, provide some explanation (manifestation of
power, disrespect, dissatisfaction with society, result of sexual
abuse when young, hostility to women, and so on). Nobody
mentions the lack of respect for woman consequent upon the
change in her role.

*   *   *

This seems an appropriate point at which to make a few
observations about the matter of rape, which are
pertinent to the arguments advanced.

No one can have any sympathy for the rapists who attack
women who are unknown to them and have done nothing to
encourage them in any form: clearly such people suffer from
grave psychological deficiencies and a marked inferiority
complex. They are a disgrace to manhood and, as far as I am
concerned, they ought all to be castrated. The man who is
worthy of the label of man has no need to use physical
violence to get his way sexually with any woman since there
are other virtues and means which he can display and use,
which will result in his getting what he is seeking. For a man
to use violence to force a woman to submit to his sexual needs
is, in the philosophical sense, no different from cheating at
cards in order to win.

I must make it clear, however, that I draw a clear distinction
between the true rapist and the man who uses violence which
may amount to rape in those circumstances which, applying
terminology developed in the United States, have become

known as 'date rape': I shall return to this subject shortly. But, there is one important point I think ought to be made straight away, especially in the context of date rape: it surely cannot be right that we should have an offence of so-called *attempted rape*. A rape is either consummated or not: if not, the relevant attempt is an indecent or physical assault. The subject matter of rape is difficult enough without having to investigate the finer points relating to the difference between the use of force, on the one hand, in an attempt to commit rape; and the insistence and persuasion which are more or less normal features of any kind of courtship.

I appreciate that to convict a person of an attempt to commit a crime does entail some difficulty. But there is a problem about attempted rape, since it cannot be predicated, especially in these days of greater awareness of sexually-transmitted disease, and especially of AIDS, that a man who, so to say, pulls his trousers down is for that reason alone intent upon sexual intercourse. It could so easily be argued that there were other forms of sexual gratification that he was setting out to achieve, and it seems to me that the evidential difficulties in the way of any successful prosecution for attempted rape are so great that the offence itself is not worth having. The man can equally be punished for assault.

In any event, I accept that there are probably no circumstances in which the use of force by a man on a woman to obtain sexual favours can be countenanced. It may theoretically be conceivable that if a man and a woman were stranded on a desert island, the use of some force might in certain circumstances be necessary if the man wanted to have his way and the woman were unwilling. That might make any form of violence in the particular instance – I hesitate to use the noun 'rape' in context – more understandable, though still not excusable. So much for the more traditional forms of rape.

Turning to date rape, it seems to me that in today's consumer-orientated environment, society's present set-up is providing the consumer of sexual favours, if a heterosexual male, with a very poor deal indeed. I recall that recently someone charged with attempted rape in circumstances where he had spent a couple of hundred pounds and had seen what he thought were absolutely clear signs that the woman was willing to have sexual intercourse, expressed the view that having spent that kind of money, he ought to have got what he wanted. Such a statement, exceptionally misguided in the context of his prosecution, is un-worthy of any man; but the existence of legalized establishments would bring benefits to those who think in these terms. For example, they would save the user considerable aggravation, avoid the risk of prosecution, and probably a lot of money for, in all likelihood, some certainty of result could be achieved by paying about one-eighth of what that man just referred to expended, as well as not having to worry that the following morning the woman would complain to the police. How much better for him and the woman involved if he had visited a brothel.

In case the reader should feel that the equation of sexual services with consumer goods is extreme, I should underline the concept that I am dealing for present purposes with lustful intercourse. Intercourse of this nature has always been capable of being sold and bought.

In his book *The Myth of Male Power** the American, Warren Farrell, after dedicating over 200 pages to a very accurate if idiosyncratic analysis of the fall of man in relation to women and to society (the examples are legion but the classic is that the woman who cries 'rape' is entitled to retain her anonymity, whereas the man accused of rape is not, even before he is convicted) goes on to analyse the reasons given in the reports of what is known as 'date rape', (i.e. rape occurring between people who know each other and who at least up to the moment that the offence is said to have been committed, were on reasonably friendly terms) are escalating. He mentions the following:

Anger towards a former boyfriend, the need of younger girls to give excuses to their parents for being pregnant, spite

---

* Simon and Schuster Inc, New York, 1993

or revenge, in order to compensate for feelings of guilt or shame, to conceal an affair, to make money by claiming against well-known persons, to facilitate an abortion where laws do not allow one in the early stages of pregnancy or because the woman was intoxicated with drink, amongst other less frequently-cited reasons.

It seems to me, however, that the matter should be looked at from a totally different perspective in order to understand the increased incidence of date rapes. A woman who, even to some extent against her will – and it is exceptionally difficult to draw the line in these matters, is it not? – has indulged in sexual intercourse with a man whom she knew, whose attentions she welcomed and may even have encouraged and who may have paid for the entertainment (whether a meal, the cinema or whatever else) may well complain the following morning that she has been raped, for some or all of the reasons that Warren Farrell has recorded. But what will precipitate her complaint, and what is in fact its fundamental cause of complaint is that she has derived no satisfaction from the experience. Put differently, the performance of the man has been that of a wimp, both on the emotional and on the physical plain, with the result that she gained no pleasure from the encounter.

On the contrary, she sees herself as having been molested and humiliated, and as having derived no satisfaction from the violation: physical, in the first place, it is true, but perhaps even more importantly, emotional or psychological upset at what has occurred. The dissatisfaction with his performance is very great. 'How dare he?' must be one of the more obvious faults by reference to either puny attributes, poor technique, selfish or weak performance, or whatever. Whatever respect or liking might have been felt for that particular man – in most cases a poor specimen indeed in any event – fades away in the wholly understandable feeling of having been soiled.

Consider, however, a different situation, namely, those circumstances where some degree of persuasion was displayed, including possibly also an amount of gentle force, but the performance of the male partner was so good (whether because of the duration of his erection, his technique, or his consideration of his partner's responses) that the woman actually enjoyed herself: in such cases, the police would not be troubled. The following morning she may well kiss his hand, but she will not report him to the police. She may well feel that she has been forced into intercourse, she may even feel that technically she has been raped: but she will not complain to the police. She may even decide that she should not see him again, although I personally believe that the likelihood is that if she knows the fellow and has his phone number, she will ring him. No 'normal' woman would send to jail a man who has given her pleasure.

If this analysis is correct, and I personally have no doubt whatsoever that it is, it seems to me that what is needed is not a clearer definition of the law of rape, attempted rape, date rape, or anything else, but better education of the male in satisfying the female. And for that, an excellent school would be the brothel, where education can be acquired without causing any harm, whether physical or psychological, to one's partner. Furthermore, I believe that men who as a matter of routine frequent establishments where they can give vent to their sexual requirements or repressions, do not rape women. Firstly, they no longer have the need, since by definition their requirements are satisfied; and secondly, they are probably the type of individuals who are not obsessed by concepts of power or by the kind of perverted sexual drive where sexuality itself is diluted by the obsession to manifest dominance over women.

(iii) THE LEGALIZATION OF BROTHELS OR EQUIVALENT ESTABLISHMENTS WILL CONTRIBUTE TO STRENGTHENING THE MARRIAGE BOND AND WILL REDUCE THE NUMBER OF DIVORCES

In 1919, there were 1600 divorces in the United Kingdom; the figure rose to 3500 in 1921 and 4000 in 1929. In 1987, a total of 351,761 marriages were celebrated in the UK thus, 703,522 persons agreed, whether in Church or at the Registry

Office (367,142 in a Church and 336,380 at a Registry Office) to bind themselves to each other, according to the marriage vows at least, for life.

But in the same year there were 151,007 divorces, nearly a forty-fold increase on 1929. Accordingly, 302,014 persons (that is to say, about 43% of the number of those who had got married that year, though not necessarily the same persons) had changed their minds about being bound together in matrimony for life. These official Government figures (taken from H.M.S.O. publications series FM.2 number 14 pages 15 and 49), have already been referred to, in updated form.

Three in every 10 wives who divorced in 1987 had married at ages under 25. A quarter of all divorces in 1987 were in respect of marriages which had lasted less than five years. In 1988, 72% of all divorce decrees were granted to wives: woman is clearly the initiator in the destruction of the marital relationship, despite the fact that the number of women who married that year and had cohabited represented 48% of the total (equivalent percentages for the early and the late 1970s were 7% and 19%).

When people divorce, co-habiting between marriages is virtually the norm. Seven out of ten second marriages are preceded by a period of cohabitation; but that does not seem to help, since remarriages are at greater risk of dissolution than are first marriages. ('Family Change and Future Policy' 1990 p.15.) Of those who divorced in 1987, for one divorcing couple in 13, both spouses had already been married (or divorced, depending on how one looks at it). Put differently, 43,439 men had married an equal number of women who had already been divorced at least once, if not more often (FM.2 number 14 page 17).

Opposite is a graph showing the escalation in the rate of divorce.

These figures make depressing reading if we consider the wellbeing of the spouses. Unfortunately, the matter does not stop there. Of the 150,000 or so couples who divorced in 1987, over half had children under 16. The same data reveal

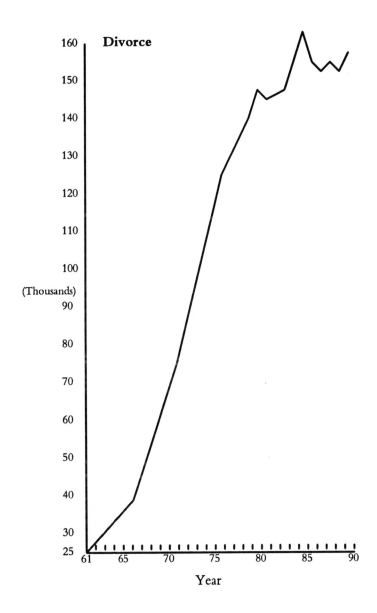

that 149,000 children aged under 16 were affected by divorce
in 1987. There is the expense to the State of such a situation.
According to the Marriage Guidance Council (now known as
'Relate') – as reported in *The Independent* of 27 September
1989 – Britain's soaring divorce rate (today, just under 50% of
marriages fail) is costing a great deal of money. The Council
has calculated that the bill to the UK taxpayer directly
attributable to divorce is 3.5 million pounds *per day*. The 'post-
divorce' payments take the form either of Income Support or
Housing Benefit or One-Parent Benefit. Updated figures, if
available, would show a much greater burden for the taxpayer.

I suppose that another way of solving the problem would be
to introduce selective or increased taxation for divorced
persons. But that might be an even worse pill for the general
public to digest than the introduction of supervized brothels.
There is also the cost of the Legal Aid fund (and, obviously, to
the spouses themselves where they do not qualify for Legal
Aid).

In passing, I would make the point that recently some
complaints have been voiced as to the justice of public funds
being used through the Legal Aid system to help people obtain
divorces, on the basis that having agreed to marry for better or
for worse, they should not seek the assistance of the State
when wishing to retract their marital vows. The precise figure
which, according to the Council, was payable by the State in
1989, let alone by the individuals, is a staggering minimum of
1.25 billion pounds a year which is made up as follows:
£850,000,000 as Income support, £220,000,000 as Housing
Benefit, £100,000,000 in One-Parent Benefit and
£80,000,000 in Legal Aid. Here again, updated figures
would show comparable increases.

The Council predicts that there will be about three million
divorces between September 1989 and the year 2000 and that
one-and-a-half million children (or about 3% of our
population) under the age of 16 will have to face the
consequences of divorce by that date.

Consider for a moment what else could be done with the

'divorce budget' of 1.25 billion pounds a year. Such a sum would purchase 62,500 kidney machines or pay for 250,000 heart by-pass surgery operations (at an average respective cost of about £20,000 and £5,000 a time).

The most damaging statistics, however, relate to the divorce rate itself, that is to say, the number of divorces per matrimonial couples. This was fairly high in 1987 (12.7, slightly above the 11.9 of 1981 and the 12 of 1984) but it rose to 12.9 in 1989, reaching 13.1 in 1990. (Population Trends 1991, HMSO) It is the highest in the Western world. The British, incidentally, only marginally beat the Danes: Denmark has a divorce rate of 12.8. The UK has been creeping up on them, however, but in 1989 we managed to take over the lead; and we have maintained the lead, indeed, increased it, for in 1991 it reached 13.6 (v. Marriage & Divorce Statistics HMSO, FM2 Series, No. 19, p.50).

It is clear that in the United Kingdom we have come to take divorce so much for granted that we have ceased to consider what its drawbacks are, especially for society and for the children. People nowadays say that they have divorced once or twice and/or have remarried, in the same way that they say they have had a toothache, or a sterilization. Whether our society is interested in reducing the number of divorces must, in the light of the statistics that have been quoted, be a moot point.

For the purposes of the present argument, however, it will be assumed that the unrestricted availability of divorce is, from both a personal and a social standpoint, a grave mistake; that the majority of those who divorce and remarry, on a statistical basis, are not necessarily any happier than they were; that people who have remarried may be tempted to divorce and marry for the third or more times, thus on the one hand endorsing the general acceptability of divorce as a normal occurrence and, on the other, creating a self-perpetuating circle of 'divorce-prone people'; that divorce has already gone a long way to destroying the family as a socio-economic unit and, if unrestrained, will cause the family even as it is normally understood in the twentieth century, to disappear completely.

Furthermore, it will also be assumed that its consequences are exceptionally grave for the children of failed marriages, well apart from having a negative and expensive effect on society as a whole, and finally, that the disappearance of the family unit is contributing to a class of people whom *I* would term 'moral imbeciles' and is a major, if not the most important, factor in the increase in crime, juvenile violence and general instability, lack of shame and of pride, and absence of standards.

If these assumptions are believed to be incorrect, then the whole of this section can safely be ignored by the reader. On the other hand, some comfort for the above views may be derived from the consideration that if one looks at British society, now that we have such a high rate of divorce, and one compares it with what it was before divorce became easier, it must be accepted that we are comparing a country which had an Empire, a role in world history, traditions which it honoured, dignity, integrity and patriotism, with one that it is incapable of understanding where its destiny, at least in the historical sense, lies, is unruly, obsessed by 'sex', violent, devoid of pride and self-contemptuous almost to the point of destruction. When the changes that have taken place are analysed, their impact is somewhat reduced by explaining that our society has become more liberal on social and sexual issues.

There are obviously some respects in which we are perhaps more tolerant of certain forms of sexual deviation, but the freedom extended to those who promised each other to remain together until death parted them, to change their minds after a mere one year of marriage, would appear to be the result, not of more liberal thinking, but of a fundamental failure to recognize the importance of the family unit.

Given these developments, there may be something to be said for the theory that the higher the rate of divorce in society, the greater that society's instability. And that is the context against which must be considered the advantages that the recognition of the need for brothels would provide.

In the first place, even within the marital relationship there is scope for the kind of sexual conduct which could be termed unnatural or abnormal or deviant. One must obviously be rather cautious in using such terminology because very often, nowadays, one sees the adjectives normal and natural applied to forms of sexual behaviour which 50 years ago would, at least at the public level, have been considered unnatural and abnormal. On the other hand, there is no doubt that there is a kind of conduct in the sexual sphere which is a deviation. Take, for example, flagellation or sado-masochistic practices. How many spouses who love each other indulge in them?

But even if we remain within the slightly less objectionable forms of sexual deviations, it must be acknowledged that most, if not all, human beings in their sexual activities manifest traits which are not always in keeping with their personality, as it is known to them and understood or believed by the world outside. Psychiatrists and doctors know of many manifestations by either men or women – there is little to choose between the sexes in this particular context except perhaps that man has greater imagination – when it comes to sexual behaviour. There is no need for us to explore this topic here: the facts of life as experienced by each of us and as recorded in medical encyclopaedias, books, novels, newspapers, magazines, films, TV, court records, etc., speak for themselves.

As mentioned earlier, in an ordinary marital situation either spouse may be reluctant or unwilling or too shy to request the other to indulge in or put up with his/her own sexual 'quirks'. To take a far-fetched but not too absurd example, few are the men who would insist upon having intercourse with their wives whilst wearing a Napoleon-style (three-cornered) hat; and few women in all likelihood would be willing to put up with such a request.

Nevertheless, there are some men who may wish to do just that. This is an extreme example which is intended to highlight the partial absurdity of any kind of request for sexual performances other than of what one considers the more conventional kind; but requests are made, tendencies do exist, needs have to be satisfied. These are not new requirements and, as we know, when it comes to the relationship between men and women there never was, there is still not and there never will be anything new under the sun. It is merely wrapped up differently at different times in history.

Thus, what can the poor husband do, who wishes to have intercourse with his wife in the manner above described? He has three choices: (1) he asks her to accommodate him and runs two risks, the one of being refused and the other of looking foolish and thus adding to the contempt his wife may already be feeling for him, as many women nowadays feel for men; (2) he does not ask, and foregoes the experience: he then feels resentful that his married life does not give him, at least at that level, all he wants; or (3) he seeks it elsewhere. There are no other solutions, it must be one of these three. If the odd or deviating tendency is there, it will either have to be satisfied by the wife, or remain unsatisfied, or be satisfied by someone else.

For present purposes we are not concerned with the first alternative. If the wife satisfies the 'deviant' need, no matter how grudgingly, or perhaps thinking, as most women do, that men will always be odd and childish, there is no official problem as far as society is concerned, except that there is a kind of humiliation of man before woman which seems to be a general feature of present-day society, or at least certainly of the Anglo-Saxon/American world, where men overall seem to enjoy humiliating themselves before women.

If we take the second alternative, namely that there is no satisfaction by the wife, then we may have some problem within the marriage. Again, for present purposes we are not concerned too much with the dissatisfaction that occurs within the marriage, although the particular difficulty will go and swell the number of other problems that occur in the marital relationship and may itself be a contributory factor in a possible neurosis of the spouse/s, especially if the resentful reaction of the husband is the result of immaturity on his part.

We are more interested at this stage with the third

alternative, namely the satisfaction of a particular tendency by someone other than his wife. In the third hypothesis, we are thrown back on the difference between sacred and profane love. The distinction is ancient, but for present purposes it should be noted that the glorification, conceptualization and representation of sacred and profane love in ancient art, is not in any sense related to pathological characters: it was merely meant to convey the idea that the same person can harbour both loving and lustful feelings and the two cannot, or need not, always be associated with the same person of the opposite sex.

When it comes to present-day society, however, there appears to be some confusion in the approach to love and marriage. Woman herself has caused and has aggravated the confusion by maintaining a certain universality for her role both within the marriage and within society, for she claims that her independence of mind, her determination, her confidence and her non-conformity are such that she can be at any time wife, mother, mistress, sister and friend. (I am not aware of any man who claims to be all these things with the same conviction as modern woman does.)

In this sense, we are quite different from our forefathers, who thought they were able to distinguish clearly between what they called sacred and profane love. They did so anyhow in their literature, in their art, particularly in paintings, and in their 'morality'. They were quite content to accept with St Augustine that a human being is capable both of looking up to heaven and of wallowing in hell; that man and woman can both look upon relationships with the opposite sex as pure or impure. These qualifications are not used in any moral sense but merely to highlight the concept that our sexuality is capable of being directed in at least two ways and consequently, is both ennobling and demeaning in the same person and at different times and, very often, also at the same time.

This fact of life is objected to, by those who disapprove of the legalization of brothels, as a pathological condition. The argument runs that, by tolerating brothels, the State would give approval to such a pathological condition. This objection was put forward most recently by Edward Glover in *The Psychopathology of Prostitution* (ISTD reprinted 1969 at pages 6 and 16) – although it is not clear whether the title considers the pathology of the prostitute or the customer. Glover took the view that the more 'drab' type of prostitute, the street-walker, was apathetic, mentally disordered or backward, prone to excessive use of alcohol and to association with criminals resulting from emotional disturbance in adolescence. It is difficult to assess how accurate these descriptions would prove for the street-walker of the nineties.

The fact remains that, even apart from any theoretical consideration of pathological factors, in the third hypothesis that has been chosen above, present-day man has the choice of either looking for a prostitute or trying to find his 'twin soul' amongst women who may be either his friends' wives or the secretary at the office or the pretty lady on the train or his research assistant.

Feminists will not have that. They say that modern woman is capable of encompassing both lewd and loving emotions and of providing a total outlet for man's sexual desires, of whichever type they may be. The Americans have gone so far as to suggest that high heels produce a happy home. Whether this means that a wife should also be a tart is a little difficult to determine from this side of the Atlantic.

One does not have to be too cynical to observe that, even if this principle worked at all, which is not conceded, it would only work when woman is young. There is something almost pathetic about a woman who has lost her looks and her figure, but still surrenders to the temptation of advertisements, to buy seductive underwear. Why not, you may say. Yet, there is surely a time and place for everything and wives should remain on the sacred side of the love-scale, well advised to leave the profane alone, on the principle that, generally speaking, no man really enjoys the thought that the mother of his children is, at heart, a prostitute.

Furthermore, there is also something amiss in the equation 'high heels, happy homes', which seems based on a misconception. If it is meant to convey the idea that a wife should always endeavour to preserve her appearance and look smart so that the husband may appreciate her more, then it is axiomatic and the saying reflects no more than what every sensible woman has known throughout the centuries. If, on the other hand, it is meant to convey the idea of a greater application by the wife to matters sexual in order to interest her husband, then it may well be that it is representative of a mentality which has failed to secure marital stability, given the high number of divorces in the USA and UK. It is conceivable that the preservation of a marriage depends much more on other, possibly more mundane virtues than the sexual.

For example, some people might be forgiven for believing that there is some truth in the statement that the key to a man's heart is his stomach and that a good cook is more likely to make a success of marriage than a good whore. To this it may be objected that the old words of wisdom are no longer applicable in the twenty-first century. Such a view is not accepted here, since human psychology, as is already self-evident from this discussion, has a degree of permanence that transcends contraception, feminism, self-assertion and permissiveness.

As has just been noted, the woman of the twentieth century believes she can be wife, mistress, mother, sister, breadwinner and friend at the same time. She can procreate, fornicate, appreciate, listen sympathetically and cater for all the passions, the failings and, at times, the deviations of her man; and earn a living. The trouble is that such an outstandingly compassionate and understanding human being has yet to be born. It is conceivable that the next millennium may see something of that kind come into existence as a result of genetic engineering: but there is at present no normal wife who has the physical, and above all, the emotional and psychological strength and ability to be all things to her husband, let alone looking after her children, if any!

This applies universally without differences of nationality, status, creed and race. The man who has known more than one woman would probably state unhesitatingly that such a creature, such a paragon of all virtues feminine, Amazon of the marital- and non-bedchamber, indefatigable and undaunting, athlete of womanhood, never tired, off-colour, irritable or irritating, always conscious of the need to please her mate at any time of day and at whatever cost to herself, is a figment of the imagination of feminists and writers of cheap novels.

If modern man does not escape to the brothel, he will escape in different ways: we shall then have the Profumo, Christine Keeler and Madame Sin types but, and this is troublesome, we shall no longer know exactly where to find them. So what does the man (or woman, for that matter) do in the third hypothesis if there are no brothels? Would it not be better for the integrity of the marriage that he should hang his hat on a coatstand in a properly supervized brothel, rather than embark upon a relationship with another woman, at the risk of damaging her marriage, if she has a spouse, and possibly his own? The great advantage of dealing with prostitutes, particularly if operating in brothels, is that the transactions are clear. They have economic and psychological transparency. A prostitute will not make the same demands that a non-prostitute may well be tempted to make of a married man who has been sleeping with her. This is a point about which I feel particularly strongly, for I believe that the absence of brothels, coupled with the reasonably free availability of unmarried women who, as modern terminology defines them, are sexually liberated, represents one of the gravest dangers for the stability of the relationship between spouses.

Taking the husband first, the point has been illustrated by a somewhat far-fetched example as to possible 'perverted' sexual tendencies by reference to an item of apparel. But the failure of the wife to provide a particular, odd form of sexual gratification is only a small example of what may go amiss in the marital relationship, since there are many more situations where friction occurs between the spouses which are not strictly related to any particular quirk by either spouse.

It is common knowledge that tensions develop within a marriage for the most multifarious reasons and that there are times when either spouse is not performing well, whether physically or emotionally, for a number of reasons (temporary inability, illness, menopausal manifestations, etc.). If in such situations either spouse has sexual relationships with a person of the opposite sex, outside the marriage, then it often becomes somewhat difficult to resist the temptation, either to compare the 'errant' relationship with the marital one or to seek outside the marriage not only sexual comfort, but also general solace and understanding.

It may be that this is more difficult to achieve for the wife than for the husband, who may content himself with a drunken session with the boys or a visit to a tart. But the greater the frequency of his visits to a mistress, the more likely, in my opinion, the development of feelings of detachment from the spouse and of appreciation and attachment for the mistress, which is a slope that in our Western society more often than not, proves very slippery, if the divorce statistics mean anything at all.

Where, however, the pressure on the husband causes him to visit a brothel, he may return home relieved and possibly even guilty and without any more serious consequences as far as the marriage is concerned. Whilst it is easier to analyse the position in the case of the adulterous husband, it becomes somewhat more difficult for the dissatisfied wife. It should be said, however, that women very often find different ways of escaping from the particular tensions to which reference has been made, and not necessarily into the arms of a lover.

Whether it is the husband or the wife who strays, if in such situations where a spouse seeks comfort with another person it is accepted that nothing can come of the new relationship, because it is not likely that either spouse would leave the marital home for a prostitute, there is more than a sporting chance that, after the crisis period is over, the visits to the brothel will cease and the spouses will resume their life together. On the other hand, where it is known that there is a let-out, the temptation in most cases is too great, the party who feels aggrieved will psychologically compound the damage or the hurt caused by the spouse's behaviour and gradually conceive the idea that, after all, the grass may be greener on the other side of the fence.

The view that prostitutes can be of help in maintaining spouses together is hotly contested by those feminists who see no difference between adultery by a husband and adultery by a wife. Unwilling to argue that wives should be able to frequent brothels where men pander to their whims in the same way as some men visit prostitutes, they adhere strictly to the view that a wife is allowed, if she wishes, to commit adultery, if her husband does. It is a tit-for-tat situation which ignores the different reactions of men and women.

In the same way as it ignores the different meanings of the word 'adultery': surely, what one may term the 'quantum' of adultery is important. One deviation from the path of marital righteousness cannot possibly have the same significance as a relationship persisted in for several years, let alone the fact that, as has already been observed elsewhere, there are some men for whom adultery, whether on a once only or more regular basis, could be said to be purely medicinal.

It must be accepted, however, that legally and morally the feminist argument is 100% correct. There is legally and morally no difference whatsoever between adultery by a husband and adultery by a wife. In practice, however, the situation is not quite so clearcut. In *Sexual Behaviour in Society* (Duckworth, 1950) Alex Comfort observed: 'Adultery today maintains far more marriages than it destroys on the principle that there can be few couples who do not experience strain over each other's foibles and fewer still who do not, if they are quite honest, sometimes desire a sexual holiday. Once the tensions have been released, however, the marriage may regain a deeper level of stability than before.'

The theory hereby propounded (that brothels should be

freely available to both men and women) may in fact endorse these remarks. The difficulty is that, nowadays, confused romantic notions straddle uninhibited sexual freedom, at the same time as there is an unwillingness on the part of both man and woman to acknowledge the possibility of a divorce between sexual activity and love.

Modern spouses appear to live in a world of make-believe which leads them to neuroticism. It is a world of fantastic images which are forced on them by films, television, advertising literature; a world, the temptations of which they find all the more difficult to resist the further removed they are, as they must be in our cities, from the realities of natural life.

One cannot ignore the fact that it may be that citizens of Finchley, near London, see things differently from those of Somerset, in the same way that there may be more uninhibited sexuality of what one may call the farmyard type in Somerset than in Finchley. But it is true to say that the removal from the realities of nature does have certain consequences, because centralized urban societies produce heightened emotional tensions that lead to a state of persistent sexual excitement, its persistence being caused by the fact that, for most of the time, the excitement remains unsatisfied. The dissatisfactions of the public with their personal sexual experiences, then have to find expression in art and entertainment, manifested as an intensive preoccupation with romantic love, sexual success and virility. The growth in that form of advertising, which depends on the promise of sexual success and virility in particular, rather than of any image of togetherness, is the best proof of this point. Brothels would provide an outlet for such dissatisfaction.

This artificial world tends to confuse images and instincts whilst at the same time certain religious fetishes and vestiges of the former morality persist. It is a situation where the roles of men and women are being confused. The traditional role of man is being redefined whilst his traditional authority and power generally are being constantly eroded; but a new role has not yet been carved out for woman.

The one advantage of brothels is to classify both men and women: the women because, by leading the kind of life that they have to lead to operate therein, they have set themselves aside from the majority of other women who are not that way inclined; the men because, frequenting those establishments, they accept that they are 'deviating' from a particular kind of conduct, if, for example, they are otherwise happily married or have a stable relationship or, in the case of more deviant behaviour or requirements, simply because they find an acknowledged outlet to those requirements. Society seems to have been conspicuously reluctant to tackle this problem; it is even more reluctant to tackle it now because the solution is unpalatable for some women.

(iv) DECRIMINALIZATION WOULD ALSO REDUCE THE RATE OF ABORTION AND ILLEGITIMACY IN WOMEN AND TEENAGE GIRLS.

The figures for abortion in the United Kingdom make depressing reading. These figures only relate to legal abortions, namely those carried out either under the National Health system, or privately by qualified medical practitioners. Nobody knows how many illegal abortions occur every year.

The jump is spectacular. From 18,000 abortions in 1968, to 179,522 in 1991 (a slight decrease of 7,390 on the 1990 figure). These are the official figures for England and Wales. The respective figures for abortions carried out on girls under the age of 16 are 3,422 for 1990 and 3,158 for 1991. The highest figures occur in the range 20–24 years, respectively 55,281 and 52,678.

One might be forgiven for believing that, insofar as these figures for abortion are far from negligible, there would be a compensation when dealing with illegitimacy which, as a result of more widespread use of contraception, should almost be a thing of the past. However, the rate of illegitimacy has also risen quite dramatically: for example, in 1939, about 4% of live births were illegitimate. From the end of the Second World War, when the figure for live births was about 9%, until 1960, Britain enjoyed a low, and even a slightly declining, illegitimacy ratio. From 1960 to 1978 the ratio of illegitimacy increased in the UK steadily, but remained modest by international standards, so much so that, as late as 1979, it was only 10.6%, one of the lowest rates in the industrial West.

Then, suddenly, in 1982, the illegitimacy ratio rose to 14.1, climbing to 18.9 in 1985 and a staggering 25.6 in 1988. (See the graph overleaf.) The increases are substantial and occurred at a time when fertility was in fact steady, if not slightly declining (1990 Birth Statistics HMSO 1992).

Some writers have suggested that the influx of 'black' and other ethnic groups have caused illegitimacy to rise. But this is far from being true. Indeed, it can be said that the overall effect of ethnic minorities living in the UK has been to reduce the size of the illegitimacy ratio since Chinese, Indians, Pakistanis, Arabs and East African women all have illegitimacy ratios that are tiny compared to those of their British counterparts. Furthermore, illegitimate children and abortions occur in what are called euphemistically 'stable relationships'. For example, of the 158,500 illegitimate births in England and Wales in 1987, 69% were jointly registered, 70% of the parents gave the same address, which would seem to suggest some kind of continuing relationship.

The position is clearly absurd because we now have freely available, reliable contraception. Indeed, our present contraceptive measures are so efficient that it can be said, without too much fear of contradiction, that they require neither intellectual nor manipulative ability above the average. It would appear that something has gone amiss in the psyche of those adult women and teenage girls who, despite the existence of contraception, persist in having children whom they intend to remain illegitimate for they seem to be going, so to say, against the grain of woman's avowed aim of being mistress of her own body.

During the same period as the number of abortions and illegitimate births has increased, we have also witnessed a rise in reported crime, as already mentioned. For example, in 1988

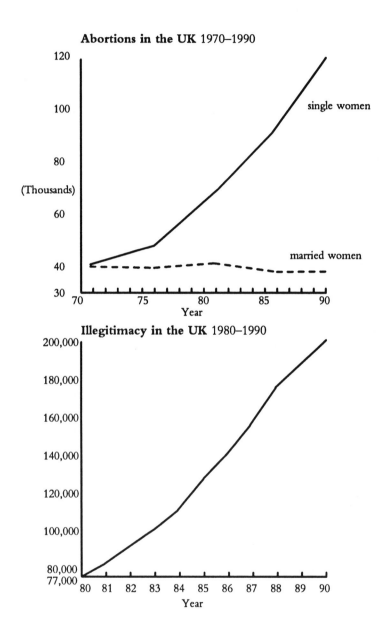

Abortions in the UK 1970–1990

England had 1,623 reported burglaries per 100,000 population. The equivalent figure for the United States was 1,309.
Motor vehicle theft is also higher in the UK than in the
United States. During the period from 1980 to 1989 crime
generally increased in England and Wales at an average rate of
5%. It then jumped to 17%. In 1990 in England and Wales,
the police recorded some 4.5 million notifiable offences and
5.1 million in 1992. Over the same period the increase in the
number of offence of theft and handling stolen goods was 18%
and in that of burglary it was 22%.

There seems to be a correlation between the rise in abortion
and illegitimacy and that in crime. Students of society will no
doubt draw different conclusions from these figures, but it is
possible that the greater pressure on young girls and women to
have intercourse at an increasingly earlier age, and with greater
frequency, is upsetting the natural balance of society and
possibly woman's own psyche. If there were licensed brothels,
such pressures would lessen and their reduction would
inevitably carry with it a slowing down both in the rate of
abortions and in that of illegitimacy. After all, intercourse with
prostitutes is, as a matter of principle and practice, most
unlikely to give rise to births, legitimate or otherwise.

(v) DECRIMINALIZATION WOULD PRODUCE A SUBSTANTIAL REDUC-
TION IN VENEREAL AND RELATED DISEASES GENERALLY AND ALSO
CONTRIBUTE TO LIMIT THE SPREAD OF AIDS.

The connection between prostitutes and venereal disease is
a long established one. In 1564 the Italian scientist,
Gabriele Falloppio, published in Padua his book *De Morbo
Gallico* where he describes the use of sheaths made in Italy, of
fine linen firstly, and at a later date of isinglass, as well as of the
caecum intestine of the lamb.

Apart from being the most illustrious of sixteenth-century
anatomists, Falloppio was concerned with the spread of
syphilis, which had been brought over to Europe by the
Spaniards who discovered America with Columbus. It was
round about this time, when syphilis was claiming a heavy toll

in Italy and elsewhere in Europe, that a feeling of marked antipathy towards prostitutes became fairly widespread. This resulted in stringent measures being taken to suppress the activities of prostitutes, to close down brothels which had been tolerated until then and to penalize the women themselves.

It was fear that motivated the persecution of prostitutes in Italy and elsewhere in the early part of the Renaissance; in the same way it was fear that caused the Contagious Diseases Acts to be passed in nineteenth-century England; and similarly, it is fear of AIDS that may bring about a reappraisal of the usefulness of prostitutes. The distinction between the street-walker and the call-girl is of fundamental importance by reference to drug use and, because of that, to AIDS.

It is to be acknowledged that the street-walker is more likely to have little respect for her body than the call-girl and, accordingly, more likely to be a drug injector. It is also acknowledged, by those who have studied the spread of drug use among prostitutes, that smaller proportions of drug-injectors are to be found among non-street-walker-type prostitutes.

Indeed, in a study by Neil McKeganey and others (of the Public Health Research Unit at Glasgow University – June 1990), it is recorded that their Glasgow project showed that 59% of all Glasgow prostitutes contacted by them were drug-injectors. The report states: 'This figure represents a much higher proportion of injectors than has recently been reported among female prostitutes in other British cities', quoting in support of this statement the 155 reported for Birmingham by Hilary Kinnel in 1989, the 14% reported by Day and others for London in 1988 and the 205 reported by Ruth Morgan Thomas and others for Edinburgh in 1989. The number of street prostitutes in Glasgow in a six-month period in 1989/90 was calculated at 304 (172 drug-injectors and 132 non-injectors).

Quite clearly, the picture that emerges of street-walkers in the United Kingdom is that they are drug addicts in varying percentages. They are therefore more likely to develop HIV. Indeed, as has been observed (*British Journal of Addiction* 1991–86 at page 1477): 'The recent association between HIV infection and drug injecting has served to place even greater emphasis on the importance of identifying the size of the drug-injecting population.'

The street-walker is by far the more dangerous kind of prostitute as far as the spread of disease is concerned. It has been calculated (*British Journal of Addiction* 1991–86 at page 1480) that prostitutes who are also drug-injectors work more nights and/or longer hours than other women prostitutes. The reason is obvious: they need more money to satisfy their craving for drugs. Equally obvious, however, is the fact that their repeat contacts are more likely to contribute to the spread of disease. Although it has been found that drug-injectors form a much higher proportion of repeat contacts than new contacts – 725 as opposed to 59% – the fact remains that even with a repeat contact, the greater frequency of intercourse increases the chances of spreading disease.

It should be recorded, however, that the same study (page 1482) is not too pessimistic about the transmission of the HIV virus: 'The balance of current evidence suggests that female prostitution is not playing an important role in heterosexual HIV transmission.' Be that as it may, it is clear that only inadequate data are available and that it would be preferable that the street-walking type of prostitution were completely abolished.

Whilst prostitutes are not acknowledged as providing a useful service and are not, therefore, as is here being claimed should be done, legalized, supervized, licensed and medically examined, there is probably a greater risk of an adulterous husband contracting venereal disease by intercourse with women who are not officially capable of being classed as prostitutes but who are nevertheless willing to offer their services, either in return for friendship, advancement, dining out, gifts or maybe even mutual enjoyment and, possibly, love. The promiscuous element of the population in the nineteen nineties may be at greater risk from venereal diseases generally than from prostitutes operating in a controlled environment.

The extent to which prostitutes spread sexually-transmitted diseases must be a matter of argument; but there can be no doubt that they make a contribution: this contribution has been assessed as quite substantial in the United States. In Colorado Springs, for example, 635 of 89 female prostitutes were found to be infected with gonorrhea during a 13-month period in the late nineteen seventies. In Fresno County, 21.75% of 512 female prostitutes tested during the same period had gonorrhea. In Atlanta, 19.8% of 237 women thought to be prostitutes and tested in 1978 also had gonorrhea. Spread across the board, 10.6% of the women had trichomoniasis, 3.4% had syphilis, 2.1% had monoliasis and 14.7% had non-specific uretritis (from *Sexually Transmitted Diseases* edited by Y.M. Felman).

The Americans have always believed that female prostitutes have accounted for a disproportionate share of venereal disease but it is clear that all their data relating to the matter have been obtained from street-walkers. According to the american point of view, the cumulative incidence of STDs in female prostitutes, even if working in brothels, may be 20 times higher than among other sexually active women.

It is not particularly clear how these figures relate to England and there is not much by way of reliable data for the rest of Europe. It is obvious that the greater the frequency of contact, the more likely one is to contract a sexually-transmitted disease: it needs neither a Royal Commission nor learned tomes to reach such a conclusion. Equally, however, the likelihood of contracting most kinds of sexually-transmitted diseases by the effective and proper use of condoms is dramatically reduced. In an American study carried out between 1971 and 1976 it was found that the rates of gonorrhea in American women aged 15–19 years, who were sexually active (not prostitutes) dropped 40% when condoms were used, and increased 110% where the contraceptive pill was used. Ultimately, it is a matter of education and hygiene. And nowhere do education and hygiene play a greater role, in my view, than in the contracting of cervical cancer. It is now well established (see recent pronouncements – February 1994 – by, for example, Dr Joan Macnab, Senior Scientist with the Medical Research Council's Virology Unit at the University of Glasgow, or Professor Peter Beverley of the Imperial Cancer Research Fund at University College, London), that cervical cancer appears to be a serious threat to the health of teenage girls who, well apart from indulging in under-age sex, take on multiple partners.

Until recently, it was believed it would take up to forty years for the disease to manifest itself, but it now appears that doctors are seeing younger women where cancerous cells have developed after only a few years.

Whether this increased risk factor is a result of the fact that sexual intercourse at a very early age can damage the cervix in such a way that it becomes more vulnerable to infectious agents, or because younger girls are having an increased number of sexual partners, or as a result of the combination of the two factors, the human papilloma virus is affecting a greater number of women than ever before.

If younger girls were under less sexual pressure because boys and men could satisfy their sexual requirements in brothels, I have little doubt that the incidence of cervical cancer would reduce proportionately to the availability of the facilities which are here advocated.

* * *

Environmental advantages

(c)(i) DECRIMINALIZATION WILL REDUCE THE TRADE IN PORNOGRAPHY AND THE PROLIFERATION OF WRITING BY DIRTY LITTLE BOYS AND GIRLS MASQUERADING AS 'LITERATURE', OR BY SEXUAL INSTRUCTION

In 1989 Faber & Faber published *Porn Gold* by David Hebditch and Nick Anning, which provides some very interesting comments and information on the kind of monetary rewards that can be reaped from pornography. Although it is quite impossible to be specific as to the precise quantities, because purveyors of this kind of literature do not release figures, it is estimated by Hebditch and Anning that the total monthly sale of 'girlie' magazines in Britain is at least 2.5 million copies. (Their book, by the way, is not included in the 'dirty-little-boys'-type of writing to which the sub-heading refers.)

The profits are very substantial indeed, as anyone wading through the records of the companies concerned at Companies House would be able to ascertain. And one is dealing here with minimum profits. In 1989 at least 45 million calls were made to telephone sex lines in the UK. The trade in these telephone calls is also very substantial, since the gross revenue for this kind of market is said to have grown from £2 million in 1984 to £130 million in 1989.

These are obviously approximate figures since nobody is prepared to boast about the greatness of their successes in the field; but it is clearly a reflection on the society in which we live that certain persons should be so sick or ill-adjusted as to wish to squander away money on services that are pathetic. These data highlight the fact that there must be something dramatically wrong in the relations between the sexes if such a stage of deviancy has been reached so quickly. The figures relate in the main to what is termed 'male' pornography, that is to say, the display of women for male titillation. But the past few years have seen a noticeable increase in female pornography, that is to say, the display of male models, etc. for female titillation.

The problem is not confined to the UK. Pornography is rampant throughout Western society. For example, it is estimated that the porn industry in the USA produced 1600 new titles of pornographic videos in 1992 with 500 million rentals of them. More recently (June 1992) a book has been published, a modern *Kama Sutra*, which purports to illustrate in graphic form the numerous positions that can be adopted for the purposes of intercourse. Also in 1992, in addition to the German, Dutch and Danish satellite channels that are available in the UK, we have pornographic films on the regular channels available to those who are willing to view them.

One of the explanations for the increase in pornography is to be found on pages 70 to 73 of Alex Comfort's *Sexual Behaviour in Society* (Duckworth, 1950): 'Genuine pornography is to the erotic literature of sexually-balanced cultures as prostitution is to marriages: it is a substitute for more concrete satisfactions, a projection of sexuality into another medium, which may be explicitly sexual or not. Civilized cultures produce little pornography of this type and regard it as a condiment; asocial cultures produce much and employ it as a diet.'

According to the Home Office, in 1991 a total of 180,000 sexual offences including rape were committed on women and if one reads newspapers and magazines, one becomes aware of constant complaints, often in angry terms, both from men and women about the ever-increasing rate of sexual violence upon women and, indeed, more recently, also about the sexual assaults and rapes by men on other men. Such complaints are, of course, perfectly justified: it is a disgrace that a woman should no longer feel free to walk the streets of the United Kingdom, should now have to resent being looked at admiringly by men, should really live in fear that she might be molested or seriously assaulted, and that young men should be similarly concerned that they in turn might be sexually assaulted and/or raped by other men.

These complaints, however, lie somewhat uncomfortably in the mouths of those men and women who at the same time maintain that prostitutes should be treated as anti-social pollutants and brothels should be illegal, but who nevertheless would not restrict the free availability of pornographic material on the basis of freedom of information. It is clear to me, beyond a shadow of doubt, that some connection exists between the free availability of pornographic material and the increase in sexual violence and rape: proof, however, is very difficult to come by. But if such a connection exists, before trying to search for a rationale, one should look at the motivation for pornography in the first instance since, by eliminating the cause, the effect would also be eliminated.

Everyone complains about pornography and its effects on women and men but few people wish to stop and ponder why it has spread so virulently. It is conceivable, if not indeed probable, that the spread has been facilitated on the one hand by the marked change that our Western society has seen in its perception of woman's function; and on the other hand, by the abolition of brothels. As regards the former, attention has already been drawn to the fact that woman's function is no longer considered the obvious, natural and long-established one of procreation; the primary function is that of sexual satisfaction and enjoyment. The spread and free availability of reliable contraception controlled by woman has ensured that such a result is attained. It is this change in perception that has caused sexual violence, rather than any increase in passion.

On the other hand, as we have already seen, woman herself has become more interested in the multifarious manifestations of her sexuality. It is no longer the prerogative of man to depersonalize the female body which he may be renting and, as women take on more masculine roles, so they will take on more masculine features; and these will include seeking male prostitutes or using pornographic material.

It is often said that there are some people who may be helped, by the use of pornographic material, to discharge or dilute their violent feelings towards persons of the opposite sex. That is exactly what brothels try and cater for; but with brothels, there would be containment whereas, now, pornography is all around us. One need only enter any public 'phone booth in London and see the pornographic messages contained in the business cards and other notices that fill the space. The need to display such would be dramatically reduced, given officially-approved brothels.

Above all, if individuals of both sexes took a more practical rather than theoretical view of matters sexual, they would have less need to be titillated by the kind of writing that abounds which is proffered as literature and which has no merit, literary or otherwise, whatsoever. We see persons in the public eye writing books that pander to the requirements of the population of the United Kingdom by adding titillation or prurient episodes which, as in one case, are totally irrelevant to the plot of a thriller; or by producing novels containing explicit sexual scenes, preferably of rape or related violence, in order to make their serialization for television more probable; and so on. It would be tiresome to list too many examples of writers who are nothing else but dirty little boys and girls, eager to make money by exploiting the frustration and the ignorance of a general public which, fed by social and sexual hypocrisy and pseudo-religious beliefs, is willing, gullible prey to muck of the worst possible kind. Much more speculative is the determination of the extent to which the legalization of brothels, both for men and for women, would reduce the ever-increasing amount of female pornographic material which is palmed off as erotic writing.

Not too long ago, a short (70-page) novella which claims to have sold more than 500,000 copies and to have been translated into 15 languages, was actually nominated for the Prix Goncourt. It is now said that women can write about passion and love and women, and not be punished for it, the guiding criterion being that women should be writing about women candidly and convincingly. When tackled about this newly-acquired freedom, women writers claim that since there are no taboos in literature for men, so there should be none for women, and some of them even claim to justify the portrayal of sexual intercourse in the oddest positions and locations, for example, on a butcher's slab, as well as sex with animals and all kinds of sado-masochistic practices.

There no longer seems to be any real difference between men and women in the field of pornography. The last resort argument, that it is subjective evaluation of writing which determines whether it be pornography or literature, is applied nowadays with equal conviction by women as it is by men. One can understand why women should suddenly feel that, just as they have been emancipated in every respect, so they should have their own D.H. Lawrence, Henry Miller and Marquise de Sade. But then, it is difficult to see what all the fuss is about when, over the last hundred years or so, women had 'pioneering' characters to advance the frontiers, George Sand, Colette and Anais Nin or even Benoite Groult.

Presumably, if there were brothels where men made themselves available for foreplay, titillation and intercourse with women, there would be less need for the kind of written stimulation which is making a fortune for a limited number of women and of publishers, but which ultimately is indistinguishable from the kind of rubbish that dirty little boys and girls have been writing for decades on the walls of toilets and elsewhere. The erotic/pornographic type of book by women is symptomatic of the new manifestations of female sexuality. It is the same kind of cant which men have put forward for centuries to justify their own kind of pornographic rubbish. Female passion and female fantasies are nothing new; all that is new is their uninhibited printed portrayal. Much better for these 'frustrated' females to visit a brothel, surely.

To blame it all on the Victorian heritage, as is often done in Britain, is wrong. What has so far prevented women from writing the kind of muck that men have indulged in has nothing to do with Victorian ideas, but merely with the view of life and her place in it that woman herself adopted. All that the feminine revival of erotic/pornographic writing reveals is that women are looking upon themselves in a different light; that they are sick and tired of being described in literature as creatures who are either basically corrupt or are punished for having been too much in love with their men; Tolstoy and Balzac no longer mean much to modern woman, who prefers Shere Hite and Nancy Friday.

It must be readily accepted that pornography written by women for women is qualitatively different from that aimed at men and is to be seen also through different eyes. However, it is certainly not different when it comes to the effects that it has upon its recipients. I have always thought that the justification for pornography is a fallacious one. It runs more or less along the lines that there are some people for whom, in certain situations, pornographic material may be of use. This cannot be denied. What no society has ever succeeded in determining is how many people can actually benefit from, what I term, theoretical sexuality. The trouble is that the same thing has happened to pornography as happens from time to time to certain foods or surgical interventions. One bright day someone discovers that carrot juice has a helpful effect on the body. No doubt a moderate consumption of carrot juice cannot be harmful and indeed may be beneficial. The discovery, however, is then turned into a rule of life. Drink as much carrot juice as you can, if you wish to remain healthy and young. Because carrot juice may be helpful to some people who are deficient in Beta-carotene, carrot juice is than said to be helpful to everybody.

I have never followed this kind of argument. I think I am sufficiently broad-minded to acknowledge that, for some people in particular circumstances, pornography may have limited uses. But it cannot possibly be preferred to the real thing and, to me at least, it has two great drawbacks. (1) it demeans, even further than is already the case, the figure of woman, and (2) it encourages a voyeuristic approach to matters sexual which I find totally abhorrent.

The two points that have just been made can be tested if one considers the effect of pornography on men and on women.

Clearly, the man who uses pornographic material on a regular basis to stimulate his mind or body, can only form a view of woman as a means to an end. The image that is created in his mind is one of lust and not of love. Much more serious, however, is the argument that such use provokes voyeurism and masturbatory practices: a lonely and anti-social activity, pursued very often in solitary circumstances and wholly dissociated from any thoughts of tenderness and consideration for women. Furthermore, the women that take part in pornographic representations are usually poor speci- mens in physical terms and, in his eyes, sluts. Masturbation seems an unnecessary way of giving vent to sexual feelings in a society like the Western one where woman is quite liberated and free, if not eager, to hop into bed.

One might be tempted to believe that the matter is less serious when considering the effect of pornography on women. But that may be a mistaken view. Not only do the same considerations apply to woman as to man; a more important objection is that pornography aimed at women all too often results in much attention being paid to the purely physical i.e. muscular, attributes of man. That is regrettable because it affects woman's instinctive reaction to her future mate. Every prostitute and some experienced philanderers know very well that physique and muscular strength are almost invariably in indirect ratio to the size and strength of the male sexual organ. This is a belief which is very well established in Mediterranean countries but which Anglo-American culture has yet to acknowledge in all its implications. For the woman, however, there is the further consideration that the component of loneliness which exists in voyeurism tends to highlight clitoral rather than vaginal enjoyment and prompts girls to masturbate at a much earlier age than they need. In my experience, it is almost invariably true that the earlier the age at which a girl enjoys masturbation, the more likely she is to be promiscuous in later life.

However that may be, in the case of both men and women, pornography moves the sexual drive away from normal intercourse; a result that is to be deprecated because it tends to dull the reproductive instinct. It is hardly a coincidence that modern man and modern woman are said to be less fertile in the 1990s than they were, say 50 years ago, despite their improved diet. This might of itself be a matter of indifference, except for the fact that it is also a contributory factor in the disorder in sexual relations referred to earlier.

The English language uses the word 'sex' in a connotation quite different from that of any other non-English speaking country: we have sex, that is to the point, concrete, simple and precise. I cannot think of any equivalent which expresses the concept so positively. Pornography, on the other hand, is theory and nothing but theory and those who use it believing that it will be of aid to their sexual drive misunderstand what sexual relations are about. It is surely no coincidence that alongside the spread of pornography is the great increase in the number of those men who have problems with their erectile tissues.

Ultimately, we are thrown back on the concept of power. When men held the power, and the cock ruled the roost, pornography was written and inspired by men; now that the balance has shifted and the hen has acquired a more raucous voice, she wants to be on top, and wants to have it her way. But to claim either originality or literary merit for the ever-increasing amount of pornographic literature by women is as foolhardy as to hope that a woman will succeed as a weightlifter. If she wishes to remain a woman, she will not try and develop the kind of muscles which detract from poise, style and femininity. How successful brothels catering to purely female requirements can be in today's world is considered later.

(c)(ii) THE CONTAINMENT OF PROSTITUTION IN BROTHELS WILL HAVE ENVIRONMENTAL ADVANTAGES BY CONFINING THEIR ACTIVITIES TO SPECIAL DISTRICTS.

It has been the practice throughout history to confine the activities of prostitutes to certain areas. In earlier times they may not have been allowed within the walls of the city, or they may have been confined to special quarters. The decision to impose this isolation was in part the result of the Church's approach to them, namely that they were a necessary evil and that their activities should be equated with cesspits, and partly the desire to underline the distinction between the whore and the respectable woman.

Closer to modern times, the decision may also have been dictated by sound commercial reasons. In the same way that shops selling a particular type of goods tend to be found in special locations (such as industrial estates), so prostitutes announced their availability to the general public by practically providing a guarantee that they could always be found in certain districts. In the case of London, Soho was the classic example.

There came a time, soon after the Second World War, when there were so many prostitutes in Soho that the general public either decided or were told that such an overwhelming presence was objectionable. Hence the appointment of the Wolfenden Committee in 1954 with the avowed aim of cleaning up the area. This did not please the Police Federation one bit, for they could see how prostitutes and their pimps and criminals operating on the fringes of prostitution activities, were disappearing from their knowledge and, effectively, their grasp as they scattered throughout central London. Much better to see what Joan or Jane were up to, who their protectors were, and who their clients were.

A more enlightened and more modern approach to the obvious problems posed by prostitutes has been adopted in Germany and Holland. Whilst both countries' attitudes are considered in detail in Chapter 7, suffice it to say for the present that in German cities, particularly ports, like Hamburg (St Pauli district), red light districts have been established. Prostitutes are allowed to operate from there and, within such districts, if they confine themselves to their professional activities, they are basically left undisturbed. The same applies in Holland, e.g. in Amsterdam and Rotterdam. In fact, Holland has gone further – in Amsterdam a whole parking area has been set aside for prostitutes to carry on their business in their clients' motor vehicles; in Utrecht, a 'Toleration Zone' has been established near the outskirts of the city.

If, therefore, sex establishments were described by a different name such as sex therapy clinics or whatever, it might even be possible to identify them by references in the telephone directory. There would then be no need for telephone booths and public telephones to be littered with cards advertising different types of sexual services and the general environment would be the better for their absence. If you, the reader, are in any doubt as to the wisdom of confining all prostitutes firstly in well-defined areas and secondly, and preferably, in buildings set aside for the purpose, you should go for a stroll through the King's Cross area of London in the early morning, before the cleaners have set to work. Doorsteps and pavements show quite clearly what has gone on during the night.

You should also enquire of any of the local women (not prostitutes) how happy they are at being constantly propositioned by clients who, because they associate the area with prostitution, can no longer distinguish between the respectable woman and the tart. You should ask local mothers whether they are pleased that their children should play in the neighbouring streets or, for example, in the garden of Argyle Square. You should enquire of the local authority and police how content they are with the resultant corruption and violence. And in areas such as King's Cross (and there are many in the principal cities of the UK) the 'harlot's cry from street to street' of yesteryear has been replaced by the slamming of car doors.

There were complaints in the early 1980s when the local MP, Frank Dobson, put forward, as a solution to the obvious problems, the legalization of brothels. Proposals of this nature recur. The Labour MP for Birmingham Selly Oak, Lynne Jones, has recently (September 1992) proposed a 'zone of tolerance' on the lines of the Utrecht one, for Birmingham, to find an answer to the nuisance and public offence caused by prostitutes in some parts of that city, especially in Balsall Heath, which is claimed to be Britain's 'unofficial' answer to Amsterdam. In Balsall Heath it is said that parks and lock-up garages have taken the place of brothels and that the visions of women in stockings and suspenders sitting behind windows in their own homes is anything but unusual. How much better an official, professionally organized, supervized and sanitized brothel would be.

The collectives that prostitutes have set up to safeguard their interests do not like the idea. The trouble about the view that prostitution should be decriminalized but that there should not be licensed brothels, is that, to date, nobody has come forward with any proposal as to what should be done once the activity of prostitutes is, in fact, decriminalized. It is wishful thinking to believe that once the activities of prostitutes were decriminalized, they would cease to frequent the King's Cross area or equivalent. Quite the contrary. They would congregate there in even greater numbers because they would be free from any kind of harassment on the part of the police. The so-called Prostitute Defence Groups are keen to influence public opinion so that the law may be changed and prostitutes should cease to be persecuted; the case they make for decriminalization is by no means wrong and is to be supported. But no single suggestion of any kind has been put forward as regards alternative forms of control.

They try to project a picture of the prostitute which is totally false, namely that she has such a sense of social responsibility, such a sensitive conscience and so great an aesthetic sense that the moment her activities are decriminalized, everything will change for the better. My argument throughout, however, is that decriminalization will only work if it is done in conjunction with the licensing of brothels.. Put differently, prostitutes should cease to be, potentially at least, criminals, and should become professionals or social workers/ sex therapists. I am not too troubled by the argument that the value of houses for acres around the area would deteriorate. I am certain that it is not beyond the ingenuity of our planners and social workers to find suitable locations.

It is beyond any reasoning man's comprehension how a society which, in effect, encourages sleaziness and promiscuity by artificially stimulating a demand for it in magazines, newspapers and especially television, as well as by clamouring for the abolition of all boundaries to decency and restrictions on behaviour, and by attempting constantly to increase sexual awareness for moneymaking purposes; a society which has permitted sex shops in the High Street not only of the major urban centres but even, at times, in comparatively small provincial communities; a society whose obscenity, vulgarity in language and manners, and absolute reliance on profit as the standard of success and reward, finds no comparison in the whole of our history; a society where 'performers' like Madonna and others too numerous to list, are glamourized, if not idealized; a society, in short, where the good, the beautiful and the true have ceased to have any significance for the majority of our people, can bury its head in the sand when it hears the word 'brothel'. But more of that later.

Finally, I see no contradiction at all between my disapproval of certain aspects of present-day Western society and my endorsement of brothels. I am not enamoured of such establishments, but they are, in my opinion, a necessity.

(vi) BY REDUCING THE NUMBER OF DIVORCES, DECRIMINALIZATION WILL CONTRIBUTE TO STRENGTHENING THE PRESENTLY CRUMBLING FAMILY UNIT, AND THUS REDUCE JUVENILE CRIME.

That today's juveniles are alienated from society cannot really be disputed. Such alienation manifests itself not only in violent behaviour, mostly inexplicable, but also in the fact that many youngsters manifest patterns of behaviour which are not only anti-social in the broad sense but are also damaging to their health. In a publication of February 1993, 'Young People in 1992', the School Health Education Unit evaluated 20,218 questionnaires completed by pupils aged 11 to 14 frequenting 132 schools in England in 1992.

A detailed analysis of the findings is beyond the scope of this book except to record that as many as 30% of our youngsters, boys and girls, smoke or drink and more than 13% had taken some kind of hallucinogenic drug. Even at age 11, the survey shows that 22% of the boys drink alcohol every week and at least 5% of the 14-year-olds are drinking more than the safe limit for adults. But much more importantly, one in four of the children in the study came from a broken home and just under 29% of them were troubled by fear of family break-up (25.1% boys, 32.7% girls).

Commenting on the findings, Richard Whitfield, Chairman of the National Family Trust said: 'Things such as joy-riding or ram-raiding, let alone more sensational cases such as we have had in Liverpool, are just the tip of an iceberg of youth alienation and insecurity.'

Divorce creates instability, insecurity and disorder, and therefore is a primary cause of juvenile crime. If the arguments outlined in (iii) above are valid, and if it is true that even in our so-called progressive society brothels contribute to keeping marriages going, it follows that the resultant greater stability of the family will reduce the alienation and insecurity which leads our youngsters to crime.

Some authors (Jack Dominion, for example) have found a close relationship between broken home and psychiatric illnesses and personality disorders. He claims that significant correlations have been established between suicidal behaviour later in life of the child that comes from a broken home, which in turn may be a causative element in crime. He quotes a Swedish study made in 1967 of delinquent boys, their parents and grandparents. The study considered 305 delinquent boys and compared them with 500 attending child-guidance clinics and 22 non-delinquent normal children. It was found that 42% of the delinquent boys were sons of divorced parents as against only 13% of non-delinquent boys.

In an earlier study, *Social Science and Social Pathology* (Allen & Unwin, 1969), Barbara Wootton makes the following point: 'The majority of our 21 investigations are thus in agreement in showing high rates of broken homes amongst delinquents; various British studies place anything from 22% to 57% of their delinquents in this category, whereas control figures, when available, range only from11% to 18%. It is therefore clear that the loss of a father increases the risk that a child, particularly if he is a boy, will become a delinquent by a factor of approximately two. Lack or inadequacy of parental support is a very determining consideration. There is a connection between emotional disturbance in childhood and delinquent behaviour.'

Of course, this is not to say that every boy without a father becomes a delinquent and it must be admitted that the consequences to children of being brought up in a home where, whether as a result of divorce or otherwise, there is no father, have not yet been fully analysed and understood. But it must be common sense that a child who lacks the guidance of a father runs a greater risk of becoming a delinquent than a boy who is brought up in what is generally regarded as a normally constituted family. It is within my own personal and professional experience that boys who are brought up solely by a mother become either effeminate and turn to homosexuality, or are surly and resentful.

Terman and his colleagues concluded that children who are strongly attached to their parents and have little conflict with them are more likely than others to be happy in marriage when they become men and women. 'Marital happiness appears to be a condition that tends to run in families.' This finding endorses in scientific form the commonly-held belief that children of divorced parents are more likely to divorce in their turn than those who come from stable families. There seems to be little doubt that the increased rate of juvenile violence, whether amongst soccer fans or in other of its manifestations, has coincided with very high rates of divorce and family breakdown.

Chapter Nine

Prostitution in the USA

Elsewhere in this work, I make many references to the question of prostitution in the United States. Here, however, is a general overview which is by no means intended to be comprehensive, together with some observations on the recent Chicago University study.

Not unexpectedly, there are clear analogies between the United Kingdom and the United States of America, in the respective approaches to prostitution. As a general statement, it should be said first of all that the enforcement of prostitution-control laws in the USA is erratic and, in the different States, depends completely upon the view taken as to what is the 'politically correct' stance at any one moment in time, on the attitude of the prosecuting authorities, and on the extent of complaints from the public. At the end of the day, in the United States, as in England, police forces have to determine how much of their resources should be committed to dealing with a problem which they know only too well they will never be able to solve, simply because there is not an overall framework within which any individual State or national policy is to operate.

Officially, it is only in Nevada that prostitution is lawful. Since 1971, it has been the position there that cities with fewer than 250,000 people are allowed to operate brothels quite lawfully. Indeed, there is even a 'Nevada Brothel Association' which ensures that prostitutes are tested at regular intervals. It is true that, even in that State, local law has been criticized because it imposes certain restrictions on official or approved prostitutes, to satisfy the moral and aesthetic objections of the remainder of the citizens, which restrictions are said to turn prostitutes into second-class citizens. But the position is not entirely clear-cut and even where limitations on freedom are in existence, and/or enforced, ultimately it is left to the woman whether she wants to abide by them. As I have observed elsewhere in this work, in 1994 it is unlikely that, in Western societies, any woman is forced to take up a life of prostitution, and it is doubtful that there are any women in Nevada who can be said to be slaves to the legal brothel system.

Elsewhere in the United States, however, brothels are not officially recognized, but equivalent establishments which provide the same services in less supervized and, in all likelihood, less hygienic conditions, are proliferating. I have in mind also, the so-called 'escort services' which can be found in the Yellow Pages and in advertisements in local papers throughout the country. This is disguised prostitution, at very expensive rates.

Then there are what are known as 'massage parlours', catering for the cheaper end of the market. It is true that these 'sex retailers' are subject to certain local and State regulations which require prior approval by what one might term 'authorized bodies'. But this merely bears out a point that I have made elsewhere, namely that the low-class prostitute is penalized all the time in most countries, whereas her upper-class sister gets away with it and becomes wealthy. Massage parlours have restrictive regulations imposed on them by USA local State law, whereas escort services escape through the net. It is true that they can justify their existence by saying that they exact higher standards from their girls; but at the end of the day, as elsewhere in the Western world, hypocrisy and the profit motive reign supreme.

Local police are as aware of the activities of escort services and massage parlours as they are of illegal brothels or streetwalkers. Whether they turn a blind eye or not depends on the considerations referred to earlier.

As in other parts of the Western world, there is considerable argument in the United States as to what percentage street prostitution represents of the total 'sex' trade. The USA consensus suggests a figure of some 2 million women and men who are engaged in prostitution. Of these, it is also believed that probably a maximum of 20% is represented by street prostitution; the remainder is taken up by escort services, massage parlours and 'nightclubs'.

The only official statistics which do not seem to be challenged is that in the whole of the United States in 1991 there were a total of 81,536 arrests for prostitution (in the general sense).

Some States are tougher than others. In Portland, Oregon, for example, a law passed in 1989 permits the city police to confiscate the motor vehicles of street crawlers or of the clients of prostitutes. (In certain northern Italian cities, notably in Milan, the same approach has been adopted recently in pursuance of municipal byelaws. Apart from the fact that it could be argued that the toughness of these regulations is wholly disproportionate to the offence committed, there are evidential difficulties and in Italy at least, a challenge has been made to such seizures on the grounds that they are unconstitutional.)

Some escort agencies have been closed down in Hertford, Connecticut, and from time to time there are drives on prostitution in Washington State. The attitude of the New York Police is believed to be uneven.

According to a survey made in 1985 and reported in the Hastings Law Journal, America's major cities 'spent an average of $12,000,000 each on controlling prostitution'. The equivalent cost for Los Angeles was estimated at one stage as being in excess of $100,000,000 a year. There has also been a serious attempt to determine the loss of revenue to individual

States arising out of the illegality of prostitution activities.

The conclusion seems to be that gone are the days when it was believed in the USA that by stopping or banning or criminalizing prostitution, one could halt the spread of venereal disease; that by quarantining prostitutes, as was the case during World War 1, the spread of syphilis amongst soldiers could be contained; that by prosecuting Lucky Luciano on pandering and prostitution charges (wrongly, as history appears to have proved) the power of the Mafia would be reduced.

The sexual revolution which started in the sixties, and which was brought about, at least in this writer's opinion, by the invention of the contraceptive pill, has ensured that prostitutes in the USA have been able to form themselves into associations and have been able to make their voice heard. The onset of AIDS has slowed down the process of decriminalization, but it has not succeeded in halting it. And although, as recently as 1989, New York City Police rounded up 88 Asian women who operated in massage parlours and charged them with performing massage without a licence, and although, as I have already recorded, Portland law allows the police to confiscate motor vehicles used for the purposes of prostitution, even in the USA there is great pressure to evolve a coherent policy towards the oldest profession.

Perhaps I am being repetitive, but coherent policy is exactly what is lacking in the Western world when dealing with matters of sex. It is all very well to pass laws, as Florida and New Jersey did in the late 1980s, making it mandatory that prostitutes should be tested for HIV. There are more than two dozen States which either require or permit officials to submit prostitutes to compulsory HIV testing.

It is the compliance with what some authors have called a form of death wish on the part of males to have unprotected intercourse with prostitutes which may contribute to the spread of AIDS, contracted from relations with prostitutes. But there is probably more than a grain of truth in the observation that, in most situations, it is the men that infect the women, and not vice versa. There seems to be adequate medical evidence to this effect. The risk clearly increases dramatically. But in the United States, as well as in England, it is becoming fairly clear that a majority of prostitutes, believed to be as high as 80% in certain cases, is insisting on the use of condoms.

The conclusion of this necessarily short overview of the USA approach to prostitution is firstly, that the same piecemeal attitude is adopted as prevails in the rest of the Western world. Prostitution is technically illegal in all States except Nevada, but substitutes are allowed for it in the form of escort agencies, massage parlours and strip-joints. Secondly, law enforcement is erratic, unreliable and, ultimately, futile. There is no overall, coherent, strategy. In a strange sense, we are all of us politicians, but none of us statesmen.

This is not a casual observation. The 'political' influence in this sphere is much more significant than most people realize. Both the American and the English Press have recently reported at some length the forthcoming publication of a survey by the University of Chicago, the results of which will appear in 'The Social Organization of Sexuality' by Laumann, Michael, Michaels and Gagnon. This is stated to be 'the first comprehensive survey since Kinsey' and is supposed to deal with the sexual lives of Americans.

Its findings are questionable, despite the fact that the authors took a random sample of nearly 3,500 Americans aged 18 to 59. (Why stop at 59? As someone who has passed that age, I find it difficult to believe that I have no further contribution to make in matters sexual . . .)

They are questionable because they run counter to everybody's experience and commonsense. For example, to find as a fact that adultery is the exception in America and not the rule, because nearly 75% of married men and 85% of married women say they have never been unfaithful, beggars belief.

To state that there are a lot fewer active homosexuals in America than the oft-repeated 1 in 10, on the basis that only 2.7% of men and 1.3% of women interviewed reported that they had had homosexual sex in the past, runs counter not only to the average person's experience of life, but also to other findings which have already been mentioned here, let alone to the divorce statistics as to the number of women committing adultery, which are also referred to elsewhere in this work.

To conclude that American men and women have found a way to come to terms with each other's sexuality, in a relationship called 'marriage', must surely be wishful thinking in a country which has one of the highest divorce rates in the world.

To say that '. . . our study clearly shows that no matter how sexually active people are before and between marriages, marriage is such a powerful social institution that, essentially, married people are all alike: they are faithful to their partners as long as the marriage is intact' is a ludicrous statement, not only because, if the approach of this work is correct, it is not borne out by the statistical data, but simply because of the qualifying clause: 'as long as the marriage is intact'. This presupposes that marriages can cease to be intact, and that people can divorce, as indeed they do. How can it be maintained in these circumstances that marriage is 'such a powerful social institution'?

The point that I am trying to make, however, is that the study started out as having nothing to do with the sexual 'mores' of heterosexual Americans. It was in fact the result of concern by American politicians about the AIDS crisis. When the research project was mooted over seven years ago, the primary purpose for which the American Government was going to make funds available, was to see how one could identify and control the spread of the AIDS virus. Government researchers wanted to have up-to-date information as to the risk element in sexual behaviour and they wanted to know what was really going on. Unfortunately for them, all they could rely upon at that time were the Kinsey Reports, and the later Masters and Johnson surveys, which were completed at a time when the AIDS epidemic was unknown.

Accordingly, as *Time International* so aptly put it (17 October 1994, Number 42): 'It was in large part to talk about homosexual activity that the study was originally proposed'. The Chicago University team had to rearrange their approach and, as the correspondents to *Time International* have observed, had to re-design their study more than once to keep conservative critics happy. They even had to go so far as to agree to curtail the interviews they were embarking upon once it became clear that the interviewee was not a person belonging to a category that was at considerable risk of contracting AIDS. In fact, it availed the Chicago Team nothing to agree to be constrained by politicians because, in any event, in September 1991 their funds were cut off. Having found private sources, they were finally able to deal with wider aspects of sexual relations.

I am not impressed by the Chicago University study. I am not saying that the interviewees did not give the information which the researchers reported and endorsed. But I simply do not believe it. In my view, it is wrong to restrict an analysis of sexual activity to men younger than 60, it is unfair that women's views were not taken into greater account and, as a cynic, I do not accept that at a moment when AIDS is spreading and is believed to be caused in the main, although not exclusively, by homosexual behaviour, people will readily admit to being homosexuals. Not many people wish publicly to acknowledge that they may be contributing to the spread of AIDS. The Chicago Team themselves admit and acknowledge this is a limiting factor.

But my major criticism is that, in general, American society behaves in such an exemplary way. Americans, we are invited to believe, do not visit prostitutes, they are faithful to their partners in marriage, they do not commit crimes of sexual violence, all of them prefer (96%, the researchers found) vaginal sex to any other option, and deviant sexual conduct is unknown to them.

All in all, we are presented with a 'politically correct' view of sexuality in America today. But a hopelessly wrong one.

NOTE

The author is indebted to the following publications in the preparation of this chapter:

1) *The Economics of Prostitution* by Helen Reynolds (Charles Thomas publishers, 1986).

2) 'Rethinking Prostitution: A Case for Uniform Regulation' *Nevada Public Affairs Review*, 1991.

3) An article by Charles Clark in the *CQ Researcher*, Volume 3, Number 22 of June 1993.

Chapter Ten

Prostitutes in other countries
[Except the UK and USA]

In most other countries, it can be said that three approaches are adopted when dealing with prostitution.

In the first place, there are countries where prostitution is illegal in every possible respect. The classic example is Eire. The same position pertains, albeit with less severity, in Iceland and Malta. Sometimes this approach is described as the 'Dallas' model, from the American city where prostitution is rather violently pursued and punished.

Elsewhere in the world, the majority of countries adopt an attitude of unenlightened toleration where, supposedly, brothels are illegal and prostitution is unlawful. In practice, however, nobody cares too much and the police from time to time turn a blind eye.

One is almost tempted to refer to this approach as the 'San Francisco' model because, although in that city prostitution is technically illegal, nobody seems to bother too much. This is the attitude adopted in countries as varied as the former Soviet Union, Finland, Norway, Portugal and Spain. The principal concern seems to be to try and punish those who exploit prostitutes rather than the girls themselves.

The third type of situation follows the pattern established, for example, in Nevada, where prostitution is lawful in the situations where a licence has been granted. This is broadly the position in Austria, Turkey, Greece and Switzerland. In these last two countries the regulation of prostitution, which is a lawful activity, is quite thorough.

The position in Australia, Holland, Germany, Italy, France and Turkey is considered in slightly more detail below.

Australia

It was announced in the summer of 1994 that a well-known brothel in Melbourne, known as the 'Daily Planet', was proposing to 'go public' and arrange for shares to be sold in the establishment.

Looking at the matter as objectively as I am capable of, it is easy to imagine the issue being over-subscribed. After all, it is the kind of business which will always thrive: to invest in a brothel is like investing in an establishment dispensing cheap food, or in a firm of morticians: they will always be around. Punters and institutional investors surely will no more hesitate to invest in brothels than they used to in tobacco companies or still do in armament manufacturers or in companies producing agricultural chemicals.

Furthermore, I hold strongly to the view that 'going public' will improve standards in the provision of sexual services, at least in the State of Victoria. Furthermore, assuming that the Daily Planet workers themselves will have the option to buy shares in the company, they will have a direct interest in its success and accordingly will work even harder to satisfy their customers.

One might almost conjecture that the customers, too, will rejoice. As far as they are concerned, they may well be relieved to think that apart from getting the sexual satisfaction they sought, they might even be said to be investing their money profitably, or at least to their advantage, in the same way that a housewife may prefer one supermarket to the other, simply because it provides air miles or the chance of a holiday.

All in all, this seems to be a development which is wholly consistent with the Western world's approach to money-making.

As regards the 'moral' implications, which will no doubt form the object of criticism and complaint from feminists and religious-minded persons, I leave the reader to peruse the chapter which deals with the arguments against decriminalization of the activities of prostitutes and the legalization of officially recognized houses of pleasure.

It may be useful to look at the situation in Australia. In the first place, brothels have been lawful in the State of Victoria since the mid-1980s. Both heterosexual and homosexual brothels are allowed, and the minimum age for prostitutes of either sex is 18.

Brothels are regulated by the local authority in the same way as other establishments, under normal planning law principles. What is known as a 'character test' is applied to the owners and the managers in the same way as equivalent tests are in force for owners of gambling establishments. There is regular police monitoring and, above all, medical control. The medical control is left to the owners. The use of drugs is wholly illegal.

The Daily Planet is situated in Hore Street, Elstonwick, and is a well-known feature in the City of Melbourne. I understand that it was recently for sale; one wonders about the practicalities for the estate agents involved of taking clients through the various rooms. Some readers may make the connection between the name of the establishment and Superman.

On a more serious note, a number of other activities are also lawful in the State of Victoria, where there are many escort agencies and massage parlours, both for men and women, which are not regulated. The legal difference between establishments like the Daily Planet and escort agencies and massage parlours is that the latter are wholly unregulated and in theory no sexual activity should occur on those premises.

As a result of the legalization of brothels, street prostitution in the traditional sense has remained illegal, although it would appear to be the case that it has not entirely been eliminated. The reason, in my view, is to be found in the fact that prostitutes who ply their trade in the streets are most likely to be on drugs.

The position in the remaining Australian States is not entirely clear-cut. For example, legislation is not always applied in some States, even though street prostitution is outlawed in all of them. An exception is to be found in the red-light districts of New South Wales where provisions for licensed brothels exist – similar to those in the State of Victoria. It is also a fact that the legislation controlling prostitution in Southern Australia, Western Australia and Tasmania is stricter than elsewhere.

For example, the position in South Australia is governed by the Summary Offences Act, 1953, Section 22. Prostitution is treated as illegal, brothels are unlawful, those who either keep or manage brothels, or permit premises to be used as such, are liable to fines or imprisonment. But the law of South Australia is draconian in this context, because Section 31 provides that upon conviction of a tenant or occupier of premises for having permitted their use as a brothel, he may be divested of the tenancy or lease. The landlord is given power to require that person to assign the lease of the premises to some other person approved by the landlord, and also to determine the lease itself.

Although technically prostitution is illegal in Queensland, the law there allows single women effectively to run brothels from their own homes.

Holland

In theory, prostitution is still illegal in the Netherlands. In practice, however, prostitution is tolerated in confined areas in a number of towns and cities such as Amsterdam, Rotterdam, The Hague and Utrecht; by this is meant that prostitutes walking the streets, as well as in brothels, are not troubled by the police. These confined areas are known as 'toleration zones' and within them prostitutes are on the whole left alone. Outside such areas, they run the risk of being prosecuted.

There is a Bill currently before the Lower Chamber of the
Netherlands Parliament which will in effect abolish the
offence of brothel-keeping as such, whilst at the same time
reinforcing the provisions of the law against those who use
force or power against potential prostitutes or traffic in human
beings. Powers to decide such matters will be left in the hands
of the Local Authority who is able to issue permits for brothels
and establishments where sexual activities are provided in any
form. These permits are issued subject to rather stringent
conditions as regards the age and the type of prostitute,
medical inspections and so on. Under the draft law it will still
be an offence to keep a brothel where a Local Authority
permit has not been granted in areas requiring a permit, or
where a Local Authority has expressly prohibited the keeping
of a brothel.

There are projects also in Holland to redeem prostitutes. A
fairly innovatory one is the Prostitution Project of The Hague
which was started in about 1989; it hopes to counsel some of
the 2,500 prostitutes who are believed to operate in The
Hague, and to direct them into different types of work. The
project seems successful; but there is a basic difficulty, namely
money. It is said that a good prostitute in The Hague can earn
as much as 1,00 gilders (about £300) a day whereas, if she
relies on National Assistance, she has to manage on 26 gilders
(about £8) a day.

In an article in *The Guardian* newspaper (6 June 1991), the
reporter (Madelaine Bunting) interviews a Dutch prostitute
who is trying to go straight (as the expression goes), and who
states in no uncertain terms that, well apart from monetary
considerations, she misses '. . . the excitement and the glamour
of the business, the companionship and the friendship' on the
basis that '. . . prostitutes are the best women there are'.
Whether one shares this prostitute's assessment of her friends,
the statement is, to say the least, symptomatic of the difficulties
that even in Holland a prostitute faces, and underlines the
concept that in some circumstances – less frequent, however,

than a lot of people may believe – prostitutes may actually enjoy the work they do.

* * *

Germany

We know that brothels were abolished in Germany in 1927. Nevertheless, State control of prostitution continued and, particularly since the Second World War, has extended beyond the initially tolerated area in the 'red' district of Hamburg. The authorities had to face increasing demands not only because of the activities connected with the port, but also locally; and accepted 'the indestructibility of prostitution'. They imposed two limitations, namely the avoidance of offence to the sensitivities of the general public and the protection of the young.

Applying these criteria, they delegated to City authorities the control and organization of prostitutes into '. . . comfortable, well-inspected quarters in discreet parts of town where they can carry on their trade in an orderly manner', concluding that only in this way would they be seen to be responding to the public's two main concerns, namely the protection of the public itself from soliciting, on the one hand, and the protection of the prostitutes from criminals and pimps, on the other.

Whilst it remains technically illegal in Germany, as it is in Britain, to live off the earnings of prostitution, it has been expressly laid down that to build a hostel which houses prostitutes and to take rents from it is not equivalent to living off the earnings of prostitution. There is quite a large one in Dusseldorf which is described as '. . . an opulent new block with many floors . . . with rooms in it for 180 girls who work there, inspected by the sanitary authorities and registered by the city police, fed from a large communal kitchen'.

* * *

Italy

As a result of the 'Merlin' law following close upon the French developments instigated by Madame Richard, brothels became illegal in Italy during the early nineteen fifties although effectively they were not finally closed down until September 1958. The number of women affected at the time is in some doubt. According to the Italian Ministry of the Interior, in 1957 there were in Italy 552 brothels with 2,584 inmates. Registered prostitutes were over 500,000, the unregistered about 10,000 and the occasional ones said to be in the region of 150,000. Figures appearing in the American press, however, show 700 brothels with some 4,000 inmates, many other thousands of street-walkers and amateur prostitutes, with a total figure close to 400,000.

In 1963, according to the Italian newspaper *Il Tempo* '. . . the number of prostitutes has shown a marked increase'. (These figures are derived from Benjamin and Masters, pages 420, 421). Anyone who knows the principal Italian cities (Rome, Turin, Milan, Florence) and especially the ports (Naples, Genoa, Leghorn and so on) knows only too well that Italy has the same problems as any other European country which has declared brothels and/or prostitution illegal. Gone are the days when one could walk peacefully in the balmy autumn evenings along the embankments of the Tiber in Rome, at the Valentino Park in Turin or in the Gardens of Boboli in Florence.

The escalation in VD cases between 1958 and 1963 has already been addressed. Nevertheless, the signs are that things are changing in Italy too. It is hardly a coincidence that in the Italian magazine *Panorama* of 23 August 1992, mention is made of a 65-year-old collector of memorabilia from brothels which he claims to have 'picked up' in 1958 at not too great a price. Amongst various items are notices that were displayed in the rooms (for example, 'Cash in advance please', 'Keep your visits short' and, no doubt, humorously, 'Keep it up').

More interesting, are some of the price lists. One of these reads as follows:-

Quarter of an hour – 30 lire
Half an hour – 75 lire
One hour – 120 lire
One day – 1,500 lire

Conversion rates are not easy to provide but the reader might like to know that the cost of a cinema ticket in 1958 was about 250 lire.

Until recently, statistical information on sexually-transmitted diseases was conspicuously lacking in Italy, as in most other countries. After the efforts made in publicizing the increase in VD following the abolition of brothels, the only data available in Italy during the past 40 years were those published by the Italian Statistical Institute (ISTAT) resulting form the compulsory notification of certain *infectious* diseases, including VD. These data were inaccurate, firstly because in terms of VD, they were and still are limited to the four most common forms and secondly because many medical practitioners, for one reason or another, did not support the requirement to notify.

Recently, the Istituto Superiore di Sanita' has embarked upon certain computerized studies which have proved beyond doubt that the ISTAT data were under-estimates by between 100% and 150%. The latest official information shows that as at 31 December 1991 the notified cases of STDs in Italy were 10,865. Of these, 57.2% used no method of contraception.

Until recent years, no study of any kind whatsoever had been made of the effect of prostitution in Italy on either STD or HIV, save that reliance was placed in general terms on information obtained, especially in African countries. The advent of, and concern for, AIDS has made necessary, if not topical, more detailed studies. Accordingly, between January 1988 and November 1990 the AIDS Centre of the Istituto Superiore di Sanita' carried out a study of the prevalence of AIDS amongst 403 prostitutes in five Italian cities (Rome, Milan, Naples, Palermo and Pordenone). Fifty appeared infected, 12.4%, and of these, 2.1% were professional full-time prostitutes and the remainder were either occasional prostitutes or prostitutes on drugs. The median age of the professional prostitutes was 33.4 years (range 19–63) whilst that of the occasional and/or drug addicts was 25.6 years (range 17–40).

The immediate reaction might be that it is not the professional prostitutes that contribute to the spread of AIDS; but it should be noted that a comparison between other studies made by the same body on professional prostitutes in 1985 and 1989, as well as the more recent ones previously referred to, show that whereas in 1985 none of the prostitutes who was tested for HIV proved positive, in 1986 1.6% of them did and in 1990 2.1%.

The AIDS problem for Italy, however, where it is calculated that today prostitutes (*puttane*) number more than 300,000, is likely to get worse, not better. In Milan alone, for example, there are said to be over 16,000 prostitutes of many nationalities, especially South American, African and, lately, Eastern European. This would appear to put Milan ahead of even New York in terms of numbers of prostitutes.

The turnover in the Italian industry has been calculated by some as being in excess of £1.5 billion. The delicate name modern Italians use to describe prostitutes who operate on the streets is '*lucciole*', or fireflies, and a tour in the early hours of the morning of the better-known areas of Milan, (Piazzale Lotto, the Cemetery, Viale Abruzzi, and Piazza Trento) has now become known as the 'Puttantour'.

Fortunately, the scandal of street prostitution may be eliminated if the bill laid before the Italian parliament in 1994 to legalize brothels and prostitution ever becomes law. According to a random sampling of opinion taken by Italian television, Channel TG4, 94% of Italians are in favour of such legalization. A referendum on the subject may take place in 1995.

If Italy decides to pass a law legalizing prostitution, however, it will first have to consider its position under the 'International Convention for the Suppression of the Traffic in Persons and of the Exploitation of the Prostitution of Others'

(United Nations Treaty Series Volume 96 page 272 – New York, 21 March 1950).

Article 2 of the Convention provides that the Parties thereto agree to punish any person who keeps or manages or knowingly finances or takes part in the financing of a brothel; and there are other provisions which effectively make it impossible for the Parties to consider brothels as legal establishments.

It is often said in Italy that it was this Convention which caused the passing of the Merlin Law (Law No. 95, dated 20 February 1958). This is not correct, because Italy acceded to the New York 1950 Convention on the 18 January 1980. The United Kingdom, however, has not ratified the 1950 Convention.

*   *   *

France

Prostitution was, and is, no less fashionable in France than in other European countries. Surprisingly, it was there that in 1946 the diplomat, Pierre Dominjon, presented to Parliament the law that was to become famous by the name of the Resistance hero who campaigned for it, Marthe Richard. Attention has already been drawn to the fact that it did not take her very long to realize that she had made a mistake. Unfortunately, she died before she could do much about putting it right, other than by expressing her views in the book to which reference has already been made.

The 1946 law abolishing the 'Maisons de Tolerance' had no effect whatsoever on prostitution other than in the sense that it closed down brothels. Prostitution is no more illegal in France than it is in Italy or England. There are offences which are related to living off the earnings of prostitution, as well as to what one might term, generally, public-order offences. But the penalties are minimal. For example, a prostitute caught in a 'provocative' posture in the street is subject to a fine ranging from £8.00 to £16.00.

It is true that when it comes to the activities of pimps and procurers, in addition to a substantial fine (from £1,000 to £20,000, and from £2,000 to £25,000 in the case of a minor), there is imprisonment from six months and two years respectively, to two years and ten years respectively. The substantial penalties imposed on procurers are explicable if one looks at the figures. In 1991 it was estimated that there were operating in France about 30,000 professional prostitutes; this means full-time tarts, and of these, at least 95% operated with the assistance of pimps. It is also estimated (*Le Quid* by Robert Lassong, Paris, 1992) that there were 60,000 'occasional' prostitutes, that is to say, part-time girls.

Most calculations as to the number of prostitutes are under-estimates in any event so that it can be said that there were at that date in France at least about 100,000 prostitutes plying their trade. In some areas, for example in Paris, the Rue St Denis quarter which is considered one of the 'hottest', it has been calculated that there were around 1,700 prostitutes operating.

The money values involved in the trade are also substantial. According to French sources, the figure could be as high as one billion pounds per annum (£1000m.). In Paris, a professional prostitute can earn as much as £3,800 a month if she is operating on the streets. The better-class whore, which even the French describe by their Anglo-American title of 'call-girl', can earn as much as £20,000 a month.

Given the combination of the two factors mentioned, namely the fact that prostitution of itself is not illegal in France and that the trade is substantial, it is not difficult to understand why applying their practical sense, the French long ago decided that a prostitute is subject to tax, whether she is full-time or part-time, on her earnings and indeed to any other tax which applies to individuals, as well as to VAT at 18.6%. . . . . She is also liable to make yearly tax declarations, in default of which the French Revenue levies assessments.

The French seem to have gone beyond most other

nationalities in finding descriptions for their prostitutes. For the reader's amusement, the majority of these are appended with their English equivalent:-

1. *La Chandelle* (the candle). As the description implies, she stands quite stationary.
2. *La Marcheuse* describes the girl who walks up and down on the pavement (usually about 100 steps before turning round).
3. *L'Echassiere* sits at her bar table, usually outside.
4. *L'Entraineuse* sits at a bar counter, inside.
5. *La Zonarde* (otherwise *La Bucolique*) operates in woods and parks.
6. *La Serveuse Montante* operates in certain hotels. It is noteworthy that although brothels are illegal in France, the hotel tart is officially recognized; girls who operate in hotels have to pay their social insurance contributions.
7. *L'Amazone* drives a car.
8. *La Caravelle* is usually to be found at airports and air terminals.
9. *L'Etoile Filante* (the falling star) is the occasional prostitute who rounds up her monthly salary by plying her trade on odd days.
10 *La Michetonneuse* also operates from bars and cafes.

For those girls who operate from their own flats mainly by telephone, the French use almost exclusively the expression 'call-girl'. An assessment has also been made of the average prices charged. It has been calculated that the girls in groups 1–6 charge from a minimum of £6.00 to a maximum of £40.00. The other, more expensive types of prostitute charge from a minimum of £60.00 to a maximum of £350.00 per night.

It is interesting to recall here that in the early years of this century there was published in Paris *La Guide Rose* which was a list of all the brothels operating within the Paris area, indicating the kind of activities in which they specialized and the prices charged. In the UK, we followed this example with the 'infamous' *Ladies Directory* which was published in 1959, the publisher subsequently being prosecuted. Good precedents, one would suggest, for allowing brothels to have adequate entries in Yellow Pages directories if the Western world should decide to officially recognize their existence.

I hasten to say that there is nothing new here, as elsewhere when dealing with matters sexual. In Venice, in the sixteenth century, one could find printed, and openly circulating, lists which gave names, addresses, prices and type of service, for prostitutes of varying numbers, and of different age groups. Obviously, the lists presupposed some organization and financial standing, so that they related exclusively to the upper-class whore, the 'cortegiana', to whom reference has already been made.

Turkey

The position in Turkey is broadly similar to that which prevailed in France and Italy prior to abolitionist legislation.

Prostitution is officially recognized. The present system of supervision and control dates back to the early 1960s and entails, as is to be expected, registration for prostitutes and compulsory regular and thorough medical checks.

Male prostitutes are not recognized officially, and women who take up the trade can operate only from officially approved and supervized premises, where police intervention is fairly frequent.

These legal brothels are to be found throughout Turkey. At the same time, there co-exists a system of unofficial prostitution which, whilst no doubt extremely profitable for those raqueteers who control it (in much the same way as it is exploited, for example, in the United States) is clearly illegal. Its principal drawbacks would appear to relate to venereal disease.

The complaint is often heard that the official system of prostitution encourages the coercion or at least the trickery of women either from poor backgrounds or with little education. It is argued that, once they enter the official system, it is very difficult for them to escape without suffering the risk of violence or, more likely, given the norms of society, of criticism and possibly ostracism on the part of members of the woman's own family.

The same criticisms, however, can equally, and more forcibly, be levelled at prostitution outside the government-recognized system. Whether the recent election in Turkey of a woman Prime Minister will have any effect on the present set-up, at least for the time being, must be a moot point. There seems to be little doubt, however, that the increasing westernization of Turkey with its concomitant increase in feminism will sooner or later create the same, social but above all psychological, conditions that will result in consideration being given to a greater liberalization of sexual 'mores' in what is still a Muslim country, albeit governed as a secular state. The present failure to officially recognize male prostitution is evidence of the fairly primitive approach that still prevails. On the other hand, although reliable statistics are hard to come by, it is probably correct to state that the incidence of sexual abuse of women and children in Turkey appears to be considerably lower than in the UK.

Chapter Eleven

Brothels in general

'Prisons are built with stones of law, brothels with bricks of religion.'
[WILLIAM BLAKE].

The name 'brothel' conjures up pictures that vary from society to society and century to century and which are often dependent upon the viewpoint of the person who provides the description. It causes different reactions in different people in the same way as the noun 'prostitute' does. Furthermore, the picture projected in films and television, such as sleazy South American establishments, or the faded images of windows in the red light districts of Amsterdam and Hamburg, are not always accurate.

Even in literature, the attitude of the writer to the brothel will be governed by his society's possibly double-edged and rather equivocal attitude towards a prostitute. Here is an extract from Tolstoy's *Resurrection* where he describes the life of Máslova – one of his protagonists:

'Heavy sleep until late in the afternoon followed the orgies of the night. Between three and four o'clock came the weary getting up from a dirty bed, soda water, coffee, listless pacing up and down the room in bedgowns and dressing jackets, lazy gazing out of the windows from behind the drawn curtains, indolent disputes with one another; then washing, perfuming and anointing of the body and hair, trying on of dresses, disputes about them with the mistress of the house, surveying of one's self in looking glasses, painting the face, the eyebrows; fat, sweet food; then dressing in gaudy silks, exposing much of the body, and coming down into the ornamented and brilliantly illuminated drawing-room; then the arrival of visitors, music, dancing, sexual connection with old and young and middle aged, with half children and decrepit old men, bachelors, married men, merchants, clerks, Armenians, Jews, Tartars: rich and poor, sick and healthy, tipsy and sober, rough and tender, military men and civilians, students and mere schoolboys – of all classes, ages and characters. And shouts and jokes, and brawls and music and tobacco and wine, and wine and tobacco, from evening until daylight, no relief till morning, and then heavy sleep; the same every day and all the week. Then at the end of the week came the visit to the police station, as instituted by the Government, where doctors – men in the service of the Government – sometimes seriously and strictly, sometimes with playful levity, examined these women, completely destroying the modesty given as a protection not only to human beings but also to animals, and gave them written permissions to continue in the sins they and their accomplices had been committing all the week. Then followed another week of the same kind: always the same every night, summer and winter, working days and holidays. And in this manner Katusha Máslova lived seven years. . . . .'

Turning to England, it is difficult to see why there should be such objections to brothels which had, until not too long ago, a glorious, if not royal tradition. The masses of foreign tourists walking down London's Jermyn Street, admiring the goods on display in the rather nice shops there, would find it difficult to believe that a great part of it and practically the whole of the St James's area, up to almost the end of the

nineteenth century, was dedicated to whoring. The following
jingle or limerick may give the flavour:

> *It almost broke the family heart*
> *When Lady Jane became a tart*
> *But rank is rank and race is race and so*
> *To save the family face*
> *They bought for her a shady beat*
> *On the sunny side of Jermyn Street.*

It is self-evidently no coincidence that the famous
'Gentlemen's Clubs' of Pall Mall and St James's Street were
established in close proximity to the whore grounds of St
James's. More than one tart was heard to remark that the
frequenters of such establishments were anything but gentle
and very many of them were not even men.

Prostitutes were first encouraged to this particular locality of
course because of the existence of the Royal Palace of St
James's. Apart from the 'nunneries' opposite the Palace (where
young country girls were taught, sometimes very violently and
clumsily, the rudiments of sexual life), and the 'bagnios'
(initially Turkish-style bathing establishments that then
became dens of sexual corruption), many of the houses and
buildings in the St James's area now occupied by respectable
shopkeepers, trading companies, institutions and professional
people, were brothels of a more or less high class.

Rosa Lewis ran a brothel in Jermyn Street from premises
then known as the Cavendish Hotel; she went down in
history as 'the Duchess of Jermyn Street'. There were brothels,
too, scattered through Covent Garden, less fashionable but no
less frequented than those in St James's. The reader who is in
any doubt as to the extent of whoredom in the St James's and
Covent Garden areas of London is referred to *Royal St James's*
by E.J. Burford (Robert Hale, London, 1988) and *Wits,
Wenchers and Wantons* by the same author (Robert Hale,
London, 1986).

A Mrs Collett, who operated from premises in Tavistock

Court, Covent Garden, had one of the most famous eighteenth-century flagellating brothels in the whole of Britain. She also operated from Portland Place and Bedford Street. Queenie Gerald ran brothels in Haymarket, Maddox Street and Duke Street: and there were other operators of whore houses, such as Mary Wilson, Mrs Mitchell, Mrs James, Mrs Jones, Mr Aubrey, Mrs Berkely, Mrs Price and Mrs Phillips whose activities centred on addresses like Waterloo Road, Kennington, Soho, Upper Belgrave Place, Charlotte Street, St Pancras, Hartford Street, Fitzroy Square, York Square, Burton Crescent and Seymour Place. And there were brothels elsewhere – in Clerkenwell, Whitechapel and Shoreditch.

Flagellating brothels were all the craze in England during the eighteenth and nineteenth centuries and in them 'governesses', as they were called (and are still called today), administered the kind of pain for which the English have always been famous – flagellation, as already noted, being termed 'the English disease'. (There is even an earlier reference to them in Thomas Shadwell's [1642–1692] *The Virtuoso*, written in 1676.)

Standards of decor, and of the service rendered, at all of these premises, varied, as did the price payable. But some establishments were very elegant and could vie with the premises of the American Polly Adler which were said to be furnished in Louis XVI style with panelled walls, jade lamps, antique leather and bedrooms and bathrooms painted 'in peach and apple green'. Modern brothels are probably not quite so smart but the notion that is common, of the whore house as disorganized and dirty, must be promptly dispelled.

In some languages, the equivalent of the noun 'brothel' is used to identify, at a less than elegant level, confusion and disorder, though nothing could be further from the truth. On the whole, brothels are run very efficiently and almost upon military lines. Sexual services are dispensed as quickly and efficiently as food is from modern eating establishments, whether super-efficient Italian restaurants at lunch-time or fast-food premises, throughout the day.

The sleaziness, dirt and stench often described in literature and shown on films, particularly for South American brothels, is no longer to be found. Modern ventilation, air-conditioning and deodorizing techniques have purified the air that formerly reeked of sweat and semen. Indeed, some modern establishments are quite well organized. There is a well-known one in a major Spanish city with a waiting-room which is not that unpleasant, displaying fairly inoffensive prints, artificial plants, and a drinks-dispensing machine.

Of course, depending on the nature of the society's moralizing attitude prevailing at any given time, governments may take action to abolish brothels. Some details have already been provided on the history of prostitution. There are times, however, when Government intervention can be quite specific. For example, in the early years of this century it was decided in the USA that the Barbary Coast, which was well known as a den of iniquity, should be cleaned up. The Red Light Abatement Act 1914 was passed and it can be said that by the end of 1917 the Barbary Coast was dead as the Las Vegas of brotheldom.

Nor is this the only example of Government intervention in matters sexual. It is interesting to note, for instance, that in the France of the 1920s the sale of contraceptives was actually banned. This was not done to encourage promiscuity or the spread of disease. It merely happened that at the time France had a falling birth rate and it was decided that de-population had to be stopped. Seventy years later, in France, Spain and England, for example, we find advertisements on television, in the press and elsewhere, advocating the use of condoms. Admittedly, this is done to restrict the spread of AIDS. Sadly, however, it is a fact that the fear of disease has never been a deterrent to sexual activity. Indeed, in March 1993, there was a suggestion put forward that machines dispensing condoms should be installed in schools.

There is, in fact, no reason whatsoever why the State should not decide that it is in its interests and in those of society as a whole, that prostitutes should only operate from brothels. If the local authorities ever took control of premises used as brothels, they could impose the same minimum requirements as to cleaning, heating, fire-escapes etc. which are to be found in legislation applicable to other premises (Fire Precautions Act 1968, Offices, Shops and Railway Premises Act 1963). Cosmetically, a brothel need not be too different from any other office or residential building. Still, there is no doubt that the word 'brothel' conjures up visions of disorganization, corruption and vice.

Nevertheless some men – but their number is reducing as a result of the passage of time – may look back almost nostalgically to the days when brothels were lawful; whereas some women – and their number is increasing – may look upon them as one of the last bastions of male chauvinism. But both views are too extreme and totally divorced from reality. The existence of establishments, no matter what they may be called, where men and women gather for the purpose of giving vent to frustrated, deviant or compelling sexual desires, is eminently desirable. Our society has poured into the cauldron of sexuality too many components; and the Street Offences Act, 1959, has put the lid on. But it is like a pressure-cooker without a safety valve: it is bound to explode.

For some women, legalized brothels may be an escape from a life of poverty, drudgery, drug-addiction and crime; for men, the brothel is an escape into a world of fantasy. Neither statement should be understood as a glorification of the activities carried on in brothels, for nobody can derive any joy from the fact that there are women who are prepared to give their bodies and to provide sexual favours, perverted or otherwise, in return for money, just as there are men who, for whatever reason, are prepared to be their partners in doing so. The truth is that most human beings prefer to shut their eyes to the less-pleasant aspects of human activity. One is tempted to wonder how many people, when they use their bathroom, spare any thought for the trouble that is taken in disposing of or in re-utilizing the product of human waste.

Josephine Butler did not agree. She was convinced that she

was doing the world much good by tirelessly claiming at meetings and in her writings, indeed throughout her life (1828–1906) that all forms of hygienic measures represented by brothels were merely excuses for the further degradation of women: she, in common with the Wolfenden Committee, did not like the establishment of a double standard in life. What she overlooked, however, was the fact noted earlier, that there are two fundamental polarizations of women, namely the honest woman or 'matron', and the whore, and that these are fairly fundamental female prototypes who, in a sense, have been fighting each other throughout the centuries.

That much was not accepted by early feminists like Josephine Butler and before her, Mary Wollstonecraft because, offended by the concept that some women were prostitutes (this is one element in the man/woman equation which really hurts for those persons who assert the superiority of women to men), they propounded to the view that, ultimately, there was no real difference between a prostitute and a wife, because they both had to work for a man; and that the only possible difference between them was the way in which they were treated by men. As a more modern feminist has put it (Dale Spender, page 480), women's work '. . . was to trade their bodies on a casual basis (prostitute), a semi-permanent basis (mistress) or a permanent basis (wife)'.

We are entitled to wonder how the mistresses and wives of this world react to such an argument; and in any event, given the more recent statistics on divorce, the status of wife seems hardly a permanent one; nevertheless, much greater sympathy can be felt for the early feminists and their approach to brothels, than for modern ones. At least, in the eighteenth and nineteenth centuries it was undeniable that prostitution was primarily a sexual and economic form of exploitation of woman by man since woman had not then achieved the equality, the social and political respectability and, above all, the power that distinguish her in the twentieth century.

In his *Satyricon*, Petronius records rather brilliantly how rotten things were in the later days of the Roman Empire. The old order, political and moral, was breaking down; standards were disappearing; sexuality and gluttony were out of control. There seems to be a similarity between the conditions prevailing then and the present-day manifestations of sexual escape in our society; pornography, blue films, obscene telephone calls, hot lines, paedophily, rape and sexual violence.

It is sometimes said that all these developments stem from the fact that since everything is now on display, there is no longer any need to fantasize. This is a point to which attention has already been drawn when quoting Maupassant. But it cannot be the whole explanation. Our desire for self-destruction cannot arise solely because everything is on show. Many of those who have studied the matter have inclined to the view that a good 40% of all those who have visited prostitutes before the Second World War were sexually abnormal, at least in the sense that what they were seeking in the girls was their own mother, or their father, or their sister, and that is why they often asked prostitutes to act parts. Their wives knew nothing of their unnatural behaviour because the appalling demands were made outside the home by apparently prosperous and respected citizens, husbands, fathers, lawyers, doctors, members of parliament – all mentally sick.

One wonders where all these men have gone now that brothels do not exist. Some have died, that is true, but the demand may still be there. Brothels represented, at least for those men, a safety-valve and it may be that the increase in sexual crimes and child abuse within the family, which is occurring more and more frequently in the 1990s, is a direct consequence of the absence of such a safety valve.

One cannot help feeling, too, that the objection to the legalization of brothels is the result of moral and personal prejudices. The matter can be tested this way: the reader is asked to assume that the advantages that heve previously been set out would, in fact, flow from the legalization of the activities of prostitutes, and of brothels. And then, to ask himself, or herself, trying to be as free as possible from principle, prejudice and hypocrisy, whether the answer to the decriminalization of such activities would not be in the affirmative. The reader is further asked to assume that the answer would be in the affirmative. At that point everything would become quite simple.

The local authorities in the UK, in the same way as they now do in Holland and Germany, would license a brothel as they license many other types of premises (from bingo halls to massage parlours). They would stipulate minimum age and health requirements for the inmates of such establishments, the absence of a criminal record, of drug-taking, a training in basic preventative measures in respect of sexually-transmitted disease. They would impose minimum standards for the premises and for the hours of work. Social security contributions would have to be paid so that the prostitute herself and her family if any, would be safeguarded in terms of health, pension, etc. There might be private medical schemes and private pension schemes. In other words, there should be no differentiation between the employee of the brothel and any other employed person.

There would be, at the expense of the establishment, weekly or fortnightly medicals and, particularly in the days of AIDS, it would be illegal for prostitutes operating in brothels to indulge in unprotected sexual intercourse. The provision of flagellation and other masochistic services would be allowed. The client would frequent the establishment in the knowledge that he/she would not be molested, robbed, blackmailed, or considered in any sense a criminal who has to hide activities or propensities.

It seems to the writer that the only people entitled to complain about such a set-up are journalists and writers of erotica, since they would be deprived of a considerable source of income. The number of men who could no longer be termed 'dirty old men' simply because, perhaps, they wanted to be reminded of the days of their youth by mixing with younger girls, would decrease dramatically. The tabloid press might even begin to feel that it would be more profitable to write about more important social issues than about a well-known film-maker who declared his love for the daughter of his mistress, or a political leader who had a fling with his secretary: the examples that spring to mind are much too numerous to record. And this would happen regardless of whether there were a law of privacy, as exits at present in France, or not, as is the position at present in the UK.

A further consideration, which is far from negligible, is that there usually is not, and in any event there need not be, any emotional commitment by a man to a prostitute. Because it is a financial (commercial) transaction, he ensures that all he gives of himself, apart from his body, is money. But then, this is inevitable because nothing else could be given. Certainly, not affection, sympathy or love, all feelings which can develop when one is dealing with 'the other woman' rather than with a prostitute.

The simplicity of the relationship between man and prostitute has always been difficult for feminists to stomach. Deep down, the honest woman has fought the prostitute, the enmity going back in time and arising both from the fact that prostitutes let the female sex down and from the reluctance of the respectable woman to accept that man may prefer something more objectionable and less clean. This reluctance is understandable as a matter of practice, but is illogical as a matter of psychology and ignores the distinction between male and female sexuality.

Havelock Ellis has shown almost conclusively that man's tendency towards prostitutes originates in his psyche and can be traced back to the orgies of earlier days: there are some men who feel the need to debase themselves by going with a prostitute. Whatever may be the moral judgement of such men, it is a fact of life that they exist.

One of the other objections raised by moralists and feminists to the legalization of brothels is that effectively prostitution caters only for the male. If the points that have been made earlier as regards brothels catering to female 'incontinence' have any validity, then this objection loses much of its impact.

Nor should it be thought that high-class brothels were only fashionable in nineteenth-century Britain. Many were to be found in other principal European cities as well as in New York and Boston.

One of the other objections that is sometimes voiced is that establishments of this kind will do nothing to satisfy the requirements of youngsters of, say, 15 and 16 who are still at school and therefore may not have the money that is needed to frequent them. A number of answers can be given, depending on one's leanings. The first is that a certain amount of relief is always available, even to youngsters of 15 and 16, whether such establishments are legalized or not, which costs nothing: the second is that perhaps such youngsters would do better to concentrate on their studies; the third is that no-one suggests that the solution which is proposed would be a cure for all the needs of all age groups within a given society. It may well be that such establishments, if legalized, would be closed to teenagers who had no money; but this does not in any way distract from their usefulness to others who could afford to frequent them.

The preservation of anonymity provided by legalized brothels is a most important consideration. With it goes the absolute textual transparency of the relationship, both parties understanding exactly what they want from the other. Indeed, it is probably true to say that in no other relationship between man and woman is there such clarity of commitment and finalities as in that between a prostitute and her client.

The reluctance on the part of Western society to acknowledge the inevitability of licensed brothels is in turn the result of a romantic approach to life. We in Britain are still living with the ideals of bygone ages. We consider ourselves as Christians long after we have ceased to take an interest in religion; we would like to look upon the United Kingdom as a world power, long after we have ceased to have any substantive say in world affairs; we still consider that we are a free country, at the same time as on the one hand there are no less than 11 categories of individuals, 252 different authorities granting powers of entry to inspectors (Salmon & Heuston, The Law of Torts, London, 1987, p. 316) and a total of 3,887 persons entitled to enter private premises without a specific search warrant (*An Inspector at the Door*, London, 1979, p. 10) who can override the right of the Englishman to prevent access to his castle and, on the other, we are campaigning desperately to curb the freedom of the Press; both men and women still cling to an idealized view of womanhood whilst failing completely to see the changes that woman's newly-acquired freedom and independence has wrought in her psyche; we hanker desperately after ideals of integrity, dignity, self-respect, hard work and patriotism, mindless of the dishonesty, servility, sleaziness and self-destruction which surround us.

Where there are no officially-recognized brothels, a trade on information, if not mis-information, is established which is a concomitant of the different ways in which the modern prostitute operates. Nowadays, she is to be found as a more or less recognized adjunct in escort agencies, gambling clubs, night clubs, saunas, massage parlours and so on. There are several fairly well known hotels in central London where middle- to upper-class prostitutes are in fact almost part of the establishment. The hotel porters, if asked, will discreetly draw the customer's attention to the lady in the bar or in the lounge. Speaking for myself (and, I hope, for my family) I would prefer to know that there existed brothels recognized by the State, than to see projected on television the kind of soft-porn images which are to our present-day society the equivalent of the brothels of Jermyn Street and St James's.

As for the argument that nobody need watch television, I find it dishonest when what I call pornographic representations (meaningless to inveterate sinners, but prurient and damaging to inexperienced or young viewers) suddenly occur in so-called serious documentaries or modern recreations of period works, whose authors ought to be turning in their graves at the offence thus caused to their integrity and their style. Cynics might even say that the whole country is now a brothel; and not a high-class one at that.

Going back to the sex trade itself, however, it is a fact that in certain parts of Kensington, London, there are, to the author's personal knowledge, prostitutes operating from premises which they themselves own. At least two of them signal their availability by displaying a sign in the window. Prostitutes are used now much more frequently than before by psychologists to assist some clients with their problems. There are Harley Street doctors who know exactly whom to approach when the services of a prostitute are required for therapeutic purposes.

These are facts of life. And yet, the tax inspector, the accountant, the man in the street, the family man or woman become coy when the word 'prostitute' is mentioned. For a great many people, prostitution is something that should not be discussed. Those women who, whilst maintaining that the criminal law should cease to apply to the activities of prostitutes, nevertheless cannot find it in their hearts to go the whole hog and support the legalization/licensing of brothels, appear to be troubled by the clarity of the relationship between a prostitute and her client.

Finally, one should not overlook the fact that the man who goes with a prostitute does not have to say more than he wants to, need not concern himself with what he does, is not bothered by any standards of performance, can let himself go without fear of reprimand, can if he is so minded transcend all limits imposed by common sense, good manners and indeed certain absurd limitations of the criminal law, does not have to be nice, entertaining, witty, considerate, does not have to lie, or profess feelings of love which he does not have. All he has to do is pay.

On her part, the woman does not have to be anything but a technician. She provides accommodation, he provides cash: there is a clarity that is incontestable, almost frightening. The same applies to the woman who frequents a man prostitute, except that, as already discussed, the effort required of the man to produce satisfaction is infinitely greater than that required of the woman. It is this clinical approach to matters sexual that is the main factor in the objections of women to the legalization of brothels. The equation 'sexual service equals money', which most women in their own way understand only too well, is too stark for a lot of honest women to digest. And yet, their salvation almost lies in this depersonalization of sexual relations; but they do not see it.

How many women read with disgust in the daily press about the abuses to which men and women are subjected in sexual terms. The employer who molests his secretaries, the father who commits incest, the driving instructor who keeps his hands elsewhere than on the examination board, the minister of religion or of State who is caught with his pants down (in more senses than one), the newspaper editor who promotes a hackette, the news of rapes committed on women and, nowadays, also on men. *Mutatis mutandis*, the same applies to a woman. Would it not have been much better for them and for society and, indeed, for their families, if they had quietly visited a brothel and discharged there whatever surplus sexual or psychological energy was troubling them at the time?

It would be a very sad day, of course, if that were to happen for some people: the providers of titillating news, psycho-analysts, agony aunts, pornographers, those pseudo-writers who obtain publicity by inserting titillating items in works of precious little, if any, literary merit; in short, all those who thrive on the twisted sexuality of the Western world: many of them would be out of a job, surely, if men and women could give vent to their surfeit sexuality and psychological frustrations in licensed establishments, the frequenting of which would be no more objectionable or newsworthy than a visit to one's GP or psychotherapist.

One further consideration to be borne in mind in connection with the hygienic advantages of brothels is that it has been found in the UK, by the few researchers to whom reference has already been made, that the prostitutes themselves are very conscious, particularly nowadays because of AIDS, of the need to use condoms. It is the client who, in pursuit of his unfettered enjoyment and sometimes motivated by an odd type of death wish, almost as though he were playing Russian roulette, the penis replacing the revolver, wishes to have unprotected intercourse; it is the client who wishes to have intercourse in a doorway, or with trans-sexuals, or in dank, dark, squalid surroundings. Often, his wish is supported by his willingness to pay more, sometimes two or three times the going rate for unprotected intercourse.

Whilst prostitutes are walking the streets, the temptation is very great to give in to such requests. In the brothel, however, they could be resisted so much more easily by the prostitute sheltering behind the rule of the house and, for example, insisting that unprotected intercourse is not permitted.

*   *   *

Lest the reader should feel that if the activities of prostitutes were decriminalized and brothels were made legal, they would be found cropping up everywhere like wine bars or fast-food establishments, it should be pointed out that the German and Dutch experience shows that controls are most efficient. The opening of a brothel would be deemed to constitute development within the definition of the Town & Country Planning Legislation, which would be amended accordingly. Therefore, application would have to be made for outline planning permission in the first place; and that would be granted applying the same criteria (need, suitability of location, environmental considerations etc.) as apply to any other planning decision.

The application for detailed consent/bye-law approval would then follow and amongst the details to be specified would be included all those matters which are relevant to ensure that the establishment does not become either an eyesore or a nuisance. The local authority, in conjunction with the Department of Health and the British Medical Association, could be trusted to deal with such applications with a sufficiently critical eye to ensure that all interests, especially those of the neighbourhood, were safeguarded.

It is often said that the medical regulation of brothels cannot work and a number of reasons are proffered in support of such a statement. The first reason is said to be that compulsory medical check-ups of prostitutes on a weekly or fortnightly basis interfere with the rights of the individual. This is quite a nonsensical observation, since no-one is forced to become a prostitute. If a prostitute wishes to operate from a brothel, she has to submit to a medical; after all, many other people have to submit to medicals for one reason or another, and increasingly today, in connection with career advancement. If I require a life insurance policy, I submit to a medical; if I am claiming benefit under a sickness policy, I have to submit to more than one medical and sometimes at regular intervals. It is now suggested that there should be compulsory testing for AIDS. There seems to be nothing unusual in ensuring that a person is free of disease.

A second argument is that medicals do not work, for a prostitute may be free of disease one day and infected the next. Whilst the objection is theoretically true, it ceases to have any validity once it is made a rule of any licensed establishment that only protected intercourse can take place. A further criticism is that regular check-ups tend to make both prostitutes and clients careless. This is a variation on the same theme; and whilst it may be true that a false sense of security is bred by the concept of regular check-ups, in some cases, it cannot possibly be true as a generalization. If it were, it would be tantamount to arguing that the provision of insurance makes a car-driver careless.

Those who argue that medical check-ups are ineffective, are in the main the same people who wish prostitution to disappear. The safety argument then becomes a rationalization of their moral stance on the basis that, since prostitution cannot be made entirely 'safe', then it should be abolished. Benjamin and Masters have demolished this particular argument with the following comment (page 407): 'One could ask whether the automobile traffic is safe? But if one tried to abolish the automobile because of its danger (and seemed at all likely to succeed) he might quickly find himself under psychiatric supervision. Instead of suppressing the automobile, we educate the driver, build better roads, and keep working at he invention of new safety devices. We apply reason and scientific methods.' Reason and scientific methods are exactly what seems to be lacking in the UK's approach, indeed the Western world's approach in general, to prostitution.

Chapter Twelve

Heterosexual brothels
for women

This is a subject about which little is known, for a combination of factors. It has always been assumed that it was men who required the services of female prostitutes to satisfy either their lust or their deviant tendencies, or because of temporary or even long-term difficulties in obtaining an outlet for their perfectly ordinary sexual drives. Women were supposed to grin and put up with intercourse, or, as the expression goes, to 'think of England', if of nothing else, when indulging in it. All the more so because it was believed that the sexual drive of women was not so strong, or at least not so immediate, as that of men.

It is perfectly true that there are well-known and long-established differences between the sexes in their approach to intercourse. But there should be no doubt whatsoever as to the strength of woman's sexual drive, which is much greater than men ever conceive. On the other hand, the way and the intensity by which it is manifested is clearly different from man's. It is, in a strange sense, wider and more diffused through the body than in a man and yet, in an odd way, it is less energetic. It is sedate, whilst man's is restless. It is diffused whilst man's is concentrated; ultimately, it is on the whole passive rather than active.

Ardent feminists do not like this type of definition of

woman's sexuality; and yet, to criticize it is tantamount to
failure to recognize what occurs in nature. It was Professor
Sash who remarked that wherever we are able to observe an
external difference between the male and the female
reproductive cells of plants, the male cells behave actively in
the union, and the females, passively: from this he went on to
draw an analogy between plants and animals. It is difficult to
see why feminists should object so strongly to the
differentiation between man and woman based on 'passiv-
·ity', actual or alleged, of the latter. The different physical
conformations speak for themselves.

In any event, wealthy women have always been able to
satisfy their sexual needs by finding younger men willing to
please, whether for money or for other reasons; and it seems
now inevitable that the equality which woman has quite
rightly claimed and obtained vis-a-vis men will have
consequences at the practical level which will affect her
sexual needs.

It is obvious, for example, that if a woman performs the
same job as a man and therefore has the same responsibilities,
remuneration and career prospects as her male counterpart,
it is not because of a great love or liking for her on the part
of the male sex, but simply because she has been found
capable of doing that job as well as, if not better than, a man.
Natural selection in the market-place will soon eliminate
those women who are incapable of attaining certain
standards or at least the same standards as men obtain, and
will favour those women who are more capable of taking on
masculine roles.

Inevitably, there will be a price that women will have to pay
for the attainment of those standards: that price is the
development of those traits which made it easier until now for
men to succeed in jobs whilst women were staying at home. It
is axiomatic that, only by developing those traits, will woman
be able effectively to compete with man. If, for example, she
wishes to be a weightlifter, she will have to develop strong
muscles.

By becoming more like man, however, she will inevitably suffer from all the ailments that have eluded her so far, at the same time as she will develop those needs, including sexual activity, for relaxation or relief without commitment. One can see this happening already. There are ambitious young men who, reversing the roles of hackettes and starlets, offer themselves, almost as amateur prostitutes, to those older women who have power either to award them contracts or jobs or ensure their promotion. What these men are doing is no different from what woman has done throughout her life, namely to use the body as a bargaining tool. Whether we call them 'toy boys' or 'hustlers' matters not; they are male prostitutes of a kind.

The women who receive these offers are some of the very same creatures whom one comes across in any wine bar in the City of London at lunchtime, either smoking or drinking or both, possibly talking with raised voices and sitting or standing in postures which are not always feminine. All this is inevitable and follows as night the day, because woman's body will have to adapt to the new requirements of a totally different work environment and to the attainment of goals that, for woman at least, are comparatively new.

One remarks in passing that from the newly-found independence and power must follow certain health drawbacks. For example, between 1978 and 1987 women's alcoholic intake increased by 14%. Single women drink consistently more than either their married, widowed or divorced counterparts, as observed. Fifty per cent more women died from lung cancer in 1988 than in 1974. This more than suggested that the number of women smokers has continued to rise; alternatively, that women are smoking much more (*The Independent*, 15 February 1990).

It is a fairly well recognized fact – at least recognized by the very women who have attained high office in business and in the professions – that to some extent their sexuality is diminished because men do not view them as sexual, warm women and they find it more difficult to establish sexual

relations. In fact, unfair though it may be, a dilemma faces
successful women: men who are successful and even some
men who, as a result of their more sedentary life and greater
financial independence, develop a slight paunch, find that
power and money opens sexual doors for them and, in a sense,
boosts their sexuality, whereas power, money and success
appear to have the opposite effect for women. This is so for at
least three reasons: the first is that a successful woman, almost
by definition, loses her femininity; secondly, because her very
status is sufficient to put a number of men off; and thirdly,
because if they are truly successful, women develop an
intimidating manner which runs counter to the establishment
of sexual tension and excitement.

Apart from other considerations, they are probably quite
tired when they get back home in the evening and the last
thing they want to do is to embark upon relationships which
need cultivating. For this reason, toy boys have become a
frequent occurrence and, for the very same reason, it might be
useful for some women to visit establishments where sexual
proclivities can be dealt with, so to say, on demand, and
without great emotional commitment. In addition, their style
of life having affected their health, as previously indicated, it
may be less troublesome to visit a brothel than nurture a close
or intimate relationship.

It is too easy to maintain, that the reason why women
have so far lived longer and appeared tougher than men is
because they are in fact stronger than men. That is true only
to a very limited extent, namely that they have led a different
life from men, inasmuch as they have been subjected to
different pressures and varied requirements which were
consistent with the development of different characteristics.
There seems no doubt that the moment woman starts
behaving like a man and attaining his same performance, she
must develop not only his characteristics but also his very
same ailments. The major consequence will be a certain
defeminization which will not be confined to woman's place
in business, or on the career ladder. And inevitably, her

sexual requirements and her approach to sexual relations generally will alter.

In the first place, she will be more inclined to fantasize and to depersonalize man; and that is a first step towards sexual intercourse motivated purely by lust and not love. In the second place, it will cease to be true that women indulge in sexual intercourse only for love and, as was recently said, that women will experience the 'one night stand' as the 'one night romance'.

Women will have need for recourse to male prostitutes. It is obvious that such need will not immediately be on the same scale as that of men: but it will come. We now have erotic publications, (see for example *Playgirl* magazine), aimed exclusively at women; there are meeting places in the United States and in Japan where young men are available for women who can afford to take them out to dinner and, if required, to bed.

The Americans, who have investigated this aspect of the matter much better than anyone else, appear to have established that only about a quarter of porn films are rented by women and that, accordingly, it is unlikely that the female sex industry would develop along the same lines as the male one. But these statistics are misleading, for they do not take into account that changes cannot occur almost overnight and that the newly-found independence of women only spans about a generation-and-a-half, whereas man's treatment of some women as prostitutes spans millenia.

Therefore, I believe that there is no logical reason why, given the way woman is travelling, she should not develop the same sexual needs as men. Accordingly, one must consider whether the State should take an interest in brothels for women who have heterosexual leanings. The rules that govern sexual behaviour in our society have changed dramatically over two generations and will no doubt change even further. We have already reviewed the extent to which modern woman has been prepared to engage in adultery whilst married. This is partly the result of a more independent spirit, but, mainly, of great dissatisfaction with her husband.

Indeed, in the 1990s it is most unlikely that where the wife is living apart from the husband or is separated from him by consent, she has not committed adultery in the technical sense. The modern ethos and the independence of woman dictates that this should be so, since in situations of marital conflict woman asserts her independence from her husband principally by sleeping with another man: this is an understandable, psychological reaction.

However, what this means in effect is that in about 40% of divorce cases in 1987, the wife was not satisfied with the husband's behaviour, generally; and specifically with his sexual performance. It has to be said that since for every adultery there are two parties, the figures may show that it is equally true to say that some men commit adultery because they are dissatisfied with their wives' performance. However, the fact remains that the percentage of women who commit adultery is greater than the percentage of men who do so and, in any event, the indications given as to the ability of the average Western male to satisfy his female companion must always be borne in mind.

And here one is not merely considering what might be termed 'casual' adultery, since even in those situations where the wife alleges adultery by the man, there may have been a wrong appreciation of the nature of the matrimonial offence. (In 1987 out of 107,556 divorce petitions by the wife, 26,944 so alleged this to be the case and 55,844 complained of the husband's behaviour generally; the remaining near 19,000 are on the ground of separation: there are others but are less significant). Furthermore, 72% of the divorce decrees awarded to one partner in 1987 were granted to the wife, 52% on the ground of the husband's adultery.

Statistics are usually symptomatic. If woman's newly-established freedom gives her the edge in taking the initiative because of dissatisfaction with her partner and if, as is true, she is not terribly fussed about committing adultery, there is no reason why she should be deterred from frequenting a brothel. After all, woman has pressed hard for her freedom of choice, extending it even to the taking of life in abortion. Why should she not consider herself free to frequent a male brothel?

There is a further consideration of some importance, namely the difference in the intrinsic merit, as individuals, of present-day spouses. It would appear that there is an imbalance in the qualities of men and women today which is now very marked and which, if we ignore physical differences and handicaps, results in woman being the better of the species. She is clearly in the ascendant and man is under pressure, if not following a downward slope. It would, in fact, appear that man has exhausted both his historical and his natural function.

With the onset of reliable contraception, woman has emancipated herself not only historically but also naturally. There is ample evidence that she is now in the forefront, she has clearer ideas; and knows, or thinks she knows (which for present purposes is the same thing) where she is going. Compare her with modern man, who has lost his sense of direction and, if Kinsey is to be believed, his sense of erection. Woman nowadays is capable of tackling practically every job a man does and the qualities that previously made her a good mother, or housekeeper, or tactician in the matrimonial home, are serving her in very good stead in her other occupations. As a generalization, she emerges as more loyal, hardworking and more positive than modern man. Some employers go so far as to maintain that nowadays, if one wants anything done, one should ask a woman to do it.

Furthermore, it is now quite possible for woman to be impregnated without even having had intercourse and to be a mother without there being a father, to be head of a family without there being a family in the traditional sense. The less likely woman is to consort with men, the more likely it is that she will turn to lesbianism. In lesbian relations, it is said that woman will find greater affinity to replace incompatibility, better understanding to replace dullness, heightened sensitivity to replace oafishness, unselfishness to replace egoism and dedication to replace chauvinism. She will find plenty of subjects of conversation that are common and which can be talked about with ease instead of being restricted to cricket or soccer.

Sexually, if she feels no need for the kind of satisfaction that intercourse with a man would provide, she may find herself just at ease with non-penetrative techniques. The different sexual requirements of a woman, it is said, do not necessitate, as a matter of course, relationship with a man. However, that is a very uncertain argument and not supported by the evidence of recent increases in sales of dildos, vibrators and analogous implements that facilitate the simulation of heterosexual intercourse.

This statement could be objected to on the grounds that the implements referred to are merely aids to masturbation and stimulation of the clitoris which, in itself, is an alternative to rather than a simulation of heterosexual intercourse. I personally discount this argument for the following reasons. Firstly, it does not matter how sexual stimulation is attained, although different ways of achieving that objective provide different sensations: it is the end product that counts. Secondly, for some women clitoral stimulation is less significant and less likely to occur than vaginal excitement. It is probably true to say that the number of such women is reducing with the greater emphasis placed by Western society on non-penetrative sexual activities: nevertheless, there are surely a great many women for whom vaginal stimulation continues to be infinitely more meaningful than clitoral. Thirdly, regarding the performance of men, if the Kinsey figures referred to earlier are to be accepted as providing realistic guidelines, clearly, they bear no comparison to the greater satisfaction that can be derived from the use of artificial aids to excitement. I also add in passing that this may help to explain the increase in lesbian activity.

At the same time, however, the need for change and variety will not be tempered by the community of feeling arising from a family set-up and will make recourse to 'adultery' in the strict etymological sense, namely a move towards another person, as normal for modern woman as it is for man. Hence her likely recourse to brothels, if they are made legitimate.

It seems to me that woman is emerging as a twenty-first century Boadicea – riding astride the steer of freedom with a sword in her hand. Perhaps, the description is not entirely appropriate, for Boadicea was resisting the Romans who were to bring civilization to Britain's shores, whereas modern woman is endeavouring to replace masculine culture, which seems exhausted, with a feminist creed, which is exhausting.

The number of women who bring up children on their own is evidence of this fact and the statistics that have been quoted show that men are not living up to women's expectations. It does not require a Royal Commission to tell us that modern woman knows what she wants and how to get it and, above all, she knows where she is going. Her stride is lengthening and its pride is increasing proportionately; and quite rightly, too, because present-day woman displays better qualities than her male counterpart. In most families she is also a breadwinner and in many families the principal one.

But this difference in quality, and in the requirements of the society in which we live, is affecting woman's psychological heritage. It must be acknowledged that in certain situations the more typically feminine requirements are transmuted into a different type of activity: but whilst this diversion of energies and finalities is a manifestation of our increasing technical expertise, they anticipate a change of approach which is highly damaging for the woman's psyche. It is difficult to see how this change of direction and emphasis can be redressed, save possibly within the framework of a totally different and new social system, which would not be too difficult to achieve as a matter of social policy, especially since we cannot easily and, above all, with impunity throw overboard our psychological heritage. It is in reality our moral baggage, without which we would not know how to travel through life or, at least, would find the journey much more perilous.

It is the distillation of the accumulated experience of all our ancestors through the previous few hundred or thousand years (who knows?). It is the little voice that warns human beings when they are about to do something that is not in keeping with our innermost nature. It is the feeling that, sometimes, all is not right, which human beings do not always recognize but that often enough makes them feel uneasy. It is our conscience, our subconscious, and all our potential neuroses. Different psychologists have called it by various names but no matter what the correct terminology may be, depending on the school of psychological thought to which one subscribes, this moral baggage is part of us all and we all have to come to terms with it.

It is like a huge jigsaw puzzle, made up of thousands of pieces which our experience of life teaches us to slot into position with a view to forming the picture which we project to the world and which is composed of our temperament, character, personality and outlook on life. We ignore our psychological heritage at our peril, for every time we do not behave in accordance with its expectations, we feel out of place in the same way as a piece of the jigsaw, when wrongly positioned, distorts the picture we are trying to form.

On the other hand, every time we take a decision which is in accord with, or at least not obviously in antithesis to, our moral baggage, we dislodge the relevant piece from our subconscious and fit it into a clear-cut conscious pattern which makes it easier for us to understand the world about us and which undoubtedly gives us confidence in our actions and in our beliefs. This analogy with the jigsaw is not far-fetched and can be applied to personal relations both by man and woman, albeit with different consequences and for a variety of reasons.

Consider, then, for a moment how woman is forced to react to modern pressures. First, she no longer has to be a mother if she does not wish to. Secondly, she is allowed by contraception to thwart the preordained aim of sexual activity: in other words, she comes together with the male on an even footing and society recognizes – indeed, nowadays demands –

this equality. But her psyche is not yet ready for this; the little pieces of the jigsaw cannot be slotted in quite so easily. Tension is thus created in woman's mind, which is aggravated by her struggle for parity in the home and in the workplace. Hence her dissatisfaction with herself, her mate and her role. Hence, too, her lack of fulfilment in sexual intercourse. We are told by those psychologists who have dedicated a lifetime to this kind of investigation, that the frequency of women's orgasms is constantly diminishing or they are becoming more and more difficult to attain. This is evidenced by her numerous sexual partners, her divorces, her unhappiness and her neuroses.

Woman is becoming more like man. And she will have need for recourse to the sexual services of men if they can be bought for cash. All the reasons that have been proffered to explain and/or justify the usefulness of prostitutes, can apply to men who sell their bodies to women. Of course, it is not only independent-minded or highly-sexed women who *may* have recourse to male prostitutes. There are those widows who, regardless of age, may not wish to remarry or establish a more permanent relationship with another man (whether because they still treasure their first husband's memory or because they do not wish to give their children a stepfather, or for whatever other reason), and may find a useful outlet there; or wives whose husbands are in jail, or away for long periods, assuming such wives would have need of a man and prefer not to take a lover.

There are also those women, with children, who have never married. According to the 1994 Home Office analysis, there are now just over a million one-parent families in Britain. This figure obviously includes single mothers, single fathers and widowed, divorced or separated mothers; and that 1 in 6 families with dependent children are single-parent families. And, as noted earlier, the number of single-parent families has grown by almost 80% between 1971 and 1986. On the basis that 98% of children live with their natural mother, there are a number of women, with children, who may have need for sexual satisfaction of one kind or the other. One could argue that it is probably better, if they do not wish to establish a permanent relationship, that, rather than being promiscuous, they have recourse to male prostitutes instead of relying on either masturbatory or lesbian outlets for their sexuality.

Having said all this for the sake of completeness and logical consistency, one envisages some problems when considering the practical aspect. A woman prostitute can gratify man's appetite without too much effort. That is clear. One need only consider, on the one hand, the statistics already quoted from the Kinsey Report concerning the power of modern man and, on the other hand, woman's psychological make-up, to see how accurate such a statement is. But it is the very physiology of the male that makes his ability to serve as a full-time prostitute very doubtful indeed. A woman may be lacking in sexual desire, as most prostitutes are, she may be nervous or afraid as to the type of encounter, as some prostitutes are at the beginning of their activity, she may be worried or tired or generally out of sorts; but despite all this she can still satisfy a man's lust most of the time. A man cannot do likewise, no matter what purveyors of titillating sexual material would have us believe. The limitations that nature has imposed on man's ability to copulate at will are too well known to require elaboration.

That, ultimately, is the principal reason why the male prostitute who offers heterosexual services will never become either as numerically or as qualitatively significant as his female counterpart. Although, as a matter of theory and logic, if the State were to license brothels where women prostitutes operated, it could not resist requests to license premises where male prostitutes operated, it must be said that in the case of males who wish to satisfy females, no matter how great the demand, the offer will be on the whole negligible, at least until such time as science has devised methods of ensuring that man's ability to satisfy woman is coterminus with woman's ability to satisfy man.

Interestingly enough, at the beginning of the nineteenth century, brothels where men made themselves available to women were quite well known in London. They are described in Volume 3 of Dr Fernando Henriques's *Modern Sexuality* (London, McGibbon and Keene, 1968) but were mainly for ladies of wealth who had to contribute such sums as a 100 guineas subscription which entitled them to choose any man for any period of time. Anonymity was preserved by women wearing a masque.

References in literature to male brothels are rare and Dr Fernando Henriques explains such scarcity on the basis that, firstly, women hardly had any freedom of action in a male-dominated world; secondly, on the widespread Victorian assumption that women do not have the libidinous appetite of men; and thirdly, that sexual expertise was the province of the whore and not the wife. There is truth in all of these observations but the real reason for the scarcity of male brothels is the practical one of the inability of the male to perform on demand.

Chapter Thirteen

Lesbian brothels

L ike homosexuality and prostitution, lesbianism has always
been with us. The word itself is linked to the Greek island
of Lesbos where the poetess Sappho is said to have indulged in
certain practices.

Although male homosexuality was always fairly well known
and openly discussed and received considerable attention on
the part both of psychologists and legislators, lesbianism was
not a topic of normal conversation until quite recently. It was
only during the First World War, with the sensational
Pemberton Billing trial, that it came into the public arena;
in the nineteen twenties, it became even more of a public
issue. Just as homosexuals began to boast about their leanings,
so, albeit hesitantly at first, lesbians began to assert their right to
their own brand of sexuality. *The Well of Loneliness* by
Radclyffe Hall dealt very openly with the problems that
lesbianism posed and, understandably, given the views
prevailing at the time, was prosecuted for obscenity.

One should also mention at this stage the activities (antics?)
of Vita Sackville-West and her lovers (Virginia Woolf,
Violette Trefusis, Rosamund Grosvenor and Mary Camp-
bell) and other members of the Bloomsbury Set.

The climate of sexual permissiveness that resulted from the
Second World War caused both male and female homosexuals

to come forward to be counted and, on the principle that a woman's body was her own, some women were at last free to adopt their real sexual role. The most literate exponent of this view was Shere Hite who, in 1977, argued quite openly for lesbians. Many others followed, extolling woman's sensitive imagination and the pleasures to be derived from embraces other than of the (dominant) male kind.

Self-identification, at least in sexual terms, became all important; the isolation and guilt of centuries was thrown overboard. The Women's Liberation Movement was formed in the early 1970s in imitation of the Gay Liberation Front, and in 1976 an Action for Lesbian Parents' Group was established. Now, in the mid 1990s, it could be argued that, generally speaking, we have reached the point where people are no longer shy, afraid and certainly not guilty of publicly acknowledging (and discussing) their homosexuality, male or female. Indeed, both groups even have their own niche in TV programming.

In too many cases in modern times the male of the species emerges as helpless, useless, and soft, an insensitive oaf for whom any woman of intelligence, initiative and courage can have nothing but contempt. If it is correct to record the displeasure of modern woman with man brought about by man's inability to satisfy her, both on the physical and the intellectual plane, then it seems likely that the number of women who will turn to members of their own sex for that very kind of satisfaction can but increase.

There is a further consideration. Ultimately, it must be acknowledged that what woman appreciates most of all in a man are those manifestations which, in one form or the other, are of power. It may be physical, moral or intellectual power, depending on the type of woman and man involved: but in all cases where a woman looks up to a man it is because of the power that the man is capable of exerting as far as she is concerned; it may be the power of his prowess as a lover, his high moral stance, his great intellectual ability, his financial success, or even his craft skills. Woman wants, and indeed needs to look up to a man; and when she does, what she appreciates most in him is power, whatever ardent feminists may say.

As Havelock Ellis put it (*Studies in the Psychology of Sex* Volume 3 page 140) the hymen is the anatomical expression of that admiration of force which marks the female in her choice of mate, since it is an obstacle to the impregnation of the young female by immature, aged or feeble males.

It is interesting that one of the most authoritative proponents of the rights of women, the author of *A Vindication of the Rights of a Woman* (1972), Mary Wollstencraft, herself tackles the subject of power. Her approach is expressed in the well-known quotation: 'I do not wish women to have power over men; but over themselves.' This sounds good enough but is based on the misconception that people who acquire power, will not use it. Those who have power over themselves normally end up by exercising their power over others. In the case of women, if they acquire power, they will use it over men. Power is not something that one puts in the safe and looks at once a year.

This appreciation of power has existed since the dawn of history. The moment man first dragged woman by her hair into a cave he asserted his dominance over her; millennia of psychological heritage of this kind cannot be thrown overboard in one or two generations. Without wishing to delve into the detail of the subject matter which is covered to the point of nausea in the numerous text books and manuals dealing with sexuality, it is clear that man's power over woman is in particular reflected in certain sexual manifestations or practices. From the gentlest to the sado-masochistic, it is established that woman wishes to be conquered and to receive some gentle pain in the act of conquest; hence the old adage that there is no love without pain.

I am not here concerned with the sexual manifestations of such a tendency, which are in any event only of interest to the theoreticians of matters sexual. Practitioners of such matters have no inclination and, above all, no need to rationalize and systematize in the way that mostly impotent sexologists do. The relevance of the observation as to power, however, is the fact that the dissatisfaction which woman finds with man in the twentieth century is also due to the balance of power between the sexes having shifted dramatically.

Gone are the days when the threat of pregnancy made woman the practical slave of man. The moment she was handed control over her reproductive cycle, it was inevitable that the balance of power should shift. Save in the most far-fetched hypotheses, there is no way that today's man can ensure that his woman carries his child if she does not wish to do so. That gives woman incredible leverage in the relationship, at least if it is of lasting duration, for it deprives man of an heir if woman does not concur. It is as though he has submitted to a sterilization operation.

If reliable contraception controlled by woman did not suffice, however, man, displaying either absolute lack of wisdom, or a total inability to understand the long-term effects of what he was doing, has allowed his seed to be encapsulated for future use by woman. A pinprick is all that is needed for conception and man's presence is no longer required.

In terms of power, there are some who maintain that modern man is surplus to requirements. In the same way as woman has learnt openly to restate her femininity and sexuality, so she can give effect to her newly-found power. She is more demanding than at any time in history. She is not only there to satisfy her companion but she herself wishes – and quite rightly so – to be satisfied.

Ignoring the long-term effects for humanity of the ever-reducing number of women who wish to be mothers (some scientists may well argue that the motherly instinct will be bred our of women, in the same way as the brooding instinct has effectively been bred out of some breeds of chicken), in the short term one will have to pose the question into which channels woman's sexuality will be directed, once it has been divorced from manhood and motherhood. The answer seems to be that it will be directed towards persons of the same sex.

It follows, therefore, that there is no reason whatsoever why, once it were decided that the State or the local authority could license brothels, there should not also be included, in such permission, establishments where women offered themselves for sale to other women. There is nothing new, of course, in this type of relationship even at present. Many prostitutes end up by behaving according to lesbian criteria either because of their friendship with fellow prostitutes or because some clients require them to perform female homosexual acts or, occasionally, because some women require them so to act. The number of women who use the services of female homosexual prostitutes is, however, small, simply because of the way prostitution is set up in the UK. Kerb-crawling by women seeking female prostitutes is unknown. The number of women who telephone massage parlours to enquire as to the provision of lesbian services is very small indeed. One has never heard the English Collective of Prostitutes arguing for the right to perform lesbian services.

Lesbianism, like prostitution, is not a crime; but the provision of lesbian services is no more encouraged than the provision of brothels. Lesbian brothels, traditionally known as 'Temples of Sappho', have not had such attention lavished on them as their male counterparts. Benjamin & Masters deal with them almost in passing and it is left to Cross (*The Lust Market*) to provide the essential texts and descriptions of activities. The view that lesbian brothels are essentially curiosities and are not worthy of detailed consideration either by the sociologist or the legislator may have been maintainable until the early sixties; but it no longer suffices in the 1990s to ignore the requirements of a section of the population whose numbers are increasing at a very fast rate.

It is said that the lesbians who operate in the 'Temples of Sappho' are mainly active lesbians and consequently their clients are mainly passive types. It is believed that this is an over-simplification, since once the concept is accepted that licensed premises are available for the purposes of the sale of lesbian services, it is inevitable that the clients of such brothels will be both active and passive types and accordingly, unless the same girl is prepared to satisfy both sets of requirements, a lesbian brothel will include prostitutes of both types.

There is nothing unusual in this either; in a heterosexual-type brothel, there are some prostitutes who are known for performing certain types of services of the kind that have been described above by a number identification. There are also prostitutes who indulge in other practices of a sadistic or masochistic kind, or are prepared to pander to coprophilia and are known to be willing to provide such services. There is no reason why, with suitable adjustments to cater for different sexual and psychological needs, the same should not happen in a lesbian brothel.

There is nothing that cannot be provided in this kind of brothel to satisfy lesbian tendencies. Dr Cross (pages 211, 229 and 230) has explored the matter in considerable detail. For our purposes, it will suffice to list the six basic lesbian activities which lesbian prostitutes could offer: 1. Cunnilingus – simultaneous or reciprocal; 2. Handling of breasts; 3. Divers body kisses. (The second Kinsey Report on female sexuality found that these represented 91% of all lesbian activities.) 4. Reciprocal rubbing of female genitalia, technically known as tribadism; 5. Mutual masturbation; 6. Artificial phalluses and vibrators. Dr Cross describes in considerable detail at least two kinds of the former and the keen reader is referred to his work.

There is little doubt that if the State ever were to look upon legalization of brothels with a more tolerant and enlightened eye, it would have to consider the provision of lesbian services. Clearly, there would be an outcry on the part of the homosexual population if in such an event there were not provision for male homosexual brothels; by the same token it is difficult to believe that the lesbian section of the UK population would not seek equal rights in the matter. The alternative would be for heterosexual brothels to include prostitutes willing to perform, for payment, lesbian services. But that would not be so efficient because a lesbian would be less willing to frequent the same establishment as men for the very same reason that she is a lesbian, namely that she dislikes men and is less keen to associate with them. On this basis, one may see a spread of lesbian brothels if heterosexual brothels were legalized.

Furthermore, it is conceivable that in the interests of profits, some such brothels may extend their sphere of operation by satisfying the voyeuristic tendencies of certain men by means of displays of female homosexual practices, a facility sometimes afforded by heterosexual brothels to their own more exacting or deviant clients.

Chapter Fourteen

Male homosexual
brothels

This is not the place to consider the various theories and factors propounded to explain, justify or classify male homosexuality, save to say that none of these theories and factors is either completely right or completely wrong.

Whether one believes in the psychological justification (with its possessive, seduction and non-conformity of gender theories), or in the functional/hormonal view, or in the social/environmental approach to homosexuality, it is a fact that the number of homosexuals in the Western world is rapidly increasing as a result of a strict application of the individual's unfettered right to self-determination and choice, our greater leniency towards sexual irregularity, because of the weakening of the family as a unit (emotional insecurity, community instability, one-parent families) or, finally, because of environmental factors, including hormonal changes in the foetus brought about by increased oestrogen levels resulting from the mother's use of the contraceptive pill. (See Sharpe and Shakkebaek in *The Lancet*, June 1993 on the feminizing effect of high oestrogen levels in the water supply. It cannot be a coincidence that in the 1940s a sperm count of 60 million per millilitre of semen was considered normal, whereas today a standard of 'normality' in man is 20 million.)

If space were not limited, one could dedicate several pages to each of these possible, and in some cases, most probable, causes.

At this point I would simply like to say that it is hardly a coincidence, that in 1989 the Danes established a landmark in the campaign to assert the individual's right to self-determination when they codified into law the 'marriage' of homosexuals. Of course, it is not called 'marriage' since conceptual hypocrisy does not always equate with terminological accuracy. The relationship is called a registered partnership and it purports to follow the example set by France a little earlier, when they had regulated relationships between lesbians.

Both the French and the Danish legislation on homosexuality give recognition to individual freedom, in theory; in practice, they are the result of pressures by a sufficient number of people whose voice could not be ignored. Kinsey found in 1952 that 4% of American males were homosexuals. This figure was considered even at that time a gross under-estimate. The 1990 update of the Kinsey Report finds that 25% of American males are wholly homosexual. This represents a sixfold increase in 40 years from the 1948 figure.

At the same time it claims (p.139) that '. . . between 62% and 79% of men who label themselves homosexual have had sex with women'. What we are not told by Kinsey is what these women thought of such 'bisexual' performances. Kinsey also notes that '. . . approximately one-third of all males are thought to have had at least one same-sex experience leading to orgasm since puberty'.

Furthermore, the Wolfenden Report does not cite the totality of the Kinsey Report findings on homosexuality. The figures given in the 1990 update of the Kinsey findings (*The Kinsey Institute New Report on Sex* – June Reinitch and Ruth Beasley Pelican 1990 p.140) have already been quoted. Given a population of about 250 million people in the USA. it is self-evident that the scale of the homosexual group in that country is not just big, it is enormous.

One may go further and assume that given also the similarity in culture and in outlook between the United

Kingdom and the United States, the figure for the United Kingdom homosexuals could also be quite easily 25%. The obvious difficulty in forming any reliable assessment of the numbers involved stems from 'the fact that no in-depth studies have been made to find out exactly how many homosexuals there are. The matter is further complicated by the consideration that homosexuality is both actual and potential, since there are human beings who, whilst not practising homosexuals, manifest a natural predisposition towards homosexual behaviour. What they may not have experienced is the type of circumstance which would precipitate them into homosexual activity.

Similarly, it is almost impossible to determine what is the number of those beings who are not homosexuals, since the burden of proving a negative cannot easily be discharged. As a result of my experience of life, both personal and professional, I am firmly of the opinion that the number of homosexuals, both male and female, in present-day British society, is substantially greater than most people believe.

There may be other reasons; there may be more people now who are more openly bi-sexual, and we have to accept the fact that there has been a substantial loosening of our moral code. Since the Wolfenden Report, the country has developed a more tolerant attitude towards homosexuals generally.

Furthermore, the male prison population has also increased over the years and, with that, the number of homosexuals in prison is now so great that condoms are made available in penal establishments, partly though not entirely as a result of AIDS.

But it should not be thought that homosexual male prostitution is confined to the USA and the UK. The male 'hustler' is well known in Europe (especially Germany, France, Holland, Italy and Spain) and also in the Scandinavian countries.

One gets the feeling that the number of homosexuals is increasing at a rate which is not proportionate with a straight population increase: figures are not available to show this. It may be that, simply because homosexuals are now freer to manifest themselves, they are in effect more visible to the general public, and since they have their own programmes on radio and television and in newspapers, one may tend to feel that there are more of them around. On balance, the view is taken here that the number of homosexuals *is* increasing disproportionately to the population of the Western world.

For this, if for no other reason, the provision of brothels that cater for homosexual requirements is as inevitable as that for lesbians. We have already considered how the unavailability of prostitutes may have a determining effect, especially on the young male, in marginal cases. Historically, there is nothing new about male homosexual prostitution which, as far as anyone can tell, is as ancient as the female variety. Homosexual prostitutes, some very young boys, were known to exist amongst the Hebrews, the Egyptians, the Persians, the Indians, in Greece, Rome, the Middle East and the Far East. Young boys were very popular in Persia, China, Japan and Rome and it was not an unusual occurrence for the Europeans, when they colonized Africa and the East, to go looking for boy prostitutes. These days we have the 'hustler' and the paedophile, endorsing the long-held view (which I insist on repeating) that there is nothing new under the sun in matters sexual.

Homosexuals, whether male or female, object strongly when their attitude is termed 'deviant' and this is not a qualification that will be adopted here. Deviant or not, homosexual needs have to be provided for in the same way as heterosexual ones. When objection was taken earlier on to the ever-increasing rate of violent sexual attacks on women, it was coupled with a consideration of similar attacks on men. Just as the 'deviant' heterosexual needs an officially recognized outlet for his violence, so do homosexual males. And what better place than a licensed brothel.

Indeed, there is no reason why one of the services rendered in homosexual brothels should not be the administration of violence, if one can put it that way. There is nothing unusual about flagellation, anyhow. Amongst the Asians, Galen had thought that a modest amount of whipping toned the body. The use of leafy twigs is routine in Finnish, Russian and other hydro-therapy institutes and, as a matter of routine, has now been extended to most saunas. If male homosexuals wish to use or receive violence, what better place than a controlled and supervised environment?

A major drawback of male prostitution is that at present male prostitutes are more likely to be transmitting AIDS than female prostitutes. There are two reasons for this: firstly, the use of condoms between male prostitutes and their clients is much less widespread; secondly, because many male prostitutes and their clients report 'private (i.e. non-commercial) sexual relationships with females'. See AIDS Care – pages 17 and 24.

If English law should ultimately decide to 'recognize' prostitution, both male and female, certain changes would be necessary. For example, it has now been decided (Queen's Bench Division 5 May 1994) that the term 'common prostitute' to which we have already drawn attention and which is embodied in Section 1 of the Street Offences Act 1959, is confined to female prostitutes and excludes from its scope the activities of male prostitutes. The Court pointed out that the term 'common prostitute' was ordinarily applied to women and that it was improbable that Parliament had intended to create by the 1959 Act a new 'male' offence which was technically different from what was still embodied in Section 32 of the Sexual Offences Act 1956.

Chapter Fifteen

The Wolfenden Report

On 27 August 1954, the Government appointed a Committee chaired by Sir John Wolfenden, CBE '. . . to consider the law and practice relating to homosexual offences and to offences against the criminal law in connection with prostitution and solicitation for immoral purposes'.

The Committee reported in September 1957 and its report (Report of the Committee on Homosexual Offences and Prostitution Command 247/1957) represents the high water-mark in Britain's approach to prostitution and prostitutes. The Committee consisted initially of 15 members, 12 men and three women. Two men resigned before the Committee could report. The first point to note about this is the imbalance between men and women. Insofar as the Committee had to consider the activities of both men and women (homosexuality and prostitution), one might be forgiven for believing that both sexes should at best be represented on the Committee in even numbers, or at least that the percentage of women should have been greater.

Much more to the point, is the fact that the interested parties themselves were apparently nowhere (officially) represented on the Committee. One can only speculate as to how many, if any, of the men who sat on the Committee, all highly respected members of the community (a Scottish magistrate, a future High Court Judge, a successful solicitor, a lady chairman of the Scottish Association of Girl Clubs, etc.) were practising homosexuals or not. One may be forgiven for believing that, perhaps, none of them was. Certainly, the three eminently respectable women members of the Committee were not prostitutes. Put differently, whilst one appreciates how difficult it may have been to have a self-confessed homosexual or a prostitute sitting together with highly-respected members of the community, it remains a fact that the voices of the parties who were going to be affected by the recommendations of the Committee were not heard at any time during the decision-making process.

It is not expressly stated, either in the list of the individual witnesses whose evidence was taken either orally or in writing, or from the statements made in paragraph 4 ('Acknowledgements') of the Report, that the Committee took evidence from prostitutes. It is true that there is a reference to witnesses putting themselves '. . . in a position of delicacy in order to assist us in our enquiry', but that is known to be a reference to the few homosexuals who did, in fact, give evidence to the Committee. No prostitutes as such were interviewed. Indeed, given the recommendations of the Report as regards prostitution, it is not likely that anybody heard what the women themselves, who plied their trade in central London, had to say. If they had, it is conceivable that the three women members would not have differed from the majority when they unsuccessfully recommended that the penalty for loitering should be increased to five years imprisonment instead of three.

Here, two key points have to be made. Firstly, that the women members of the Committee were inclined to impose greater penalties upon prostitutes than the men. The maximum proposed by the three women members of the Committee, five years imprisonment, instead of three, for a simple loitering offence, underlines what was said earlier concerning the hatred between the matron and the whore. Secondly, we must resist the temptation to say that if, for example, the Wolfenden Report had been considering the advance of AIDS or heroin addiction, it surely would not have been sensible to argue that infected people or heroin addicts should have been included amongst the members of the Committee; or that, if it had been considering the law of theft or of murder, murderers and thieves ought to have sat on the committee.

The apparent attraction of this argument belies its fallacy. In the first place, there is no doubt whatsoever that prostitutes were not interviewed at all, let alone allowed to sit on the Committee. The writer contacted Lord Mishcon who, as Victor Mishcon, an eminently respectable solicitor, was one of the members of the Wolfenden Committee: he has confirmed that no evidence whatever was taken from prostitutes. Secondly, if the Wolfenden Committee had been considering theft or murder, it would have been sitting in judgement on existing offences, well known to the criminal law. Prostitution, however, under English law is not a criminal offence; nobody can be punished for being a prostitute.

Whichever way one looks at the matter, it remains a fact that the report paid much greater attention to homosexuality than it did to prostitution. The structure of the report itself makes this clear: of a total of 116 pages, 76 are dedicated to homosexuality and less than half, 35, to prostitution. The Committee took evidence from 35 professional and public bodies (the Churches, British Medical Association, Law Society etc.), six Government departments and 31 individual witnesses consisting of Judges, Magistrates, JPs, Medical Officers, etc. Only three such witnesses appear to have had no official or authoritative post, two men and a married woman. In addition, it considered written memoranda from 11 public and professional bodies and Government departments, and 15 individuals. Of these, only six did not have some professional qualification or official position and of the six, only two were women.

It could be argued that a great deal of the evidence before the Committee came from those members of society who were least likely to have any direct and personal knowledge of prostitutes and brothels. Furthermore, although the Committee purported to take into account the findings of the Kinsey Reports, it quoted Kinsey only when dealing with homosexuality and not when dealing with prostitution. Eight case histories are given for homosexuals but none for prostitution. And that is clearly significant. The Committee made a total of 30 recommendations, 18 of which relate to homosexuality and 12 to prostitution. There are 13 pages of statistical tables relating to homosexuality but only six pages of statistical data relating to prostitution. One cannot help the feeling of a middle-to-upper-class bias not only in the composition but also in the findings of the Wolfenden Committee. Furthermore, it is clear that the Committee took the view that the law relating to homosexuality was perhaps more intricate and serious than that relating to prostitution. But that shows a crass misunderstanding of the significance, for society, of prostitutes.

However, these are not the principal criticisms of the Wolfenden Report. The accusation of a hypocritical stance in its dealing with prostitution is much more fundamental. What Wolfenden ultimately recommended was that whilst prostitution as such was not a crime, it should be made more difficult for the prostitutes to ply their trade openly in the streets. Whereas, under previous law, one had to establish annoyance by the prostitute of her client (potential or actual) or of the general public, Wolfenden recommended that the law should be formulated so as to eliminate the requirement of annoyance, that maximum penalties for street offences should be increased and a system of progressively higher penalties for repeated offences should be introduced.

In other words, the Committee endorsed the view that we should try and get the prostitutes off the streets, by sweeping them under the carpet. The objections of the Police Federation to this concept of protecting appearances without tackling the substance were brushed aside. The Committee also decided that the licensing, or at least the official toleration of brothels by the State, was not acceptable since it would proceed from the premise that the State recognized prostitution as a social necessity.

It is easy to appreciate the Committee's view on this aspect of the matter: nobody wants to acknowledge immorality, let alone be seen to condone it. In fact, prostitution *is*, at least in the mind of the writer, a social necessity, not only because prostitutes have existed for as long as society has, but also because even assuming that the point had any legal validity, such an approach was hardly appropriate for a Committee which effectively made homosexual behaviour easier, whilst attempting to discourage heterosexual behaviour. I fully realize that, technically, what the Committee did was not officially to make homosexual behaviour easier but merely to take homosexual conduct between consenting adults in private outside the sphere of the criminal law. But there is no doubt that the moment an activity ceases to be illegal, people are likely to indulge in it more frequently than if it were illegal.

This is not meant as a criticism of the Wolfenden Committee's findings on the need to liberalize the laws relating to adult homosexual behaviour in private, since these were inspired by humanitarian needs and were long overdue. But insofar as prostitution itself is not illegal in English law, it is difficult to see why the activities of those who practise it should be illegal. What was at the back of the Committee's mind was the fear that the existence of brothels would encourage promiscuity. This, of course, is nonsense because the elimination of brothels results in more women spread throughout society having to make themselves available, willingly or unwillingly, for the purposes of sexual gratification.

But the most objectionable reason for not recognizing the suitability and need for an official system of licensing brothels is stated by the Committee to be that there was no guarantee that the control of prostitutes, insofar as it would entail medical supervision on at least a weekly basis, would do anything to discourage venereal disease. As has been pointed out by Benjamin & Masters (*Prostitution & Morality*, Souvenir Press, London, 1962): 'Here we have the remarkable but often heard argument that if you cannot prevent *all* infection, then there is no point in preventing *any* infection.'

The statistics that have been quoted (Chapter 6) concerning the rise in reported cases of venereal diseases in Italy from 1958 to 1962 show how spurious such an argument is. All in all, it could be argued that the implementation of the Wolfenden Report did more harm than good, certainly as regards prostitution. In the first few months following its publication, commentators went to town on its findings concerning homosexuality; but prostitution was hardly discussed.

Whether the legalizing of homosexual acts in private gave rise to an increase in the homosexual population seems a moot point. It may well be that because the number of homosexuals was already substantially on the increase, there was no choice but to make legal a pattern of behaviour which was prevalent and to declare no longer applicable those provisions of the criminal law that were clearly not being enforced. But the suspicion remains that decriminalizing homosexuality has contributed to greater numbers of 'gays' coming to the fore, and to a greater virulence in the explosion of homosexual beliefs and practices; and probably, to an easier spread of AIDS.

As regards prostitution, the Street Offences Act 1959, which was a direct result of the recommendations of the Report, gave the police power to achieve the theoretical result of driving prostitutes off the streets. But anyone who knows certain areas of the principal cities in the United Kingdom realizes that prostitutes are still walking the same streets, and many more new ones, and have been doing so for some three decades. That particular recommendation was incapable of being given effect on the ground.

The unsatisfactory state of English law in matters sexual, is surely further highlighted by the consideration that half way between the date of appointment of the Wolfenden Report (September 1954) and the publication of its recommendations

(September 1957), the Sexual Offences Act 1956 was passed which purported to consolidate the statute law of England and Wales relating to sexual crimes, to the abduction, procuration and prostitution of women, as well as to 'kindred offences'. In other words, without even waiting for the result of the Committee's deliberations, the 1956 Act proceeded to tackle certain aspects of prostitution. But the point being made here is a different one.

The Sexual Offences Act 1956 restated the common law as regards the offence of buggery (sexual intercourse *per anum*) for it stated expressly that it is an offence for a person to commit buggery with another person (or with an animal). One year later, the Wolfenden Committee, in effect, recommended that buggery should cease to be a criminal offence if committed by *male* consenting adults in private and this recommendation received express statutory endorsement in section 1(1) of the Sexual Offences Act 1967 which states: 'Notwithstanding any statutory or common law provision, . . . , a homosexual act in private shall not be an offence provided that the parties consent thereto and have attained the age of 21 years.' The reader may be left wondering why, if anal intercourse is permitted between two willing parties of the same sex, it should be forbidden between man and woman: this is clearly discriminatory and sexually naïve. One wonders, too, how many men and women, married or not, who take pleasure from this particular type of intercourse, would sleep less comfortably at night if they really knew what theoretical English law has to say about their behaviour. Fortunately for them, even the most intrusive policeman would experience difficulty in finding sufficient evidence to prosecute for sodomy between willing males and females.

Chapter Sixteen

Child prostitutes

In ancient times, child prostitutes of both sexes were popular but they served the function of catering to a more perverse taste in sexual relations than the normal. The extent of the problem in those days was not great and although young boys and girls were made available throughout history in one form or the other to satisfy the male ego and, occasionally, the female, by their very nature they represented a fairly exceptional form of perversion, for the availability of which the client paid a high price.

It is a matter of record that in ancient Persia young boys were used for these purposes, being taught from an early age to use the anal muscles to advantage. Similarly, young girls were employed with equal success, given the contractability of vaginal muscles. The inclination to take advantage of children for prostitution purposes has always been very great. In the UK for example, in the early part of the nineteenth century, there were brothels (in the vicinity of London's Bryanston Square) which provided very young girls for their clients. The girls were principally from France and Italy and were offered to both English and foreign clients; the venture seems to have been quite successful.

The 1885 revelations by W.T. Stead in the *Pall Mall Gazette* are well known. The existence of child prostitutes is associated with man's leaning towards virginity; another factor relating to their existence, whilst not directly brought about by hygienic considerations, may be the thought that apart from syphilis, which is inherited, until modern days, with the advent of AIDS, there were no other sexually-transmitted diseases that could be passed on by a girl or a woman who had not had previous intercourse with another man. In the eighteenth century it was not unusual, for example, for unmarried men actually to go and buy young girls in order to avoid having to share the women of other men.

Even such a liberal character as the philosopher, Jean Jacques Rousseau, did exactly that together with his friend, Carrio, when he was working at the French Embassy in Venice in 1743/44. The young Venetian girl they jointly bought was only 11 years old. It is true that he, Rousseau, did not have intercourse with her, firstly because he soon developed paternal feeling towards her, but mainly because he left Venice about a year after he had 'purchased' her. What his friend, Carrio, did with her is not known. (J.J. Rousseau, *Confessions* – years 1743/44). But then, perhaps we should take what Rousseau says in matters of sex with more than a pinch of salt, since his sexuality was suspect, he being a most frank and frustrated masochist.

Certainly, virginity has been much prized by man, at least until recent times, and may become fashionable once more. It is often said that the preference for virgins is due to man's selfishness. This must be admitted since the defloration of a woman to some men provides the same sensation as the climbing of Everest for the first time to others: there was no-one there before him. In certain civilizations, particularly around the Mediterranean, it was until recently unheard of that a man could marry anything but a virgin.

There may well have been reasons for this other than the question of hygiene. The most important seems to be the need to establish paternity beyond any shadow of doubt. There is also the matter of the rationalization of an instinct to the effect that the woman who has not had previous sexual experience is less capable of analyzing the ability of her partner. This not only makes it easier for the man because his performance is subject to less stringent standards and criticisms, but it also provides greater peace of mind for the woman for she cannot miss what she has never had and to that extent it may, although it need not, even strengthen the marital bond.

This approach was far too easy when man looked upon woman as a chattel because obviously he would prefer to have a new car rather than a second-hand one, at least on the basis that any machine which has been used by more than one person may well develop the faults that a particular user inevitably brings to it. But with the emancipation of woman, it is claimed that it is her feelings and her personality that are to be considered rather than the state of her hymen. Be that as it may, the defloration of a child almost inevitably turned that child towards a life of sexual laxity and of prostitution. This is quite tragic. Unfortunately, whereas in olden times the child prostitute was not numerically significant, in the nineteen eighties and nineties a very nasty trade has been flourishing. From paedophile clubs and rings to the child prostitutes of Thailand and Cambodia, the plight of abused children is a blot on the so-called civilization of modern man, or more correctly, Western man. For example, it has recently been estimated that in Sri Lanka alone there are about 15,000 child prostitutes (usually in the age group 11 to 17 years of age). They are mainly boys and their services are demanded almost exclusively by Americans, Belgians, Dutch and German 'tourists'.

The World Health Organization (WHO) is exceptionally conscious of the fact. Work is being done on a Convention on the rights of children and by the Commission on Slavery to address and, if possible, redress the problem. The greatest difficulty is that any investigation into child prostitution is methodologically difficult and has to rely, to a noticeable extent, on anecdotal data. It would appear that the WHO has neither the time nor the resources to put pressure on individual Governments to try and combat the spread of child prostitution. 'Defence for Children International' based in Geneva is doing its best but it does not appear that both it and other organizations concerned by the spread of child abuse are too successful.

The existence of child prostitutes is more easily understood in poor countries that have been torn apart by war, where the inherent poverty and the uncontrolled fertility of the local population is such that to sell one or two children of the family as prostitutes may in some cases be necessary for survival and in others, only marginally significant. It is much more difficult, however, to see why this type of prostitution should be on the increase also in the Western world. That can only be due to vice and perversion.

Clearly, if legalized brothels came into existence in the UK it would have to be stipulated that no minor would be allowed to work in them. The difficulty would certainly be to decide at which age a person is sufficiently mature to be a prostitute officially. The two obvious dates are the date of majority (18), or the date at which a person is permitted to marry (16). The earlier age could be justified on the grounds that some girls are quite mature sexually at 16 but as a matter of social policy it might be preferable to stipulate the age of majority, namely 18. What the State could never countenance is recognition of child prostitution as such and nothing that is said herein is to be taken as an encouragement in that direction. On the other hand, if a girl or a boy can choose a government, by having been given the vote at 18, there is no reason why they should not be allowed to choose to be prostitutes. Many of them, already long before that age, dispose of their bodies for purposes other than procreation and love. The fact that they would do so for money seems totally irrelevant.

Chapter Seventeen

Conclusions

Whatever view may be formed about prostitutes and prostitution generally, and specifically in the 1990s, on one matter it may be easier to find a consensus and that is that in present-day Western society there is a great deal of discordant thinking about matters sexual. This is the result both of man's inability to come to terms with the new role that modern woman is carving out for herself, and of the constant heavy bombardment from the mass media of communications which tends to highlight the more titillating and less settled developments and ideas, causing utter confusion in the minds of adults and youngsters alike.

It is true to say that the more extravagant a notion, the more far-fetched a hypothesis, the more extreme an expectation and the more unorthodox the behaviour which is reported upon, especially if it has sexual overtones, the greater the indiscriminate publicity that is given to it. The noise of the bombardment is deafening and it is hardly surprising that the mind finds it more and more difficult to cope.

If there were parameters to judge the news, the theory or whatever else is being thrown at the people, it might not matter so much; but these are conspicuously lacking. Religious belief, honesty, integrity, patriotism, the family, the good, the beautiful, the true are all values to which our society seems, incredibly, to attach little and certainly decreasing significance. At the same time that parameters and standards of behaviour are disappearing, the myth of personal freedom is converted into freedom to do what one likes without any moral or social constraints. The glorification of this kind of laxity does not square up with the abolition of such freedom when it comes to prostitutes and prostitution.

But there is worse to come, at least in the sense that the concept of individual freedom lacks at the same time realism and practical sense. It fails completely to acknowledge that human beings, in common with other animals, need controls and rules to their behaviour if society is to survive. What is more, our civil liberties have been gradually eroded over the years. From the early 1970s the processes of erosion have been particularly marked. Indeed, there are some who have argued that it has become more pronounced over the last ten years or so (see *Freedom under Thatcher – Civil Liberties in Modern Britain* by K.D. Ewing and C.A. Geardy, Clarendon Press, Oxford, 1990). Coupled with this erosion of personal freedom whilst proclaiming the absolute right of the individual to behave and pontificate as he considers fit, we find a marked inability or unwillingness to confront fundamental issues. We are not prepared to distinguish between love and lust. Our forefathers were much better at this than we are.

It is because of this inability to distinguish between love and lust that it is so easy to say that, if one tolerates prostitution, one gives social approval to what is by definition a pathological condition. As with Edward Glover, it is not easy to determine whether sociologists, when they express themselves in this manner, refer to the pathology of the prostitute or of the customer. Perhaps they have both in mind; but whichever way one looks at it, such a view is mistaken.

The trouble about considering either the prostitute or her customer, or both, as pathological characters, is that it ignores reality. Whereas it is undoubtedly true that certain frequenters of brothels may well have an unbalanced personality, or otherwise have a twisted sexuality, it is equally true that a great number of so-called 'normal' individuals frequent prostitutes (one need only think of Boswell, Samuel Pepys, Palmerston, Lloyd George, Pushkin, Toulouse Lautrec, etc.). It is often argued in this context that whereas it may have been perfectly acceptable for Boswell and Pushkin to visit prostitutes and Toulouse Lautrec actually to live and paint in a brothel, we ourselves, in the twentieth century, have changed. This is a spurious argument since the requirements of human beings, and the need for some men to self-abasement, which we have already discussed at some length, have not only remained the same, but have in fact grown worse. The moral pollution brought about by the indiscriminate display on television and in print of intimate sexual details is infinitely more abominable, in the eyes of the writer, than the provision of a modern, controlled and reasonably aseptic brothel. Nothing has changed, except that the ability immediately to project images of titillation, is being exploited in a manner which was not available in the days of Boswell and Lloyd George.

Most reasonable people nowadays complain about standards of sexual behaviour or 'immorality', are upset at the ever increasing number of divorces, are puzzled by inexplicable manifestations of violence by youngsters sometimes as young as 11 years of age, claim to uphold virtue in their personal lives and, when confronted with the modern reality of unruly behaviour in all spheres of life, quite comfortably if not piously, express the hope that the pendulum will swing back. For them, the day will come when marriage will once more be sanctified, we shall not have to lock our cars and our doors, our wives and daughters will be able to walk the streets unmolested whether during the day or at night, etc., etc. It seems to me that these are the very people who have allowed our society to get to present extremes such as those referred to. The reason why a pendulum swings back is normally because there is either a reliable 'regulator' or someone who, at stated intervals, winds the clock up by pulling the chains and/or the weights to ensure that the pendulum, as the hallowed expression goes, will in fact swing back. The swing may occur in political terms but it very seldom does in social terms. The new freedom of woman will not be curtailed.

Nor should it be forgotten that from the psychological point of view prostitutes may remedy the deficiencies which a number of men, for one reason or the other, experience within the framework either of their marriage or of their broader relationships with persons of the opposite sex; to this type of man, the prostitute certainly renders a service.

No amount of wishful thinking will cause prostitutes to disappear since the only set of circumstances in which prostitution might be eliminated, at least as a matter of theory, would be in a society where a system of 'free' love were established and maintained by the State. Apart from the fact that this is an extremely far-fetched hypothesis as matters stand at present, it is doubtful whether, even in that kind of situation, prostitution would totally disappear since there is something satisfying for some men about paying for sexual favours; in that way their contempt of woman is appeased or their shyness overcome or their enjoyment made greater.

In the same way, there are some women who are essentially contemptuous of men or inclined to lesbianism or frigidity or both: they would certainly make better prostitutes than they would wives or mothers. One may even go so far as to say that, from the point of view of society's needs, it would be better if that particular type of woman never married, or procreated. The truth is that, as both Alex Comfort and Benjamin and Masters have observed, the best way of dealing with prostitution is to improve the standards of entry to the 'profession', and of performance. We would be more honest if we took sexual relations for what they are worth,namely that they are not always aimed at procreation; and as a form of enjoyment, so that just as we have singers, old-time dancers, jazz bands, orchestras and similar types of performers, we could have prostitutes who would advertise their different services. Alex Comfort put it thus: 'If sexual virtuosity were to acquire a different valuation in our society, the problem of prostitution would disappear and its personnel would change very markedly – in particular, many of those who now constitute an offence to society by being prostitutes would have to find other ways of offending it.'

It maybe that Comfort was joking when he made such a statement but it is clear that he was identifying the cure for one of the ills of our society, namely the need to acknowledge that certain sexual instincts have to be catered for. Once that conclusion is reached, we might as well cater for them as healthily, hygienically and efficiently as possible. If we were prepared to accept more readily and more clearly the distinction between love and lust, we would find it a lot easier to adjust to the difference between the matron and the whore.

Nobody can be enamoured of the idea that brothels should be established or re-established: the concept is manifestly not a happy one. But then, nobody can be enamoured of sewage works either, or of the existence of entry 'phones, locks, surveillance systems, the police and every other means of prevention and control which our society has had to establish to protect itself. As I have already said, in an ideal world, we would have no need for brothels. We would, however, still require some sexual activity to ensure the perpetuation of the species. Regrettably, our world is anything but ideal and is getting less and less so with the passage of time. Our present social system is not working out very well: it is accompanied by violence and dirt and their indiscriminate spread through society: the way in which these trends have developed is damaging not only to society as a whole, but interferes to a very noticeable degree with the psychological make-up of both men and women.

We should spend a little more time reflecting on the difference between sacred and profane love, the distinction between the two being very clearly acknowledged in art and literature. Each type of love satisfies different needs in human beings but particularly in the man where those needs are more obvious and, above all, more violent and immediate than in woman. It is far too easy to speculate that the difference between the sacred and the profane is merely a convenient representation for artistic purposes. It exists in a very stout form also in reality. Some writers maintain that it is only man's love for God that (theologically and philosophically) is sacred; and any other kind of love is profane. But this is too subtle a distinction for the purposes of everyday life, for, if all men loved God, there would be no need for brothels any more than there would be need for a system of criminal law and sanctions for its breaches.

Undoubtedly, man often finds satisfaction in forms which are different from those which are sacred and hallowed. There is a tendency in man to seek debasement and humiliation which, on the whole, woman does not follow either at all or to such a marked degree. But there are signs that she is now starting to go down that road, such as in the degrading dirty books and pornographic literature women are now prepared to publish, and this is clashing with her motherly instinct, if not causing it to atrophy completely. When that instinct is totally bred out, woman may well be a true Amazon in bed; but by then, it may not avail her very much, because man will have been destroyed.

The belief of present-day woman that she can be and achieve anything, leads her also to the belief that she can reconcile both the sacred and the profane. This is an impossible task. No matter how much her orgasms may be glorified, her primary function is the reproductive one and for that, orgasms are not even needed; for that, no satisfaction is required, not even intercourse, but merely a pindrop injection.

The signs, however, are there to indicate a slight change in woman's approach in this matter. Not too long ago, a group of Danish women petitioned their Government for the legalization of brothels, since they were concerned about the evils they saw spreading through society. A number of countries that had abolished brothels and had made prostitution illegal have now changed their minds and are looking at the matter afresh.

To the average Westerner, however, all this is anathema. 'Well, if you want to re-introduce brothels, you might as well legalize drugs', is a common-enough riposte. As though there were a connection between immorality and drug-taking; although some people consider the taking of drugs immoral, from a strictly physical point of view drug-taking is no more immoral than drinking beer.

What is overlooked when considering the activities and the usefulness, or otherwise, of prostitutes is how essential a service they have provided and may still be providing for men generally. The number of persons of the male sex who have not frequented a prostitute at least once, if not more often, in their lives, is very limited indeed. Kinsey found that seven out of every 10 males in America have had intercourse with a prostitute at least once in their lives. Benjamin and Masters (page 208) believed that the correct figure is eight out of 10. No such figures exist for the United Kingdom, since no research even remotely approximating to that of either Kinsey or Benjamin and Masters was ever carried out. In Mediterranean countries, where the sexual emancipation of women has been slower than in the Anglo-American or Scandinavian world, the only outlet for male sexuality was, and sometimes still is, with prostitutes.

In the present period of the greatest sexual permissiveness ever, prostitutes are still with us and they are still very much in demand. Our society, however, has determined that prostitutes are taboo, illegal, unworthy of official acknowledgment or recognition, a blot on our so-called civilization and an offence to the dignity of woman. Whilst this attitude persists, we are surrounded by manifestations of sexuality which are extreme, absurd, abhorrent. One does not wish to belabour the words of St Augustine but his description of the 'capricious lusts' that would overtake society once we ceased looking upon prostitutes as a natural outlet for sexuality seems, in 1994, quite apt.

Dictionaries define the adjective 'capricious' as: 'impulsive, unpredictable, fickle and subject to whim'. It certainly does not seem too extreme to suggest that some of the activities we witness in Western society are deserving of the description 'capricious'. You may say that too much weight is being given to the views of St Augustine of Hippo and St Thomas Aquinas, venerable patriarchs who, however, were writing some 1500 and 750 years ago respectively. What could they have to say that was relevant to the twentieth century? There are at least three answers to such an objection. Firstly, both are saints and fathers of the Church and if one has any feeling for the Christian tradition, their words should carry some weight. Secondly, the fact that they were writing a long time ago does not make what they said, wrong. If one adopted this principle, then one might have to discount the Bible, the Gospels and the Acts of the Apostles, unless one concentrated on their 'revealed' nature rather than their age; Chaucer and Magna Carta would be worthless: and so on. But more importantly, we should remember that there are certain concepts of universal validity. When it comes to the relations between the sexes, there never was, there still is not and it is unlikely that there ever will be anything new under the sun, at least in the sense that the particular relationship has been explored in all its implications long before the intervention of the sex-obsessed writers of the present century. The basic human instincts of man and woman are unchanged. What has changed about them is the way in which they have been given effect to, and their perception: but basically, man and woman are, at the instinctive level, not too different from what they were even two thousand years ago.

A further objection could be that we have not in fact 'abolished' prostitutes; but that has only superficial validity. What St Augustine and St Thomas were referring to was the availability of prostitutes as an *acknowledged outlet* for sexuality. This is no longer so and it will not be whilst on the one hand we prefer not to know that prostitutes exist; and on the other, we continue to treat as criminal both their activities and the existence of brothels.

The relevance of the observations of St Augustine and St

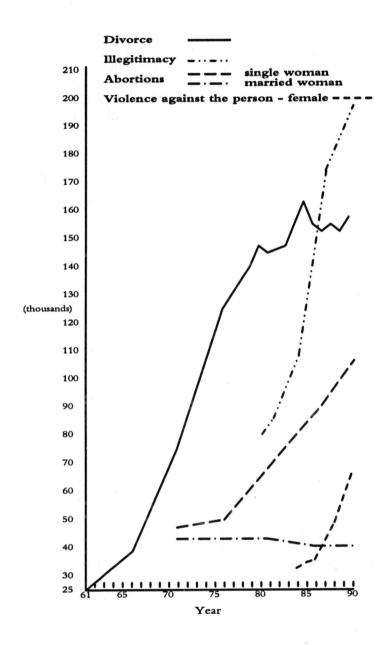

Thomas is their timelessness and universality; and prostitution is a timeless and universal activity. The reason their sayings are topical is exactly that: they are of universal application and are timeless. Nor can the sexual permissiveness prevailing in our society be of any help in trying to solve this particular sexual problem. Using an analogy with riches, it could be argued that in a society where theoretically everybody had the same amount of wealth, theft would not exist. Such an argument is probably theoretically valid. It follows from this that in a society where there is sexual permissiveness and 'sex', generally speaking, is available to everybody, there should in theory be no need for any kind of sexual violence on women.

In our Western world, however, the exact reverse is true. There is reasonably free access to sexual relations; indeed, some might say that there is greater freedom in matters sexual than in trying to make money. And yet, violence on women has increased, as the figures already quoted show only too well. The dissatisfaction of both men and women in the second half of the twentieth century with their sexual relations and with each other is very marked. (As evidence, one could cite the extreme promiscuity of both sexes, the very high rate of failure in marriages, and the unusually high rate of adultery by both men and women.) It is also reflected in the escalation in crimes of violence committed against women, in the high rate of illegitimacy and, to a lesser degree, in the high rate of abortion. The composite graph, opposite, makes this point even clearer.

It is obvious that the so-called battle of the sexes is now more marked, virulent and bloody than it probably was at any other time in our previous history, save perhaps, in the United Kingdom, for the days of the suffragette movement. There appears to be an almost constant slanging match between man and woman nowadays, the men accusing the women of wanting it all their own way, and the women retorting that men do not know how to communicate; the men increasingly unhappy at the bread-winner role of modern woman, the women insisting that men are not honest in their emotions.

There is truth in all these complaints but there is probably greater truth in those voiced by women, for it is quite clear that man is finding it much more difficult to communicate with his modern counterpart and is becoming confused, and therefore not honest, in his emotional approach to her. The reason for man's confusion is the wrong image and related messages that woman is projecting. For this, woman must bear the greater part of the blame, for her ambition to be everything to man is incapable of realization; but even if it could be realized, it would ultimately not solve the problem, because man would not wish it that way.

Man is essentially promiscuous and wants variety: this is something that very few women have ever truly understood, although the tendency of man to stray is very well recorded in history and in literature. One need only think of Shakespeare's *Much Ado About Nothing*.

> 'Sigh no more, ladies, sigh no more.
> Men were deceivers ever;
> One foot in the sea, and one on the shore.
> To one thing constant never.'

But if they applied their minds to this characteristic of the male species, they might find it easier to see that the satisfaction of the male's craving for variety would be much less damaging (in both its immediate and its long-term effects) if it were channelled along routes that are comparatively harmless. No amount of theorizing and moralizing will stop men and women from committing adultery. Clearly, in some cases there may be genuine love in the resultant sexual relationship; but in most cases, certainly as far as man is concerned, there is more likely to be lust. Accordingly, when considering to what extent it would be in the best interests of society to legalize brothels, one should appeal to women for the answer. Such an appeal to the 'weaker' sex is prompted by two eminently practical considerations: the first one is that man has lost his sense of direction and could be said to have exhausted his historical function. Furthermore, his intellectual and physical powers are reducing and he is probably not in the best condition to decide whether or not it is a good thing to legalize brothels.

The second consideration is that woman, on the whole, is much more appreciative of the risk she runs in the event that her husband or her partner wishes to stray from the path of marital righteousness. Ask any woman whether, assuming that her husband had to stray, she would prefer that he had relations with an occasional prostitute or with the wife of one of their friends, or with his secretary. It is easy to predict the answer, since a woman may forgive a husband his occasional straying with a tart but would find it much more difficult to make allowance for a different kind of relationship, because she knows instinctively that her man's commitment to a prostitute is monetary and transient, whereas his obligations in a different kind of relationship will go well beyond the cost of an occasional dinner. The woman involved will see to that, in a manner much more psychologically grasping and practically dangerous than any prostitute would.

Let us call a spade a spade. Let us acknowledge that men, and some women, require a break from the comfort and continuity of a permanent and loving relationship if for no other reason than perhaps, afterwards, they will appreciate the permanent relationship even more. When that happens, it will be infinitely better for all concerned if the errant creatures visit a brothel.

Postscript

On 8 November 1994, the *Daily Star* reported that Edinburgh was to become Britain's number one 'Sin City', referring to the fact that a number of saunas and health clubs had been inspected by Health and Safety officers as well as by the fire brigade, and had been given the go-ahead to continue their activities as 'brothels'.

This item was seized upon by the *Sunday Times* which, on 13 November, ran a half page article under the title 'Taking Prostitution off the Streets'.

There is, of course, nothing new in the concept of prostitutes operating from saunas. The first case history given in Chapter 2, that of Janice, makes it quite clear that she carries out business mainly in saunas in North London, and is pleased to do so because in that way what she termed 'greater cleanliness' is achieved. But there are some features about the Edinburgh situation that warrant closer examination, for it seems to confirm in most respects the findings in the present work.

In the first place, there is the obvious hypocrisy inherent in the 'arrangements'. The Sexual Offences (Scotland) Act 1976 applies to Scotland (as distinct from England, where the Sexual Offences Act 1956 prevails).

The Scottish Act makes it quite clear that the causing of prostitution of a woman (Section 23), the procuration of a girl under 21 (Section 24), the living on earnings of prostitution (Section 30), the keeping of a brothel (Section 33) and the letting or permitting the use of premises as a brothel (Sections 34, 35 and 36) are criminal offences, punishable summarily by varying terms of imprisonment. One wonders, therefore, how the Edinburgh licensing authorities have been able to by-pass the provisions of The Sexual Offences (Scotland) Act 1976. Presumably, this is another of those situations, to which I have already referred, where the law is being ignored. I repeat, to have on the Statute Book laws that are not enforced, as a matter of principle, tends to bring the law as a whole into disrepute.

Either massage parlours are now to be the brothels of the twentieth and twenty-first century, or they are to be massage parlours. We all know, of course, that the kind of massage offered in a number of these establishments is entirely to do with sexual gratification. In fact, my own sources tell me that there are at least two such massage parlours in the SW1 area of London, where masturbation is offered and performed as a matter of course.

But I suppose it could be said that we are dealing here with a passive, rather than an active sexual manifestation, at least on the part of the man. On the part of the woman involved, this is another way of earning money.

The second point which is of interest is that the girls involved, at least those interviewed by *The Sunday Times'* reporter, appear to be of a type which, if the reader will forgive the use of the expression, is superior to the normal street-walker. One or two even claimed to have a university degree, and other respectable jobs. This once again highlights the concept, to which attention has already been drawn, that modern woman tends routinely to use sex as a means of making money. The suggestion is made in the article that, on occasions, these girls may even enjoy, in sexual terms, the services that they provide. I am highly sceptical about this particular observation. While it is not inconceivable that very occasionally a prostitute may enjoy intercourse in the accepted sense, it is my experience that most prostitutes do not. Any enjoyment by them in this context is equivalent to that of some men who frequent prostitutes merely in order to satisfy their urge to humiliate and degrade woman. In the case of men, it is a perverted form of misogyny; in the case of the prostitute, she is getting her own back for the same psychological, warped, reasons.

I find it difficult to believe that a prostitute operating in a sauna or massage parlour can enjoy intercourse. This may apply to some nymphomaniacs, but on the whole, I think that the girls merely do it as a job. Enjoyment is not either a prerequisite or a frequent consequence.

The third respect in which this development is interesting relates to the use of words. I have already remarked on how significant the use of words is; in the sexual context, it becomes of paramount importance. The Edinburgh girls term themselves 'sex workers'. They clearly do not like the term 'prostitute' with its pejorative connotations; but neither they, nor their organizers (nor the local authority which apparently, if the article is to be believed, has actually provided licences for these establishments) like the use of the word 'brothel' either. This noun also appears to have a pejorative connotation, whereas sauna and massage parlour are much more easily accepted. Just as our rat-catcher has become a rodent exterminator and our dustman a public cleansing operative, so the brothels of yesteryear have acquired names which are either Finnish (sauna) or are associated with better physical fitness (massage parlours).

I suppose that if this is the first step towards recognition of the arguments proffered in this book, it is to be welcomed. Certainly one feature of it has indisputable benefits, as I see it, namely, that if the women in question are right in their contention that they have a more wholesome outlook on matters sexual, this can but improve the standards of entry to the profession; any such improvement is highly desirable.

Bibliography

(The criterion for selection is simply what I considered relevant to the argument; otherwise, too much has been said on radio and television and written, especially in newspapers and magazines.)

ACTON, W., *Prostitution* 1870 ed. Poeter Frye, Macgibbon, 1968

ARETINO, PIETRO, *The Education of Pippa*, 1534

ARETINO, PIETRO, *The Life of Courtesans*, 1534

BAILEY, PAUL, *The English Madam. The Life and Work of Cynthia Payne*, Jonathan Cape, 1982

BASSERMAN, LUJO, *The Oldest Profession – A History of Prostitution.* Translated by James Cleugh. Arthur Barker, London, 1967

BAUDELAIRE, *Les Fleurs du Mal*, 1857

BENJAMIN, HARRY & MASTERS, R.E.L., *Prostitution and Morality*, Souvenir Press, London, 1962

BENNION, FRANCIS ALAN R., *The Sex Code Moral for Moderns*, Weidenfeld & Nicolson, London, 1991

BERG, DR LOUIS, *Revelations of a Prison Doctor*, Minton Balch & Co., New York, 1934

BRANDON, RUTH, *The New Women and the Old Men, Love, Sex and the Woman Question*, Secker & Warburg, London, 1990

BURFORD, E.J., *Royal St James's Being a Story of Kings, Clubmen and Courtesans*, Robert Hale, London, 1988

BURFORD, E.J., *Wits, Wenchers and Wantons London's Love Life, Covent Garden in the Eighteenth Century*, Robert Hale, London, 1986

CALHOUN, A.W., *A Social History of the American Family from Colonial Times to the Present*, Cleveland, 1917

CHARNOCK, STEPHEN, *The Chief of Sinners . . .*, Thomas Nelson, London & Edinburgh, 1847

CHESSER, EUSTACE, *Is Marriage Necessary?*, W.H. Allen, London & New York, 1974

COMFORT, ALEXANDER, *Sexual Behaviour in Society*, Gerald Duckworth & Co., London, 1950

CROSS, HAROLD, *The Lust Market*, Citadel Press, New York, 1956

DICKINSON, R.L. & BEAM, LAURA, *A Thousand Marriages − a medical study of sex adjustment, etc.*, Williams & Norgate, Balliere, Tindall & Cox, London, 1932

DUMAS, ALEXANDER, *Dame Aux Camelias*, Calmann-Levy, 1961

ELLIS, ALBERT, *Sexology: Why Married Men visit Prostitutes*, January, 1959

ELLIS, HENRY HAVELOCK, *Studies in the Psychology of Sex*, Wilson & Macmillan, London, 1897

EWING, K.D. & GEARY C.A., *Freedom under Thatcher − Civil Liberties in Modern Britain*, Clarendon Press, Oxford, 1990

FALLOPPIO, GABRIELE, *De Morbo Gallico Ciber*, Patavii, EditoPrima, 1564

FELMAN, YEHUDI M., *Sexually Transmitted Diseases* (ed.) Y.M. Felman, Churchill Livingstone, 1986

FERRIS, PAUL, *Sex and the British − A Twentieth Century History*, Michael Joseph, London, 1993

FLUGEL, J.C., *The Psycho-Analytic Study of a Family*, Hogarth Press, London, 1921

FRIEDAN, BETTY, *The Feminine Mystique*, Gollancz, London, 1963

GLOVER, EDWARD GEORGE, *The Psychopathology of Prostitution*, (Second ed.), I.S.T.D., London, 1957

HALL, RADCLYFFE, *The Well of Loneliness*, Virago, London, 1982

HAYWARD, C., *The Courtesan: the part she has played in classic and modern literature and life*, The Casanova Society, London, 1926

HEBDITCH, DAVID & ANNING, NICK, *Porn Gold: Inside the Pornography Business*, Faber, London, 1988

HENRIQUES, LOUIS FERNANDO M., *Prostitution and Society*, McGibbon & Kee, London, 1962

HENRIQUES, LOUIS FERNANDO M., *Modern Sexuality*, McGibbon & Kee, London, 1968

HENRIQUES, LOUIS FERNANDO M., *The Sociology of Prostitution*, McGibbon & Kee, London, 1962

HORACE, *Horace's Complete Works* (English Text). Introduction by J. Marshall, Dent, London, 1911

ITZIN, CATHERINE (ed), *Pornography, Women, Violence & Civil Liberties*, Oxford University Press, Oxford, 1992

KINSEY, A.C. & OTHERS, *The Sexual Behaviour of the Human Male*, W.B. Saunders Co, Philadelphia & London, 1948

KINSEY, A.C. & OTHERS, *The Sexual Behaviour of the Human Female*, W.B. Saunders Co, Philadelphia, 1953

KIRKENDALL, LESTER ALLEN, *Premarital Intercourse and Interpersonal Relationships. A research study of interpersonal relationships and case histories of 668 premarital intercourse experiences reported by 200 college level males*, Julian Press, New York, 1961

KRONHAUSEN, PHYLLIS & EBERHARD, *Sexists of American College Men*, Valentine, New York, 1960

KOUPRINE, ALEXANDER I., *La Fosse Aux Filles*, Lama, Noman Tranvit, Paris, 1923

LASSONG, ROBERT, *Le Quid*, Paris, 1992

LECKY, W.E.M., *The History of European Morals from Augustus to Charlemagne*, Longman's & Co., London, 1911

LOMBROSO, C. & FERRERO, W., *La Donna Delinquente*, Turin, 1893

LYNDON, NEIL, *No More Sex War: the failure of feminism*, Sinclair-Stevenson, London, 1992

MORASSO, *Archivo di Psichiatria*, 1896

PARENT-DUCHÂTELET, *De la Prostitution dans la Ville de Paris*, Paris, 1836

PETRONIUS, ARBITER, *Satyricon*, AD 63

POLO, MARCO, *Il Milione. Travels of Marco Polo*, Dent, 1908

REINISCH, JUNE M. & BEASLEY, RUTH, *The Kinsey Institute New Report on Sex. What you must know to be sexually literate*, Penguin, London, 1990

RICHARD, MARTHE Mme, *L'Appel des Sexes*, 1951

ROUSSEAU, J.J., *The Confessions.* Translated by J.M. Cohen, Penguin, 1953

RUSSELL, BERTRAND, *Marriage and Morals*, Unwin Books, London, 1976

SALMOND & HEUSTON, *The Law of Tort*, 20th Ed. Sweet & Maxwell, London, 1992

SCHOFIELD, MICHAEL, *The Sexual Behaviour of Young People*, Penguin, Harmondsworth, 1968

SHADWELL, THOMAS, *The Virtuosos*, 1676. 'Virtuoso' ed. by M. Nicholson Arnold, Regent Restoration, 1966

SPENDER, DALE, *Women of Ideas and what men have done to them*, Routledge & Kegan Paul, London, 1982

ST CLAIR, LINDI, *The Autobiography of Miss Whiplash*, Piatkus, London, 1992

STONE, LAWRENCE, *Road to Divorce*, Clarendon, Oxford, 1990

TERMAN, LOUIS M., (et al) *Psychological Factors in Marital Happiness*, McGraw Hill Book Company, New York & London, 1938

TOLSTOY, LEO N., *Resurrection.* Translated by Rosemary Edmonds, Penguin, 1966

TREVELYAN, G.M., *English Social History – A Survey of 6 Centuries. Charles to Queen Victoria*, Longman & Co., London, 1967

TROLLOPE, A., *The Vicar of Bullhampton*, Alan Sutton, 1983

WESTERMARK, EDWARD A., *The History of Human Marriage*, Macmillan & Co., London, 1921

WILDE, OSCAR, *The Harlot's House*, Carpathian, Amsterdam, 1990

WOLLSTONECRAFT, MARY, *A Vindication of the Rights of a Woman 1792*, Gregg International, 1970

WOOTTON, BARBARA, *Social Science and Social Pathology*, George Allen & Unwin, London, 1959

WORTLEY, MONTAGUE LADY MARY, *Woman not Inferior to Man*. In Poems by eminent ladies etc. Vol. 2, 1757

PUBLICATIONS

Adam Smith Institute, 'An Inspector at the Door. An index of officials who can demand rights of entry', London, 1979

British Journal of Addiction, 1991–86

Family Policy Unit Fact Sheet No. 3, 1990

Lancet, The Sharpe and Shakkebaek, June 1993

Series FM2 Nos. 14, 16, 17 & 18 HMSO

Series FM2 No. 19 '1991 Marriage and Divorce Statistics', HMSO

'Young People in 1992'. School Health Education Unit

HASKEY, J., 'Population Trends' No. 55, 65 1989 HMSO

WOLFENDEN, SIR JOHN, 'Wolfenden Report', Command 248 of 1957

Index